Table of Contents

Illinois TAP Math
Test of Academic Proficiency - Math Preparation

Mary DeSouza Stephens

I. Introduction

I. Introduction

Introduction: About the Author

Mary Stephens (née DeSouza) graduated from MIT with a bachelor's degree and a master's degree in Computer Science and Electrical Engineering. She has over 15 years of teaching experience, including designing courses and teaching as an adjunct faculty member at UMASS Boston; TAing discrete math at MIT; and developing curriculum for and teaching classes in high school computer science, LSAT, algebra, geometry, science, humanities, and K-12 math and computers. Outside of teaching, Mary worked in engineering, product management, and strategy for companies including Edusoft and Oracle. In the past few years, she has spoken at international education conferences and has served as Professional Math Consultant at Merrimack College, founder of Omega Teaching, and Research and Development Manager at Houghton Mifflin Harcourt. She is the founder and CEO of PrepForward (www.prepforward.com), a leading provider of teacher preparation materials, and can be contacted at mary@prepforward.com. Please visit the PrepForward website to find out about other preparation offerings, including self-paced, online courses that are certified by the Illinois State Board of Education for CPDU credit.

Introduction: How to Use this Book

This book is designed to help you succeed on the mathematics subtest of the Illinois Licensure Testing System (ILTS) Test of Academic Proficiency (TAP). Each test area is given its own separate section in the book so that you can follow a study path that works best for you.

I recommend that you work through all chapters of the book at least once. Each of chapters 1 through 6 is followed by a review that will help you to gauge your level of preparedness and see which concepts require further study. Print out the formula sheet which can be found in the appendix, and get comfortable using it while you work through the problems.

You can take the diagnostic exam either prior to your preparations or it can be used as a final exam after you have completed the other chapters. Based on your results, go back and review any areas of weakness. Then, take the final exam two weeks before your test date. Make sure to use the test-taking strategies outlined in the book.

Passing the ILTS TAP exam is critical for your future role as a licensed teacher, but understanding the concepts is just as important. With this book and your commitment, you can achieve both goals. Good luck!

Introduction: About the Test

To obtain a teaching license in the state of Illinois you must pass this test which is part of the Illinois Licensure Testing System (ILTS). The Test of Academic Proficiency (TAP) replaced the Basic Skills exam, and is offered only as a computer-based test. It consists of four subtests: Reading Comprehension, Language Arts, Mathematics, and Writing.

There is an ILTS Test Attempt Limit Policy of five attempts. Each attempt of one of more of the TAP subtests will count towards this limit. You should register for all four subtests for each attempt and just focus on the subtests you need to pass. There is no penalty for skipping a subtest.

Please refer to the following website for the latest information on the ILTS TAP exam. www.il.nesinc.com

Test Structure and Scoring

The Mathematics subtest of the ILTS TAP includes 50 multiple-choice questions. These questions will cover the following standards:

Standard 14: Solve problems involving integers, fractions, decimals, and units of measurement.
Standard 15: Apply mathematical reasoning skills to analyze patterns and solve problems.
Standard 16: Solve problems involving algebra and geometry.
Standard 17: Understand concepts and procedures related to data analysis and statistics.
Standard 18: Solve applied problems using a combination of mathematical skills (including word problems involving one and two variables).

You will be provided with a sheet with Mathematics Definitions and Formulas. Please see the Appendix to see the information contained on this sheet.

There is no penalty for skipping questions. Therefore, never leave a question blank and at least attempt to answer each problem with a guess. Also, each multiple choice question is worth the same value. You will be given a scaled score between 100 and 300. You need a 240 to pass each subtest.

If you choose to take only one subtest during the session, you will be given 2 hours and 30 minutes. If you choose to take all four subtests, you will have 5 hours to complete them. You might find that you need less time, but be prepared to stay for the entire time. Use any remaining time to check your work for accuracy.

Test Objectives

The chapters of this book are mapped to the objectives of the exam. You can download a full list of the objectives from the test-makers' website at **www.il.nesinc.com.**

Registering for the TAP exam

Computer-based testing is available year-round by appointment, Monday through Saturday. Register for the exam through **www.il.nesinc.com** and you are given the opportunity to choose your date and location.

Knowing the subject matter is the best way to prepare for the ILTS TAP exam. But, test-taking strategies can make a difference to your score. Follow these tips to make the most of your performance on the day.

1. Read the Entire Question

Read the entire question carefully before you start solving the problem. Otherwise, there's a chance you will miss some crucial information.

2. Use Your Time Wisely

If you know how to solve the problem, go ahead and do it! But don't waste time on problems that cover material you don't know. Circle these problems and come back to them after you have completed the other problems. Know your strengths and weaknesses, and make decisions based on them.

3. Write It Down

Write out the steps for complex calculations instead of trying to do them in your head. Under test pressure, your ability to perform mental calculations will be put under strain. Writing things down also makes it easier to spot mistakes in your approach.

4. Leave No Blanks

Answer every question, even if that means guessing. You will not be deducted any points for incorrect answers.

5. Eliminate, Then Guess

It's to your advantage to guess on this test, but be clever about it. Eliminate any unreasonable answer choices before guessing.

6. Back Solving

Since the questions are multiple-choice, you can plug the numbers from the answer choices into the question. For example:

Which of the following values for N will make the statement true? $N \times N = N + N$

  A. 1   B. 2   C. 3   D. 4

Try each option in the statement and see which one makes it true.

7. Estimate First

If you quickly estimate the answer before looking at the choices, you are less likely to get thrown off by distractors. It will also help you determine how much work is needed to solve the problem.

8. Plugging In

"Plugging In" can be a useful time-saving strategy when dealing with formula and equation questions. Guess a number; plug it into the original problem; and then plug it into each answer choice to see what works. Make sure to plug in valid numbers. For example, if a problem is dealing with minutes, use 30 or 60, not –143.

Example: If N is an even number, which of the following products is an odd number?

  A. $(N + 1)(N - 3)$

  B. $(N + 1)(N + 2)$

  C. $N(N + 1)$

  D. $N(N - 3)$

Think of any even number, such as 4. Then, plug that number into each answer choice to see which option results in an odd number.

9. Use Formula Sheet

Ensure you are familiar with all the definitions and formulas on the sheet before you go into the exam. Refer to the sheet during the exam as opposed to relying on your memory.

10. Check Your Work

Use any remaining time to go back and review your work.

Introduction: Test Day Preparation

- Before the day of the test, make sure that you know where your test center and its parking facilities are located.

- Check the official ILTS website for a list of items allowed at the test site. Remember, a calculator is not allowed on this test.

- The day before the test, make sure to review the test-taking strategies.

- Try to relax and get a good night's sleep before the test. Performing well in this test requires critical thinking, which is best done when you are fully alert.

- Plan to get to the test center early in case there are unforeseen issues with registration or parking.

1. Number Sense

Sets of Numbers

Most likely, numbers and counting were the first things you learned about in math. You might have begun by learning about the set of **"natural" or counting numbers:** 1, 2, 3, 4... Later, your knowledge would have expanded to include all **whole numbers**, the set of natural numbers plus zero: 0, 1, 2, 3...

Integers include zero and all the positive and negative numbers that do not need to be represented with fractions or decimals. A number line is a great way of visualizing integers.

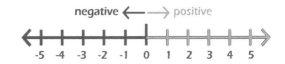

If a number can be written as a fraction, it is a **rational** number. Rational numbers include all decimals that either terminate or repeat, since those numbers can be expressed as fractions. Numbers, such as π, whose decimals do not terminate or repeat, are called **irrational** numbers. The **real** numbers include all rational and irrational numbers.

The diagram shows the relationship among the sets of numbers. For instance, the integers include the negatives and all the whole numbers, while the whole numbers include 0 and the counting numbers.

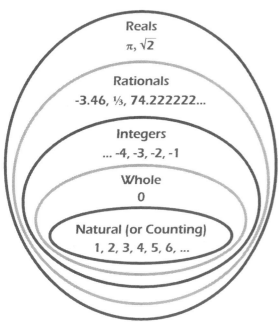

Each of these sets is infinitely large. In other words, there is not a finite number of whole numbers. You can always keep adding 1 to the largest and get another whole number.

Other common number sets include the **evens** and **odds**. Even numbers include all numbers that equal 2 times an integer, for example –6, 0, 2, 10. Odd numbers are all integers that are not even, such as –5, 1, 9, or 17.

Ordering and Comparing Numbers

The number line helps to show the order of numbers. The farther to the right a number is, the greater its value. For example, when comparing two negative numbers, the one closest to zero will be greater.

The following symbols are used to compare numbers:

= Equal to	> Greater than	≥ Greater than or equal to
≠ Not equal to	< Less than	≤ Less than or equal to

You should memorize the above symbols, but if you are ever confused, refer to the Math Definitions and Formula Sheet that will be provided to you during the exam.

Examples:

28 > 12   (28 is greater than 12)
–12 < –4   (–12 is less than –4)

Foundations: Practice

1. What is a possible value for x if 12 > x > 8?

   A. 9

   B. 20

   C. 7

   D. Not possible

2. What is a possible value for x if 12 < x < 8?

   A. 9

   B. 20

   C. 7

   D. Not possible

3. Choose all the answers that are true about 3.25:

        I. Integer

        II. Irrational

        III. Real

   A. I and III

   B. III only

   C. II and III

   D. I, II, and III

4. Which of the following numbers are irrational?

        I. $\frac{1}{3}$

        II. −12.451

        III. π

   A. None

   B. I and III

   C. III only

   D. All

5. Which answer is a list of negative integers ordered from least to greatest?

   A. −8, −9, −10, −11

   B. −8.5, −9.5, −10.5, −11.5

   C. 8, 9, 10, 11

   D. −11, −10,− 9, −8

6. How many integers are greater than −3 but less than 4?

A. 5

B. 6

C. 7

D. 8

$$-3 \quad -2 \quad -1 \quad 0 \quad 1 \quad 2 \quad 3 \quad 4$$

7. How many negative odd integers exist between −10 and 4?

A. 5

B. 6

C. 7

D. 8

$$-10 \quad -9 \quad -8 \quad -7 \quad -6 \quad -5 \quad -4 \quad -3 \quad -2 \quad -1$$

8. How many positive rational numbers are greater than −2 and less than 7?

A. 6

B. 7

C. 9

D. An infinite number

Foundations: Answer Explanations

1. A Let's look at the statement 12 > x > 8.

x must meet two different conditions:

12 must be greater than x

x must be greater than 8

Go through each answer choice and eliminate those that don't work. 12 is not greater than 20 (eliminate B). 7 is not greater than 8 (eliminate C). Answer choice A works: 12 is greater than 9, and 9 is greater than 8.

2. D Let's look at the statement 12 < x < 8.

x must meet two different conditions:

12 must be less than x

x must be less than 8

No number exists that is both bigger than 12 and less than 8. Answer D is correct.

3. B   Let's examine each property against the number 3.25:

        I. Integer – Remember, integers do not include decimals or fractions. Therefore, 3.25 is not an integer.

        II. Irrational – Irrational numbers are numbers that cannot be expressed as fractions. Numbers with terminating decimals are rational. 3.25 is rational as the decimal terminates. Another way to think about it is 3.25 can be expressed as $^{325}/100$ or $3\frac{1}{4}$, so it is rational. 3.25 is not irrational.

        III. Real – Real numbers include all rational and irrational numbers. Therefore, 3.25 is a real number.

4. C   Irrational numbers are numbers that cannot be expressed as fractions.

        I. $\frac{1}{3}$: Since this number is a fraction, it is rational.

        II. –12.451: Any number with a terminating decimal can be expressed as a fraction. In this case, $-12.451 = -^{12451}/1000$. Therefore, it is rational.

        III. π: π cannot be written as a fraction. If π is written in decimal form, it goes on forever and does not repeat. Therefore, it is the only irrational number in the list.

5. D   Negative integers do not include any decimals or fractions. That eliminates option B. Option C only includes positive numbers, therefore that is eliminated.

    Now, let's examine options A and D.

        A: –8, –9, –10, –11
        D: –11, –10, –9, –8

    When comparing two negative numbers, the one closest to zero is greater. So, –10 is greater than –11. Here, the numbers in option D are ordered from least to greatest.

6. B   List all the integers greater than –3 and less than 4. Note that the question says greater than –3, not greater than or equal to –3. Therefore, we do not want to include –3. In the same way, the question asks for integers less than 4, not less than or equal to 4. Therefore, we do not want to include 4. Also, remember to include 0:

    –2, –1, 0, 1, 2, 3

    This gives 6 numbers.

7. A   List all the negative odd integers between –10 and 4:

        –9, –7, –5, –3, –1

    This gives 5 numbers.

8. D   There is an infinite number of rational numbers between any two integers. Rationals include any number that can be made into a fraction. For example, $\frac{1}{2}$, 1.1, 1.231, and 1.42347824 are all rational numbers.

Place Value

The number 9,876,543 could be viewed simply as a string of digits. But, with an understanding of place value, you can break the number into its parts. In 9,876,543, the digit 7 stands for 70,000, and the 6 represents 6,000. Each digit is given a specific value by its place in the number. The chart shows some place values.

one millions hundred thousands ten thousands one thousands hundreds tens ones

$$9 , 8 7 6 , 5 4 3$$

Numbers can be written in expanded form, which shows the value of each digit.
For example: $9,876,543 = 9,000,000 + 800,000 + 70,000 + 6,000 + 500 + 40 + 3$

Illustrating Place Value

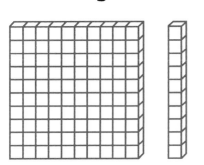

Pictures or blocks are often used to illustrate the concept of place value. A small block represents one unit. A group of ten small blocks makes a stick used to represent the tens place. This approach makes it easy to see, for instance, that 3 sticks represent 30 blocks or the number 30. The same concept applies to the hundreds and thousands of blocks.

These blocks can also be useful for visualizing redistribution, which is necessary for addition and subtraction. To imagine redistribution, think of a stick of 10 blocks broken into single units or vice versa.

Rounding and Estimation

Imagine that you drove 1,297 miles on a road trip. You would most likely tell your friends you drove 1,300 miles. Approximating numbers to the powers of ten in this way is called rounding. Rounding is useful for quickly estimating the outcome of various operations.

There are specific rules for rounding:
1. To round a number to a place value, you must look at the value of the digit to the right of the rounding digit. For example, look at the value of the digit in the tens place when rounding to the hundreds place.

2. If the digit is a number from 0 to 4, round down by keeping the rounded digit the same and make the digits to the right equal to zero. For example, to round 938 to the nearest hundred, look at the digit in the tens place. Because 3 is less than 5, round down to 900.

3. If the digit is a number from 5 to 9, round up by increasing the digit by 1 and then making all digits to the right equal to zero. For example, to round 217 to the tens place look at the digit in the ones place. It is 7, which is greater than 5, so you must round up to 220.

If the digit to be rounded up is a 9, then multiple digits of your number will be affected. For example, if you round 1,296 to the nearest ten, you would note that the 9 is in the tens place. You would then look to the right of that 9 and see that the 6 is between 5 and 9 and you must round up. First, make the 6 a zero and then round the 9 up by 1 digit to 10. This creates a problem as you can't put a two digit number into the tens place. So, redistribute, giving you 1300.

$1296 = 1000 + 200 + 90 + 6$
We round the 90 to 100 and make the 6 a zero.
$= 1000 + 200 + 100 + 0 = 1300$

Numbers & Place Value: Practice

1. What digit is in the ten–thousands place in the following number: 5,609,823 ?

    A. 6

    B. 0

    C. 9

    D. 5

2. Round 72,349 to the nearest hundred.

    A. 72,350

    B. 72,000

    C. 72,300

    D. 72,400

3. What number is shown to the right?

    A. 5

    B. 14

    C. 104

    D. 1004

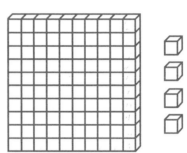

4. Choose the best answer to replace the question mark.

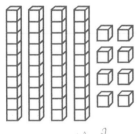

    A. >

    B. <

    C. =

    D. ≥

5. Order the following from least to greatest:

    I. 7000 + 6

    II. 800 + 90 + 9

    III. 7000 + 30

    A. I, III, II

    B. III, I, II

    C. II, I, III

    D. II, III, I

6. Round 28,956 to the nearest hundred.

A. 28,900

B. 28,960

C. 29,000

D. 29,100

7. What number is equal to 40 + 1000 + 900 + 300000 ?

A. 4193

B. 3194

C. 31,940

D. 301,940

8. What number is eight hundred forty thousand three hundred six?

A. 84,306

B. 840,306

C. 840,360

D. 80,040,306

Numbers & Place Value: Answer Explanations

1. B   5,609,823

Working from the right, the following are the place values:

3 is in the ones place.

2 is in the tens place.

8 is in the hundreds place.

9 is in the thousands place.

0 is in the ten–thousands place.

6 is in the hundred–thousands place.

5 is in the millions place.

Therefore, the answer is 0.

2. C   To round 72,349 to the hundreds place, first determine which digit is in the hundreds place. The 3 is in the hundreds place. Now, look at the digit to the right of that 3, which is the 4. If the number to the right is 5 or greater, you round the 3 up. In this case, since it is less than 5, you leave the 3 the same.

Therefore, 72,349 rounded to the nearest hundred is 72,300.

3. C   The larger box represents 100. Each of the smaller boxes represents 1.

There is 1 large box and 4 small boxes. Therefore, we want 100 and 4 = 100 + 4 = 104.

4. B   To determine which is larger, you must first figure out the value of each image.

There are 4 tens and 8 ones, which equals 48.
There are 5 tens and 1 one, which equals 51.

Therefore, since 48 is less than 51, the answer is B, <

5. C   Let's determine the value of each so that they can be ordered.

I. 7000 + 6 = 7006
II. 800 + 90 + 9 = 899
III. 7000 + 30 = 7030

Ordering from least to greatest: 899, 7006, 7030
II, I, III

6. C   To round 28,956 to the nearest hundred, first identify what digit is in the hundreds place, and then look at the digit to the right.

The 9 is in the hundreds place. Look at the digit to the right, since it is a 5, which is ≥ 5, then you must round up. So, change all the numbers to the right of the 9 to 0 and then round the 9 up to 10. Yet, you can't put a two digit number in the hundreds place, so, you have to carry it over to the next place, which is the thousands place. Therefore, round the thousands place digit, which is 8, u

Let's put all of this together. We change the 5 and 6 to zero, round the 9 to a 10, so make it a 0 and carry 1, which makes the 8 a 9. So, 28, 956 rounded to nearest hundred is 29,000.

Another way to think about it is that we know we want to round to the nearest hundred, so we look at the digit to the right of the 9 in the hundreds place, which is a 5, so we want to round up. Therefore, we think of what is the next hundred that is greater than 28,956. The next closest hundred greater than 28,956 is 29,000.

7. D   First, put the numbers in decreasing order.

40 + 1000 + 900 + 300000
= 300000 + 1000 + 900 + 40

Next, convert from expanded form to standard form.
300000 + 1000 + 900 + 40 = 301940

8. B   Take each number and put in the correct place value.

Let's take the first part: eight hundred forty thousand
This equals: 840,000

The second part: three hundred six
This equals: 306

Now, put them together:
840,000 + 306 = 840,306

Factors

A factor of a number is an integer that divides evenly into the number with no remainder. For example, 5 is a factor of 50, since 50 divided by 5 is 10 with no remainder. However, 6 is not a factor of 50, since 50 divided by 6 is 8 with a remainder of 2. A number that has only 1 and itself as factors is called a prime number. Examples of prime numbers include: 5, 17, and 23.

The greatest common factor (GCF) of two numbers is the largest factor that they both share. To explain, let's figure out the GCF of 24 and 18.

Factors of 24: 1, 2, 3, 4, 6, 8, 12, 24
Factors of 18: 1, 2, 3, 6, 9, 18
The largest factor they both share is 6.

Fundamental Theorem of Arithmetic

The fundamental theorem of arithmetic states that every positive integer can be expressed as a product of prime numbers. The theorem also states that it can be expressed in only one way, other than rearrangement. This product of the prime numbers is known as the prime factorization of the number.

Finding the prime factorization of numbers is a critical first step to many arithmetic and algebraic concepts, such as simplifying and factoring numbers, all which are covered in later lessons. One way to find the prime factorization of a number is by using a factor tree. The "leaves" at the bottom of the two factor trees here are the prime factors of the number 200. It doesn't matter that each level is different, the final prime factorization will always be the same.

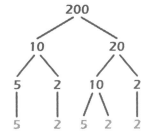 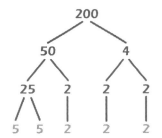

The prime factorization of 200 can be written as

$5 \times 2 \times 5 \times 2 \times 2$

$= 5 \times 5 \times 2 \times 2 \times 2$

$= 5^2 \times 2^3$

Divisibility

Divisibility is another way of stating factors of a number. There are a few tricks to easily determine the divisibility of certain numbers.

2: Only even numbers are divisible by 2. No odd numbers are divisible by 2.

3: If the sum of the digits of a number is divisible by 3, the number is also divisible by 3. For example, to determine if 4,158 is divisible by 3, add the digits: $4 + 1 + 5 + 8 = 18$. 18 is divisible by 3, so, 4,158 is divisible by 3.

4: If the last two digits of a number are divisible by 4, the whole number is divisible by 4. This works because 4 divides evenly into 100. For example, 23,924 is divisible by 4, since 24 is divisible by 4.

5: Any number that ends in 0 or 5 is divisible by 5.

6: Any number that is divisible by both 2 and 3 is divisible by 6.

8: If the last three digits of a number are divisible by 8, then the whole number is divisible by 8. For example, 984,840 is divisible by 8 since 840 is divisible by 8.

9: If the sum of the digits of a number is divisible by 9, then the number is also divisible by 9. So, 4158 is divisible by 9 since its digits add up to 18.

10: Any number that ends in 0 is divisible by 10.

Multiples

A multiple of a number is equal to that number times an integer. For example, all even numbers are multiples of 2.
2 x 0 = 0, 2 x 1 = 2, 2 x 2 = 4, 2 x 3 = 6, ...

It is often useful to find the Least Common Multiple (LCM) of two numbers, the smallest non–zero multiple that the numbers share. To find the LCM, list the multiples of each number until you find a common one.

Let's find the LCM of 8 and 6.

Multiples of 8: 8, 16, 24, ...
Multiples of 6: 6, 12, 18, 24, ...
24 is the smallest multiple that they share – in other words, 24 is the LCM.

If two numbers do not share any factors, the LCM is their product. For example, the LCM of 6 and 7 is 42.

The Least Common Multiple is used often in mathematics, especially when finding equivalent fractions, which will be reviewed in later lessons.

Factors, Multiples, Divisibility: Practice

1. Which of the following is/are factors of 36?

    I. 12
    II. 24
    III. 72

A. I only

B. III only

C. I and II

D. I, II, and III

2. Write 234 as a product of its prime factors.

A. 39 x 6

B. 13 x 2 x 3

C. $13 \times 2 \times 3^2$

D. 13 x 23

3. Find the least common multiple of 15, 25, and 6.

A. 1

B. 75

C. 150

D. 2250

4. Two teams are competing to split all the candy in a jar. If Team A wins, each member will get 6 pieces. If Team B wins, each member will get 5 pieces. Which of the following could be the total amount of candy in the jar?

A. 65

B. 36

C. 11

D. 60

5. How many positive integers less than 200 are divisible by both 7 and 3?

A. 9

B. 10

C. 20

D. 28

6. Find the prime factorization of the greatest common factor of 126 and 900.

A. 2 x 3

B. 2 x 3 x 5 x 7

C. 2 x 3^2

D. 2^2 x 3^2 x 5^2 x 7

7. What is the sum of the least common multiple and greatest common factor of 12 and 24?

A. 30

B. 36

C. 54

D. 60

8. What is the sum of the prime numbers greater than 1 and less than 20?

A. 58

B. 60

C. 75

D. 77

Factors, Multiples, Divisibility: Answer Explanations

1. A If a number is a factor of 36, then it divides evenly into 36 with no remainder.

I. 12: Since $36 \div 12 = 3$, then 12 is a factor of 36.

II. 24: Since $36 \div 24 = 1$ remainder 12, then 24 is not a factor of 36.

III. 72: 72 is a multiple of 36, not a factor. 72 does not divide evenly into 36. Factors are always less than or equal to the number.

Answer A: I only.

2. C One way to find the prime factors of a number are to create a factor tree.

The prime factors of 234 are 3 x 3 x 2 x 13. Answer C is correct.

Answer choice A: 39 x 6. Those are not prime numbers.
Answer choice B: Does not multiply to 234.
Answer choice D: Does not multiply to 234.

3. C To find the least common multiple of 25, 15, and 6, you can list out the multiples until you find the smallest multiple they share.

Multiples of 25: 25, 50, 75, 100, 125, 150...
Multiples of 15: 15, 30, 45, 60, 75, 90, 105, 120, 135, 150...
Multiples of 6: 6, 12, 18, 24, 30, 36, 42, 48, 54, 60, 66, 72, 78, 84, 90, 96, 102, 108, 114, 120, 126, 132, 138, 144, 150...

The LCM of 15, 25, and 6 is 150.

Another way to find the LCM is to find the prime factors of each number and then multiply the highest powers of each the prime factors together.

15 as product of prime factors $= 3 \times 5$
25 as product of prime factors $= 5^2$
6 as product of prime factors $= 2 \times 3$

The highest powers of the prime factors are: $2 \times 3 \times 5^2 = 150$

4. D If all the candy can be split evenly into either 6 pieces if Team A wins or 5 pieces of Team B wins, then the total amount of candy must be divisible by both 5 and 6.

60 is the only answer that is evenly divisible by 5 and 6, therefore Answer D is correct.

5. A If a number is divisible by both 7 and 3, the number is divisible by the lowest common multiple of those numbers. The lowest common multiple of 7 and 3 is 21, since that is the smallest number that both divide evenly into.

We need to figure out how many integers less than 200 are divisible by 21. If you divide 200 by 21 you get 9 11/21. That means that there are 9 different numbers that are multiples of 21 and less than 200.

6. C   Remember that the greatest common factor is the greatest number that is a factor of the original numbers. Another way to think about it is that the greatest common factor is the product of the prime factors common to two or more numbers.

To find the prime factorization of the greatest common factor of 126 and 900, first find the prime factorization of each number. The easiest method would be to use a factor tree for each.

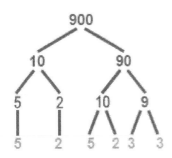 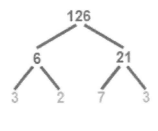

As can be seen from the factor trees:
prime factorization of 126 is 3 x 2 x 7 x 3 = $2 \times 3^2 \times 7$
prime factorization of 900 is 5 x 2 x 5 x 2 x 3 x 3 = $2^2 \times 3^2 \times 5^2$

The greatest common factor would include all the factors that evenly divide into both 126 and 900. There are three factors: 2, 3, and 3 that go into 126 and 900. Therefore, the prime factorization of the GCF of 126 and 900 is: 2×3^2.

7. B   The least common multiple is the smallest number that both 12 and 24 multiply evenly to. Since both 12 and 24 go evenly into 24, it is a common multiple. It is the least common multiple since 24 does not have any multiples that are smaller.

The greatest common factor is the biggest number that divides evenly into both 12 and 24. Since 12 divides evenly into both numbers and is the greatest factor of 12, it is the greatest common factor.

The sum of 12 and 24 is 12 + 24 = 36.

8. D   First, list out all the prime numbers that are greater than 1 and less than 20, and then add them.

2, 3, 5, 7, 11, 13, 17, 19
2 + 3 + 5 + 7 + 11 + 13 + 17 + 19 = 77

Addition

Addition is the process of combining two or more numbers to get a total. To add large numbers, line the numbers up vertically by place value and add the digits of each column, beginning with the ones place.

For example, 7,325 + 10,644 = ?

$$\begin{array}{r} 7,325 \\ +\ 10,644 \\ \hline 17,969 \end{array}$$

Sometimes adding numbers will require redistribution (see place values lesson). Adding 50 + 70 involves redistribution. You have 5 tens and 7 tens, which adds up to 12 tens. 10 of those tens can be combined or redistributed to 1 hundred, with 2 tens remaining. Therefore, the sum of 50 and 70 is 100 + 20 or 120. Here is another sample problem with redistribution. In this question, the 9 ones and the 3 ones added to 12 ones. Those were redistributed to 1 ten, leaving 2 ones.

$$\begin{array}{r} {\scriptstyle 1} \\ 4563 \\ +\ 1319 \\ \hline 5882 \end{array} \quad \xleftarrow{\ \ } 3+9=12$$

Subtraction

Subtraction is the inverse of addition and the result of a subtraction problem is called the difference of the numbers subtracted. As with addition, line up big numbers by place value to subtract, beginning with the ones place.

$$\begin{array}{r} 97,642 \\ -\ 23,120 \\ \hline 74,522 \end{array}$$

Redistribution is necessary in subtraction when the number being subtracted for a certain place value is larger than the number it is being subtracted from. In such cases, one from the place value above is broken into ten pieces.

$$\begin{array}{r} {\scriptstyle 7\ \ 11} \\ 72\cancel{8}\cancel{1} \\ -5137 \\ \hline 2144 \end{array}$$

In the ones place, 1 is smaller than 7, therefore you must redistribute.

From the tens place, you take 1 from the 8 to make it a 7, and you break that into ten ones. Those ten ones are added to the 1 to make 11.

Multiplication

Multiplication, which is repeated addition, results in the product of two or more numbers. Three multiplied by four is the same as adding four three times (3 x 4 = 4 + 4 + 4 = 12) or three four times (3 x 4 = 3 + 3 + 3 + 3 = 12).

In order to multiply large numbers, multiply each digit of one number by each digit of the other number, and sum the results.

$$\begin{array}{r} {\scriptstyle 2} \\ 2014 \\ \times\ \ 756 \\ \hline 12084 \\ +\ 100700 \\ \hline 1409800 \\ \hline 1522584 \end{array}$$

6 x 4 = 24, put the 4 in the ones place and carry the 20 to be added in with the tens place.

Remember that the 5 in 756 is actually 50. Use a placeholder 0 to account for that fact.

Division

Division is the inverse of multiplication, and the result of a division problem is called a quotient. It asks how many groups of a given number can be made out of another number. For example, how many groups of 2 can be made out of 12? $12 \div 2 = 6$; six groups of 2 can be made out of 12.

Long division is division that shows out each step of the process. Unlike all other basic operations, long division starts with the greatest place value and works back to the ones.

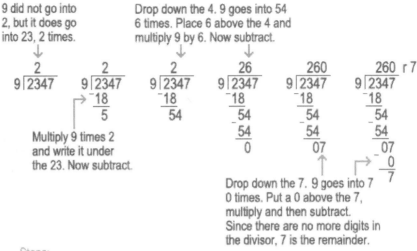

The problem to the right has a remainder of 7. It can also be thought of as 7/9. Or, you can add a decimal place and zeros to the dividend, and continue the long division process.

Steps:
1. Determine how many times the divisor (9) goes into the first part of the dividend.
2. Place that number above the line. Multiply the divisor by that number.
3. Subtract, and bring down the next digit of the divisor.
4. Determine how many times the divisor goes into that number. Repeat steps 1-3.

Order of Operations

For problems containing multiple operations, there is a standardized order in which these operations must be carried out. Without such an order, a single problem could generate multiple answers. The order is:

Parentheses

Exponents

Multiplication and **D**ivision from left to right

Addition and **S**ubtraction from left to right

A common mnemonic device for remembering the order is "Please Excuse My Dear Aunt Sally"

Example: $200 - 7 + 6 \times (2 \times 3) \div 4 =$	
$200 - 7 + 6 \times (2 \times 3) \div 4 =$	Parentheses first.
$200 - 7 + 6 \times 6 \div 4 =$	No Exponents. Multiply and Divide from left to right.
$200 - 7 + 36 \div 4 =$	Keep multiplying and dividing.
$200 - 7 + 9 =$	Now Add and Subtract from left to right.
$193 + 9 =$	The final addition step.
202	Answer.

Common mistake is that people perform multiplication always before division. It is multiplication or division from left to right, whichever comes first. $12 \div 2 \times 3 = 6 \times 3 = 18$.

Averages

The average of a set of numbers is equal to the sum of the numbers divided by the number of numbers.

For example, find the average of 3, 4, and 8.

Average $= (3 + 4 + 8) \div 3 = 5$

Averages will be covered in more detail in the Data Analysis & Statistics Chapter.

Operations: Practice

1. What is the difference between 84,763 and 27,888?

A. 56,875

B. 56,975

C. 64,985

D. 64,976

2. Nadine is totaling her accounts due and accounts payable for the month. She owes $496 to one creditor and $736 to another. She receives $1326 from one source of income and $139 from another. How much has she earned or lost this month?

A. lost $233

B. lost $333

C. gained $233

D. gained $333

3. Solve. 4 x 9 – 6 ÷ (2 + 1) =

A. 4

B. 10

C. 16

D. 34

4. Deidre went to the store and bought 5 notebooks, each cost $2. Then, she purchased 2 bags for $7 each. If she paid $30, how much change should she receive?

A. $6

B. $16

C. $24

D. $54

5. What is the product of 1408 and 321?

A. 422,400

B. 450,560

C. 423,808

D. 451,968

6. Solve equation to the right.

A. ⁵⁄₄

B. –⁵⁄₈

C. ³⁷⁄₄

D. –⁵⁄₄

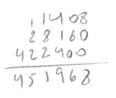

$$\frac{-3 \times 10 \div 2 - 6 + 4^2}{12 - 8 \times 2}$$

7. Solve 7958 ÷ 25 =

A. 318

B. 319

C. 318 R8

D. 319 R8

(handwritten work)
$$25 \overline{)7958}$$
31858 / 25 / 45 / 25 / 208 / 200 / 008

8. $\dfrac{(12 + 6) \div 3 \times (18 - 16)}{16 - 5 \times 2}$

(handwritten: 18, 6×, 2, 12/6 = 2, 10 = 6)

A. 2

B. ½

C. ⁵⁄₁₁

D. 18

Operations: Answer Explanations

1. A   To subtract large numbers, line up by place value. Don't forget to redistribute when necessary.

(handwritten subtraction)
$$\begin{array}{r} 84{,}763 \\ -\, 27{,}888 \\ \hline 56{,}875 \end{array}$$

2. C   First, add the total amount she earned. She received $1326 from one source of income and $139 from another. Then, find the total amount she owes. She owes one creditor $496 and another $736.

$$\begin{array}{r} 1326 \\ +\ 139 \\ \hline 1465 \end{array} \qquad \begin{array}{r} 496 \\ +\ 736 \\ \hline 1232 \end{array}$$

She owes $1232 and earned $1465. Therefore, she gained money. Subtract to find out how much she gained.

$$\begin{array}{r} 1465 \\ -\ 1232 \\ \hline 233 \end{array}$$

Gained $233.

3. D   Use order of operations. PEMDAS.

Parentheses first.

$4 \times 9 - 6 \div (2 + 1) = 4 \times 9 - 6 \div 3 =$

Multiply and Divide from left to right.

$4 \times 9 - 6 \div 3 = 36 - 6 \div 3 = 36 - 2 =$

Finally, Add and Subtract from left to right.

$36 - 2 = 34$

4. A   First, determine the total cost of what she spent. Then, subtract that from what she paid to find the change.

She bought 5 notebooks at $2 each. Multiply to find the total cost of the notebooks. 5 x $2 = $10.
She bought 2 bags at $7 each. Multiply to find total cost of bags. 2 x $7 = $14.

Now, add those two quantities to determine her total purchases. $10 + $14 = $24.

Finally, subtract the total from $30 to figure out how much change she received. $30–$24 = $6.

5. D   Line the numbers up by place value and multiply each digit of one number by each digit of the other number. Remember placeholder zeros. Then add the results.

$$
\begin{array}{r}
1408 \\
\times\ \ 321 \\
\hline
1408 \\
+\ \ 28160 \\
422400 \\
\hline
451968
\end{array}
$$

6. A

$$\frac{-3 \times 10 \div 2 - 6 + 4^2}{12 - 8 \times 2} =$$ Exponents - take 4 squared.

$$\frac{-3 \times 10 \div 2 - 6 + 16}{12 - 8 \times 2} =$$ Multiply / divide from left to right on top and bottom.

$$\frac{-30 \div 2 - 6 + 16}{12 - 16} =$$

$$\frac{-15 - 6 + 16}{12 - 16} =$$ Add / subtract from left to right on top and bottom.

$$\frac{-21 + 16}{-4} =$$

$$\frac{-5}{-4} =$$

$$\frac{5}{4}$$

7. C

$$
\begin{array}{r}
318\ \text{R8} \\
25\,\overline{)7958} \\
\underline{75} \\
45 \\
\underline{25} \\
208 \\
\underline{200} \\
8
\end{array}
$$

8. A   In the last step, you see that the fraction bar has the same meaning as divide. This will be explored further in the next chapter.

$$\frac{(12 + 6) \div 3 \times (18 - 16)}{16 - 5 \times 2} =$$

$$\frac{18 \div 3 \times 2}{16 - 5 \times 2} =$$

$$\frac{6 \times 2}{16 - 10} =$$

$$\frac{12}{16 - 10} =$$

$$\frac{12}{6} = 2$$

There are several properties of numbers, most of which you will already be aware of – even if you are unfamiliar with the names.

Associative

The associative property says that for problems containing only addition or only multiplication, grouping of numbers does not affect the result. In the cases below, it does not matter whether a and b or b and c are multiplied or added first, the result will always be the same.

$a + (b + c) = (a + b) + c$
$a(bc) = (ab)c$

For example, $3 + (4 + 5) = (3 + 4) + 5$ and $2(5 \times 4) = (2 \times 5) \times 4$.

Commutative

The commutative property states that for problems containing only multiplication or only addition, order does not matter.

$a + b = b + a$
$ab = ba$

For example, $3 + 5 = 5 + 3$ and $2 \times 6 = 6 \times 2$.

Distributive

The distributive property states:
$a(b + c) = ab + ac$

On the left hand side of the equation above, a is multiplied by the sum of b and c, and this is equivalent to the sum of a multiplied by b and a multiplied by c.

Example: $5(2 + 3 + 4) = 5(2) + 5(3) + 5(4) = 10 + 15 + 20 = 45$

Zero

The identity of addition is 0. Therefore, any number plus zero will equal itself. $17 + 0 = 17$
The product of any number and zero is 0. $17 \times 0 = 0$
Zero divided by any number is 0. $0 \div 17 = 0$
No number can be divided by 0. $17 \div 0$ can not be done.
Any number raised to the power of zero is 1. $17^0 = 1$

One

The identity of multiplication is 1. Therefore, any number times 1 will equal itself. $17 \times 1 = 17$.
Any number divided by 1 is itself. $17 \div 1 = 17$.
Any number raised to the power of 1 is itself. $17^1 = 17$

Properties of Arithmetic: Practice

1. The associative and commutative properties apply to which of the following operations?

A. Addition only

B. Addition and Multiplication

C. Adding and Subtraction

D. Addition, Subtraction, Multiplication, and Division

2. In the following problem, what properties were used from step 2 to 3 and step 3 to 4, respectively?

1. 73 x 101 + 200 =
2. 73(100 + 1) + 200 =
3. 7300 + 73 + 200 =
4. 7300 + 200 + 73 =
5. 7500 + 73 = 7573

A. Distributive, Associative

B. Associative, Commutative

C. Commutative, Distributive

D. Distributive, Commutative

3. Choose the best answer to replace the question mark.

   p(r − s)   **?**   pr − ps

A. >

B. <

C. =

D. Not enough information.

4. What is 8(9 + 6)7 ?

I. 7(9 + 6)8

II. 8x9 + 6x7

III. 8x9x7 + 8x6x7

A. I only

B. II only

C. I and III

D. I and II

5. Which property would you use to help you solve the following problem quickly in your head?

   5 x 73 x 2

A. Associative

B. Commutative

C. Inverse

D. Identity

6. Use the student work sample below to answer the question that follows.

1. 4(16 + 23) + 36 = 64 + 23 + 36
2. 64 + 23 + 36 = 64 + 36 + 23
3. 64 + 36 + 23 = 100 + 23
4. 100 + 23 = 123

What property does the student use incorrectly, and in which step?

A. Associative, Step 1

B. Distributive, Step 1

C. Distributive, Step 3

D. Commutative, Step 3

7. Which of the following statements are true about properties of addition and subtraction?
   I. The commutative property applies to addition only if a and b are both positive.
   II. The associative property applies to addition only if a, b, and c are positive
   III. The commutative and associative properties apply to subtraction.

A. I and II.

B. III only.

C. I, II, and III.

D. None of the statements.

8. Which of the following statements are true about properties of multiplication and division?
   I. The commutative property applies to multiplication only if a and b are both integers.
   II. The associative property applies to multiplication only if a, b, and c are integers.
   III. The commutative and associative properties apply to division.

A. I and II.

B. III only.

C. I, II, and III.

D. None of the statements.

Properties of Arithmetic: Answer Explanations

1. B   The associative and commutative properties only hold true for addition and multiplication. Here are some examples:

Associative
Addition: $9 + (4 + 5) = (9 + 4) + 5$, Both equal 18.
Subtraction: $9 - (4 + 5) \neq (9 - 4) + 5$, Left side = 0, Right side=10
Multiplication: $6 \times (2 \times 5) = (6 \times 2) \times 5$, Both equal 120
Division: $(12 \div 4) \div 2 \neq 12 \div (4 \div 2)$, The left side equals 1.5, right side equals 6

Commutative
Addition: $9 + 4 + 5 = 5 + 4 + 9$, Both equal 18.
Subtraction: $9 - 4 - 5 \neq 5 - 4 - 9$, Left side = 0, Right side=−8
Multiplication: $6 \times 2 \times 5 = 2 \times 6 \times 5$, Both equal 120
Division: $40 \div 4 \div 2 \neq 4 \div 40 \div 2$, The left side equals 5, right side equals 0.05

2. D   1. 73 x 101 + 200 =
           2. 73(100 + 1) + 200 =
           3. 7300 + 73 + 200 =
           4. 7300 + 200 + 73 =
           5. 7500 + 73 = 7573

In the above problem, the distributive property was used to help calculate 73 x 101. The distributive property states that a(b + c) = ab + ac.

Then, from steps 3 to 4, the order of the addition problem was changed. The commutative property states that for addition, order does not matter.
Distributive, Commutative

3. C   This is an example of the distributive property, with just different variables. Also, do not get thrown off by the minus sign. Remember, that the original definition of the distributive property has addition, but subtraction is the same as the addition of the opposite.

The distributive property states that you multiply each term on the outside by each term on the inside.
p(r − s) = pr − ps

4. C   8(9 + 6)7: To solve this problem, you would use both the commutative and distributive properties.

I. 7(9 + 6)8: This option is only different from the original because the positions of 7 and 8 are moved. The original problem is the multiplication of 3 expressions 8, 9+6, and 7. The commutative property states that you can multiply in any order and the result will still be the same. Option I is just the multiplication of those expressions in a different order. I is the same.

II. 8x9 + 6x7: This answer is not the same. Use the distributive property on the first two expressions: 8 and (9 + 6). To expand this, you multiply the 8 by every term inside the parentheses. 8(9+6) = 8x9 + 8x6. Then, you would multiply this result by 7. Even before multiplying by 7, you see that option II is different.

III. 8x9x7 + 8x6x7: To see if this one is true, perform the distributive property twice. First, with 8 and (9+6) and then take that result and multiply it by 7 by using the distributive property.
8(9+6)7 = (8x9 + 8x6)7 = 8x9x7 + 8x6x7
III is also true.

5. B   5 x 73 x 2
Multiplying 5 by 73 in your head would be quite difficult. However, multiplying 5 by 2 first would give you 10. Then, you could multiply 10 by 73 in your head to give you 730.

Instead of multiplying 5 x 73 and then that result by 2, you would multiply 5 x 2 and that result by 73.

5 x 73 x 2 = 5 x 2 x 73

Changing the order that you multiply is the commutative property.

6. B   From Step 1 to Step 2, the student attempted to use the distributive property. The distributive property states that a(b + c) = ab + ac.

In this case, the correct use of distributive property is:
4(16 + 23) + 36 = 4(16) + 4(23) + 36 = 64 + 92 + 36

The student forgot to multiply the 4 by the 23.

7. D **Commutative Property:** The commutative property of addition states that you can add elements in any order and the sum would still be the same. In terms of variables, the commutative property of addition is written: $a + b = b + a$.

There are no restrictions on whether or not the terms are positive or negative. You can add numbers in any order whether they are positive or negative, the result will always be the same.

For example, $3 + 5 = 5 + 3$ and $-4 + 7 = 7 + -4$.

The commutative property does not apply to subtraction. You can not subtract in any order and get the same result. For instance, $8 - 2 = 6$, while $2 - 8 = -6$.

Therefore, statements I and III are false.

Associative Property: The associative property for addition states that you can group terms for an addition problem in different ways but still get the same results. Written with variables: $(a + b) + c = a + (b + c)$. There are no restrictions on whether or not the terms are positive or negative.

Note that the associative property is simlar to the commutative property. For instance, in the expression: $(a + b) + c$, if you follow the order of operations, you would add $a + b$ and then add the result to c.

In the associative property, that expression equals: $a + (b + c)$. Here, add $b + c$ and then add the result to a.

You can add the three terms in different orders and get the same result. Since the commutative property has no restrictions on whether the terms are positive or negative, so does the associative property.

The associative property does not apply to subtraction. This can be seen with a counterexample:
$(12 - 4) - 2 = 8 - 2 = 6$
$12 - (4 - 2) = 12 - 2 = 10$
The results are clearly not the same. Statement II is also false.

8. D **Commutative Property:** The commutative property of multiplication states that you can multiply terms in any order and the product would still be the same. In terms of variables, the commutative property of multiplication is written: $ab = ba$.

There are no restrictions on whether or not the terms are integers. You can multiply numbers in any order whether they are fractions, decimals, integers, or any real number, the result will always be the same.
For example, $2.1 \times 3 = 3 \times 2.1 = 6.3$.

The commutative property does not apply to division. You can not divide in any order and get the same result. For instance, $8 \div 4 = 2$, while $4 \div 8 = 0.5$.
Therefore, statements I and III are false.

Associative Property: The associative property for multiplication states that you can group terms for a multiplication problem in different ways but still get the same results. Written with variables: $(ab)c = a(bc)$. There are no restrictions on whether or not the terms are integers or any real number.

Note the associative property is simlar to the commutative property. For instance, in the expression: $(ab)c$, if you follow the order of operations, you would multiply a times b and then multiply the product by c.

The associative property states that $(ab)c =$ equal to: $a(bc)$.
In this expression, you would multiply b and c and then multiply the result by a.

In other words, you can multiply the three terms in different order and get the same result. Since the commutative property has no restrictions on whether the terms are integers, so does the associative property.

The associative property does not apply to division. This can be seen with a counterexample:
$(24 \div 4) \div 2 = 6 \div 2 = 3$
$24 \div (4 \div 2) = 24 \div 2 = 12$
The results are clearly not the same. Statement II is also false.

As discussed in the "Foundations" chapter, all numbers greater than zero are positive and all numbers less than zero are negative. This can be represented on a number line. Zero is neither positive nor negative.

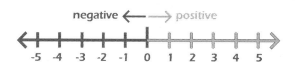

Addition and Subtraction of Signed Numbers

Use the following techniques to add and subtract signed numbers.

Add two positive numbers:

Add as normal. Example: $23 + 74 = 97$

Add two negative numbers:

Add as usual, but place a negative sign in front of the sum. Example: $-23 + -74 = -97$

Add one positive and one negative number:

Subtract the smaller number from the larger and then assign the sign of the greater number to the result.

Example: $-48 + 32$; Subtract $48-32=16$. Since 48 is greater and it was negative, the answer is negative. $-48 + 32 = -16$

Example: $-32 + 48$; Subtract $48-32=16$. Since 48 is greater and it is positive, the answer is positive. $-32 + 48 = 16$

Subtraction of a positive number:

When dealing with a combination of positive and negative numbers, treat subtraction as the addition of a negative number.

Example: $25 - 75$ is the same as $25 + -75$. Now follow the rules you learned for adding signed numbers. $75-25=50$; 75 is greater, and it is negative, so answer is negative. $25 + -75 = -50$

Example: $-25 - 75$ is the same as $-25 + -75$. Add the numbers as usual, but keep the negative sign since they are both negative. $-25 + -75 = -100$

Subtraction of a negative number:

Subtracting a negative number is equivalent to adding a positive number.

Example: $32 - -45 = 32 + 45 = 77$

Example: $-15 - -40 = -15 + 40 = 25$

Multiplication and Division of Signed Numbers

To multiply or divide by negative or positive numbers, use the following rules.

A positive times a positive is positive.

A negative times a negative is positive.

A positive times a negative is negative.

Another way to think about that, is if there are an even number of negative signs then you get a positive answer. If there are an odd number of negative signs, the result is negative.

Example: $-2 \times -3 = 6$

Example: $-1 \times -1 \times -1 = -1$

Absolute Value

The absolute value of a number is its distance from zero. Absolute value is always expressed in positive terms.

Example: $|\ 42\ | = 42$

Example: $|\ -13\ | = 13$

Signed Numbers & Absolute Value: Practice

1. Solve. −49 + 53 =

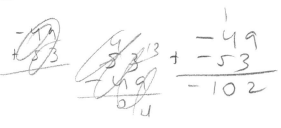

   A. −4

   B. 4

   C. 102

   D. −102

2. Choose the best answer to replace the question mark.

     20 − 70   ?   −70 + 20

   A. ≥

   B. >

   C. <

   D. =

3. Solve. 79 x −1 x −1 =

   A. −79

   B. 97

   C. 79

   D. 77

4. Two positive, odd integers and one negative, even integer are multiplied together. Which of the following could be their product?

   A. −60.5

   B. −15

   C. 100

   D. −100

5. Choose the best answer to replace the question mark.

     0   ?   All Positive Numbers

   A. >

   B. <

   C. ≤

   D. ≥

6. Solve. (−3 x 20) ÷ −4 − 40 =

   A. −55

   B. −25

   C. 25

   D. −104

7. Solve. $|20 - 33| - 17 + 6(-5) =$

A. –60 -13

B. –34 $13 - 17$

C. –10

D. 34 $-30 + -35$

8. A math teacher curves all the test scores so that the average is always a 70 on her tests. Sandra gets a 74 on her first test, and then on the next test gets a score 11 below that. She studies much harder for her 3rd test and gets 15 points higher than her 2nd test. Finally, for the 4th test which was extremely difficult, Sandra gets 22 points below her score on the 3rd test. How does Sandra's score on her 4th test compare to the class average?

1) $74 - 11$

2) 63

3) 78

4) 56

A. 18 below

B. 14 below

C. 10 below

D. Class Average

Signed Numbers & Absolute Value: Answer Explanations

1. D   Subtraction is equivalent to adding a negative number.
$-49 - 53 = -49 + -53$

To add two negative numbers, add the two numbers and give the sum a negative sign since they are both negative.
$-49 + -53 = -102$

2. D $20 - 70 = -70 + 20$

These two expressions are identical. They are simply written in a different order.

You can solve each side to see:
$20 - 70 = 20 + -70 = -50$
$-70 + 20 = -50$

3. C $79 \times -1 \times -1$

To multiply signed numbers, first multiply the numbers and the determine the signs.
$79 \times 1 \times 1 = 79$

Then count the negative signs. There are two, which is an even number, so the answer is positive.

Another way to think about it is multiply the first two numbers, and then multiply the result by the third number.
$79 \times -1 = -79$ (since positive times negative = negative)
$-79 \times -1 = 79$ (since negative times negative = positive) Answer: C = 79.

4. D   Let's examine each answer choice.

A: You know that the product of integers is always an integer, so eliminate answer choice A.

B: Even x even= even
Even x odd = even
Odd x odd = odd
In this case, we have odd x odd x even = odd x even = even
Eliminate answer choice b.

C: Positive x positive = positive
Positive x negative = negative
In this case, we have positive x positive x negative = negative
Eliminate answer choice c.

D: This is the only answer remaining, so it must be correct.
Here is one possible option.
Positive Odd x Positive Odd x Negative Even = 25 x 1 x –4 = –100

5. B   Positive numbers are all those greater than zero. Zero is neither positive nor negative. Therefore, zero is less than all positive numbers.

0 < All Positive Numbers

6. B   To solve this question, follow the order of operations and rules for signed numbers.

–3 x 20 ÷ –4 – 40 =

The first step is to multiply –3 x 20 = –60
–60 ÷ –4 – 40 =

Next, divide: –60 ÷ –4 = 15
15 – 40 =

To subtract, change the problem into the addition of a negative.
15 – 40 = 15 + –40 = –25

7. B | 20 – 33 | – 17 + 6(–5) =

Following the order of operations, first solve whats in parentheses. You can treat what is in the absolute value symbols as parentheses.

| 20 – 33 | – 17 + 6(–5) =
| –13 | – 17 + 6(–5) =
13 – 17 + 6(–5)

Next, perform the multiplication. Finally, working from left to right add or subtract.
13 – 17 + 6(–5) = 13 – 17 – 30 = –4 – 30 = –34

8. B   Sandra gets a 74 on her first test. The next test she scores 11 below that. That means the score on her 2nd test was 74 – 11 = 63. On the third test she gets 15 points higher than that = 63 + 15 = 78. Her final test was 22 points below the third. Fourth test = 78 – 22 = 56.

Now, compare 56 to the class average of 70.

70 – 56 = 14. Therefore, Sandra scored 14 points below the average on her 4th test.

Powers or Exponents

The terms powers and exponents are interchangeable. The power or exponent represents how many times a number is multiplied by itself. In the expression 2^5, the base number 2 is raised to the 5th power. When a base number is raised to a power, it is multiplied by itself a number of times equal to the power.

$2^5 = 2 \times 2 \times 2 \times 2 \times 2 = 32$
$4^3 = 4 \times 4 \times 4 = 64$

Multiplying and Dividing Exponents

When multiplying numbers with exponents, if their bases are the same, you can just add the exponents.
For example, $2^3 \times 2^4$ is equal to $(2 \times 2 \times 2) \times (2 \times 2 \times 2 \times 2) = 2^7$
or, since both numbers had a base of 2, you could just add the exponents $(3 + 4 = 7)$.

When dividing numbers with exponents, if their bases are the same, you can just subtract the exponents.
For example, $4^7 \div 4^5 = 4^2$

Negative Exponents

Numbers can also be raised to negative exponents, which indicates that the expression is a fraction with 1 as the numerator and the base raised to the power as the denominator. (See Fractions chapter for help)

$2^{-5} = 1/(2 \times 2 \times 2 \times 2 \times 2) = \frac{1}{32}$
$4^{-2} = 1/(4 \times 4) = \frac{1}{16}$

Scientific Notation

Scientific Notation is a way of writing numbers (usually very small or very large) as powers of ten. Numbers written in scientific notation take the form of coefficient x 10^{power}. The coefficient must be greater than or equal to 1 and less than 10.

$63{,}500{,}000 = 6.35 \times 10^7$
$470{,}000 = 4.7 \times 10^5$
$0.0000348 = 3.48 \times 10^{-5}$
$0.0023 = 2.3 \times 10^{-3}$

As can be seen in the examples above, first find the coefficient which will be a number between 1 and 10. To figure out the coefficient, place the decimal point after the digit in the greatest place value. Then, determine how many times you moved the decimal places, either in the positive or negative direction.

When multiplying numbers in scientific notation, use the commutative property of multiplication to rearrange the terms and then multiply the coefficients and then the powers of ten.
$(3 \times 10^8) \times (2 \times 10^{-5}) = (3 \times 2) \times (10^8 \times 10^{-5}) = 6 \times 10^3$

Roots

A root is the opposite of an exponent. Since the square of a number is a number times itself, for example $9^2 = 81$, the square root of a number is what number times itself equals that number. The square root of 81 is 9. This is written $\sqrt{81}$.

To find the third root of 64, you need to figure out what number times itself 3 times gives you 64. Since, $4 \times 4 \times 4 = 64$, the third root of 64 is 4.

Exponents & Scientific Notation: Practice

1. $(-3)^4 =$ -3 x -3 x -3 x -3
+9 -3 = -27

3/81

   A. –12

   B. 12

   C. –81

   D. 81

2. 236,900 can be written in scientific notation as:

   A. 2.369×10^2

   B. 2.369×10^5

   C. 2.369×10^6

   D. 2.369×10^{-5}

3. Write 9,000,000.00 in scientific notation.

   A. 9×10^6

   B. 9×10^7

   C. 9×10^8

   D. 9×10^9

4. 2.3×10^{-4} is equal to what number?

   A. 0.0023

   B. 0.00023

   C. 2300

   D. 23000

5. What is the product of (2×10^3) and (4×10^{-7}) ?

   A. 8×10^{10}

   B. 8×10^{-21}

   C. 8×10^{-4}

   D. 8×10^4

6. $(-2)^4 - 3^2 =$ 16-9

   A. –25

   B. –14

   C. 7

   D. 25

7. What is the quotient of 3×10^{-4} and 6×10^7 in scientific notation?

    A. 5×10^{-10}

    B. 2×10^{11}

    C. 5×10^{-12}

    D. 1.8×10^4

8. $2^5 \times 2^4 \div 2^2 =$

    A. 2^3

    B. 2^7

    C. 2^{10}

    D. 2^{11}

 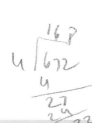

Exponents & Scientific Notation: Answer Explanations

1. D   A number raised to a power is multiplied by itself the number of times indicated by the power.

$(-3)^4 = (-3) \times (-3) \times (-3) \times (-3) = 81$

Notice that there was an even number of negative signs (four), so the answer is positive.

2. B   To write 236,900 in scientific notation, we first place a decimal point after the digit in the greatest place value: 2.369. Now, we determine how many times that decimal point would need to move to equal the original number, which is 5 times. Write the number of times the decimal point moved as a power of ten.

2.369×10^5

3. A   When writing a number in scientific notation you need to figure out how many times you are moving the decimal point.

To go from 9 to 9,000,000.00, move the decimal point 6 places in the positive direction. Therefore, 6 is the exponent of the power of 10.

$9,000,000.00 = 9 \times 10^6$

4. B   This problem asks us to take the scientific notation of a number, and write the number in standard form.

2.3×10^{-4}

The exponent in the power of ten tells you what direction and how many places to move the decimal point. In this case, we want to move the decimal point 4 places in the negative direction. This will give you 0.00023.

5. C $(2 \times 10^3) \times (4 \times 10^{-7})$

To multiply numbers in scientific notation, break the problem into two problems. First, multiply the coefficients, then multiply the powers of ten.

$2 \times 4 = 8$. Therefore, the new coefficient will be 8.

$10^3 \times 10^{-7}$: To multiply powers, add the exponents.
$10^3 \times 10^{-7} = 10^{-4}$

You can also think of this as moving the decimal point 3 places in the positive direction and then moving the decimal point 7 places in the negative direction, which is the same as moving the decimal 4 places in the negative direction.

Now combine the two products: 8×10^{-4}.

6. C $(-2)^4 - 3^2$

$(-2)^4 = (-2) \times (-2) \times (-2) \times (-2) = 16$
$3^2 = 3 \times 3 = 9$

$16 - 9 = 7$

7. C $(3 \times 10^{-4}) \div (6 \times 10^7)$

To find the quotient of two numbers in scientific notation, you should break it into smaller problems. First, divide the coefficients, then divide the powers of 10 by subtracting the exponents, and then put those results into scientific notation.

$3 \div 6 = 0.5$
$-4 - 7 = -11$

0.5×10^{-11}

Unfortunately, 0.5×10^{-11} is not in proper scientific notation since 0.5 is not between 1 and 10. So, convert 0.5 to proper scientific notation and multiply it by 10^{-11}.

$0.5 \times 10^{-11} =$
$5 \times 10^{-1} \times 10^{-11} =$
5×10^{-12}

8. B $2^5 \times 2^4 \div 2^2 =$

Let's break this problem into 2 separate problems. Let's first find the product and then take that result and find the quotient.

$2^5 \times 2^4$: When multiplying numbers with exponents, if the bases are the same, you add the exponents.

$2^5 \times 2^4 = 2^9$

Another way to think about it is that 2^5 is 2 times itself 5 times, and 2^4 is 2 times itself 4 times, therefore the product will be 2 times itself 9 times $= 2^9$.

Now, the second part. Take the 2^9 and divide it by 2^2. To divide numbers with exponents, if the bases are the same, you can subtract the exponents. Therefore, $2^9 \div 2^2 = 2^7$.

Word Problems

Solving mathematical word problems is a great way to demonstrate your deep understanding of mathematical concepts and practice applying them to real–world situations. There is no single way to approach or solve word problems, but there are several strategies you may find helpful.

Understand what the Question is asking

Read the problem carefully a few times to make sure you understand exactly what the question is asking.

Focus on Relevant Info

Once you know what you are looking for, recognize extraneous information and disregard it. For example, try to find out the relevant information from the following scenario:

Anna, Ralph, and Susan were sharing a pizza that cost $12.50. Ralph ate 1/7, Susan ate 3/8, and Anna ate 4/9. How much pizza did the two girls eat?

The price of the pizza and the amount Ralph ate are extraneous and can be ignored. To solve this question, simply add the fractions Susan and Anna ate.

Clue Words

Translate words into mathematical operations. For example, the word "of" often indicates multiplication. Examples: Fifteen percent of 20. 1/3 of the 60 students are seniors.

There is no guarantee that a certain word will always translate to the same operation; you must read the problem and think about what is actually happening. Still, the following chart provides a basic list of useful operation clue words.

Clue Words	Operation/Symbol
is, are, was, were, equals, totals	equals, =
of, by, times, product	multiplication, x
difference, less than, reduced	subtraction, –
together, more than, sum, all, total	addition, +
ratio, groups of, separated into	division, ÷

Diagrams

Another strategy for approaching word problems is to draw a picture or diagram to make the situation easier to comprehend and to help yourself see what information is missing.

Example: Carmen walked 3 miles due North and Sam walked 4 miles due East. if they started at the same point, how far apart were they when they stopped walking?

In this case, drawing a diagram helps to see that the distance between Carmen and Sam is the hypotenuse of a right triangle. (See Geometry – Triangles lesson for help)

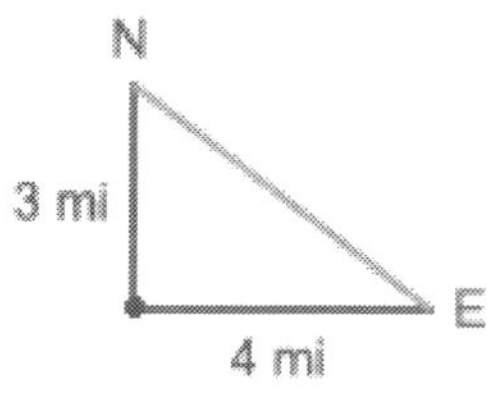

Multiple Steps

For complex word problems, it is often necessary to break a problem into multiple steps to reach the answer. Many people become confused when they do not plan out those steps before beginning calculations and when they do not separate a problem into manageable pieces.

Example: Sandra went shopping for school supplies. She bought 3 notebooks which cost $0.75 each and 2 packs of pens for $2.50 each. If she paid with a $10 bill, how much change did Sandra get?

This is a simple example of a multiple step problem. First, find the price of all 3 notebooks by multiplying 3 by $0.75. Next, determine the total cost of the pens by multiplying 2 by $2.50. Then add the cost of the notebooks and the pens to final the total cost of the items purchased. Finally, subtract the total cost from $10 to determine the change received.

Write down Information

If you have no idea how to begin a particular problem, it often helps to write down the information contained in the problem in an organized way. This may bring forward connections between pieces of information.

Connections between Operations

This section is meant to serve as a review of the different ways of looking at the four basic operations and to highlight the connections among those operations. It also introduces a few additional methods of performing these operations.

Addition and Subtraction

Addition and subtraction are a pair of inverse or opposite operations, meaning that either operation can be undone by the other. For example, $12 - 5 = 7$, $7 + 5 = 12$. Subtracting 5 from a number and then adding 5 to the result will lead back to the original number.

Adding is sometimes taught as "counting forward" from a particular number. For example, $29 + 3$ would be counting forward 3 times: 30, 31, 32. Subtraction can be thought of as counting backwards: $32 - 3$: 31, 30, 29.

Multiplication and Division

Multiplication and division make up the other set of inverse operations. Each of them can be represented in many ways, here are a few:

Multiplication is generally introduced as repeated addition: adding a number to itself the number of times indicated by the multiplier.
$4 \times 5 = 4 + 4 + 4 + 4 + 4$

Division is often shown as repeated subtraction – subtracting the divisor from the dividend until reaching zero. For repeated subtraction, the number of times the divisor is subtracted the dividend is equal to the quotient.
$12 \div 3 = ?$, $12 - 3 - 3 - 3 - 3 = 0$, $12 \div 3 = 4$

Rules for Evens and Odds

Any time two even numbers are added or subtracted, the result will be even. Examples: $4 + 8 = 12$, $22 - 6 = 16$.
Any time two odd numbers are added or subtracted, the result will be even. Examples: $13 + 5 = 18$, $21 - 7 = 14$.
When one even and one odd number are added or subtracted, the result will be odd. Examples: $13 - 2 = 11$, $5 - 8 = -3$.
When an even number is multiplied by any number, even or odd, the result will be even. Example: $2 \times 4 = 8$, $6 \times 5 = 30$
When an odd number is multiplied by an odd number, the result will be odd. Example: $3 \times 5 = 15$, $7 \times 11 = 77$.
For division, you may get remainders when dividing even and odd numbers.

Word Problems: Practice

1. Jennifer gave Vanessa half of her candy. Vanessa gave David half of the candy she received from Jennifer. David ate 6 pieces and gave the remaining 4 pieces to John. How many pieces of candy did Jennifer start with?

    A. 5

    B. 20

    C. 40

    D. 60

2. An even integer divided by an even integer could be:

    I. even

    II. odd

    III. fraction

    A. I only

    B. II only

    C. I and III

    D. I, II, and III

3. A car's gas tank holds 14 gallons. If the car had a full tank before being driven 250 miles and then was filled again, how many gallons were needed to refill the tank?

If you wanted to answer the question above, what additional piece of information is needed?

    A. Amount of time it took to drive the 250 miles.

    B. The car's average fuel consumption in miles per gallon.

    C. The price of gas when the tank was refilled.

    D. The average speed the car is driven in miles per hour.

4. If you have an average of 82 after 4 math tests, what do you need on the 5th test to increase your average to an 85?

    A. 88

    B. 92

    C. 95

    D. 97

5. If you add 17 to a number and then divide the sum by 3, how can you manipulate the result to return to the original number?

    A. subtract 17 and then multiply by 3

    B. add 17 and then divide by 3

    C. multiply by 3 and then subtract 17

    D. subtract 17 and then divide by 3

6. If the remainder of a number when divided by 7 is 2, what is the remainder when 4 times that number is divided by 7?

_14 x 4_

    A. 1

    B. 2

    C. 4

    D. 6

7. A bottle distributor is dividing bottles into equal sized groups for shipping. Each day he only uses one type of box, either boxes that hold 16 bottles, 20 bottles, or 25 bottles. On this particular day, there will be no bottles leftover regardless of which type of box he uses. What is a possible number of bottles that must be shipped today?

    A. 300

    B. 360

    C. 400

    D. 450

8. Use the following computation to answer the question.

The letters a, b, c, d, e, f, and g represent the specific digits of the numbers involved in the long division computation to the right. The letters a, b, c, d, e, f, and g are not variables.

$$\begin{array}{r} eb \\ d\overline{)abc} \\ af \\ \hline gc \\ gb \\ \hline g \end{array}$$

Which of the following equations represents the correct computation?

    A. $abc \div d = eb.g$

    B. $abc \div d = eb + g$

    C. $abc \div d = eb \; \frac{g}{d}$

    D. $abc \div d = eb \; \frac{g}{abc}$

Word Problems: Answer Explanations

1. C   This problem is best solved by working backwards.

    John: Got 4 pieces.

    David: Ate 6 pieces and gave 4 to John. 6 + 4 = 10. Got 10 pieces.

    Vanessa: Half for herself and half for David. Gave David 10 pieces. If 10 is half, then Vanessa must have received 20. Got 20 pieces.

    Jennifer: Half for herself and half for Vanessa. Gave Vanessa 20 pieces. If 20 is half, then Jennifer must have started with 40.

    You can check your work by going through the problem in order.

    Jennifer started with 40 pieces.

2. D   An even integer divided by an even could be even. For example: $20 \div 2 = 10$.

An even divided by an even can be odd. For example: $12 \div 4 = 3$.

An even divided by an even can be a fraction. For example: $6 \div 8 = 3/4$

Answer D: I, II, and III

3. B   The question asks how many gallons are needed to refill the tank. Therefore, we must figure out how many gallons were used when driving the 250 miles. If you know how much gas is consumed for every mile driven, you can calculate the amount of gas used.

The time it takes (answer A), the price (answer C), and the speed (answer D), will not help you determine the number of gallons used which is needed to figure out how many gallons are needed to refill the tank.

4. D   To calculate the average, you find the sum and then divide by the number of terms. In average problems, it is often easier to think of the problem in terms of sums.

Average = Sum / Number of numbers

Sum = Average × Number of numbers

In this problem, first find the sum of the scores on the first 4 math tests: $82 \times 4 = 328$.
Then, if you want an average of 85 on all 5 tests, the sum of your scores must be: $85 \times 5 = 425$.

If you know the sum on 4 tests and you know the sum that you want on 5 tests, if you subtract, you will find the score that you need on the 5th test. $425 - 328 = 97$.

5. C   To "undo" an operation, apply its inverse. Addition is the inverse of subtraction. Multiplication is the inverse of division.

Since division was the last operation performed, you must first do the opposite of this operation. The inverse of divide by 3 is multiply by 3.

The next operation to undo is adding 17, so you must subtract 17.

Multiply by 3 and then subtract 17.

6. A   To solve this problem, first pick a number that has a remainder of 2 when divided by 7. There are an infinite number of possible numbers to choose from, including: 2, 9, 16, and 23.

Let's choose 9. Now, the problem asks what is remainder when 4 times that number is divided by 7. Multiply 9 by 4 and divide by 7 to find remainder.

$9 \times 4 = 36$
$36 \div 7 = 5$ remainder 1

Remainder is 1.

7. C The problem states that the number of bottles can be divided evenly into any type of box. Therefore, the number of bottles must be divisible by 16, 20, and 25. There are many ways to approach this problem : you could divide each answer by 16, 20, and 25 to see which answer is evenly divisible by all three numbers; you could find the least common multiple of 16, 20, and 25 and know that the answer must be a multiple of the LCM; or, you could find the factors of 16, 20, and 25 and ensure that they go into each answer. Remember, the least common multiple is the smallest number that is divisible by the original numbers. Let's find the LCM using the factors and see if that helps us get the answer quickly. First, find the prime factorization of 16, 20, and 25.

$16 = 2 \times 2 \times 2 \times 2 = 2^4$
$20 = 2 \times 2 \times 5 = 2^2 5$
$25 = 5 \times 5 = 5^2$

Therefore, we know that the correct answer must be divisible by four 2s and two 5s, as this is the largest occurrence of each factor (there are four 2s in 16 and two 5s in 25, and 20 has a combination of the other factors).

Now, we could go through each answer and make sure it is divisible by 24 and 52 or we could find the LCM by multiplying these and then ensuring the answer choice is divisible by that number.

$2^4 5^2 = 2 \times 2 \times 2 \times 2 \times 5 \times 5 = 400$

This actually already leads us to the answer as choice C is the LCM.

8. C This is a long division problem with a remainder. The problem shows the steps and work involved with dividing abc by d.

Sometimes, when faced with questions without numbers, it is sometimes easier to write out a similar problem with actual numbers so you can see the pattern that is developed. For instance, you could write out the steps to divide 20 by 7, and you will see that you get 2 with a remainder of 6. Therefore, the computation could be written as: $20 \div 7 = 2\,\frac{6}{7}$. Now, if you think of the letters in this problem, abc would be 20, d would be 7, 2 would be eb, and the remainder g would be 6. Thus, abc $\div$ d = eb $\frac{g}{d}$, which is answer C.

Another way to approach the problem is to use reason and analyze the setup of the problem. In a long division problem, the number inside the symbol is the dividend and the number on the outside is the divisor. In this problem, abc is the dividend and d is the divisor. The result of a long division problem will always be on top of the symbol, in this case the result is eb. Then, we notice that this problem has a remainder since it doesn't have a 0 at the bottom. The remainder is g. The remainder can be expressed as a fraction, with the remainder written as the numerator and the divisor as the denominator. Therefore, the remainder is $\frac{g}{d}$.

abc $\div$ d = eb $\frac{g}{d}$

1. In a family, the oldest child is four times the sum of the younger children's ages. If the younger children are 1 and 3, what is the oldest child's age?

A. 10

B. 11

C. 13

D. 16

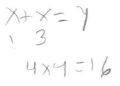

2. Choose which of the following are true about 21,936:

    I. It is divisible by 12.
    II. It is divisible by 8.
    III. It is divisible by 6.

A. I only

B. I and II

C. I and III

D. I, II, and III

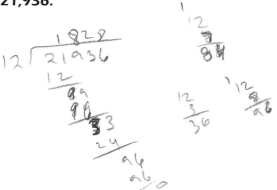

3. On an extremely cold day in Chicago, the temperature at noon was 3°. By 6PM, the temperature had dropped another 5 degrees. If the wind chill factor reduces the temperature by another 10 degrees, what does it feel like outside at 6PM factoring in the wind chill?

A. −18°

B. −12°

C. −8°

D. 8°

4. Which of the following is a set of four consecutive odd integers?

A. 1, 2, 3, 4

B. 0, 1, 3, 5

C. −9, −11, −13, −17

D. −3, −1, 1, 3

5. Which property could you use to more easily calculate the following product?

    815 x 100.1

A. associative

B. commutative

C. distributive

D. identity

6. $(-1)^6 - (-1)^5 - (-1)^4 =$

A. –3   *[handwritten]* $-1 \times -1 = 1 \times -1 = -1 \times -1 = 1 \times -1 = -1 \times -1 = 1$

B. –1

C. 1

D. 3

7. If the length of one living room is 1.2 x 10^1 meters and the length of a bacteria is 2 x 10^{-6} meters, how many times longer is the room?

A. 6×10^6 *[handwritten]* 2.2×10^{-5}

B. 6×10^8

C. 2.4×10^{-5}

D. 2.4×10^7

8. Which number line shows how to solve −3 − 4?

A.

B.

C.

D.

9. The sum of an even and an odd is:

A. always odd   *[handwritten]* $2 + 3 = 5$ $2 + 21 = 23$

B. always even   *[handwritten]* $4 + 7 = 11$

C. sometimes odd and sometimes even   *[handwritten]* $6 + 13 = 19$

D. no way to tell without actual numbers

10. If you start with an even number. Then, you add it to an odd number, multiply it by a different odd number, and then subtract the original even number, the result will be:

A. Even   *[handwritten]* $2 + 3 = 5 \times 3 = 15 - 2 = 13$

B. Odd

C. Zero

D. Not enough information.

11. Which answer choice is the largest?

A. $(-2)^0$

B. $(-2)^7$

C. $(-2)^8$

D. -2^{10}

12. Which of the following problems could be solved by finding the product of 3.5 and 6?

A. You have a string that is 6 feet long and you need pieces that are each 3.5 feet. How many pieces can you make from the string?

B. There are 6 documentaries whose average length is 3.5 hours. How many total hours of film are there?

C. You have $6 and go to a store and buy $3.50 worth of supplies. How much change do you have?

D. You are making cookies and put in 6 tablespoons of sugar. The recipe calls for an additional 3.5 tablespoons, how many total tablespoons have you put in?

13. What mistake did the student make in her calculations?

1.	$14 - 3 \times 5(12 \div 2 \times 3)$
2.	$14 - 3 \times 5(12 \div 6)$
3.	$14 - 3 \times 5(2)$
4.	$14 - 15(2)$
5.	$14 - 30$
6.	-16

A. Step 1 to 2. She should have calculated $12 \div 2$ first.

B. Step 2 to 3. She should have performed the distributive property next.

C. Step 3 to 4. She should have calculated 5(2) next.

D. No mistakes. Student got correct answer.

14. Order the following from least to greatest:

I. 300,000 + 80,000

II. 30,000 + 9000 + 900

III. 300,000 + 70,000 + 900 + 90

A. I, II, III

B. II, I, III

C. III, II, I

D. II, III, I

15. How many integers between 1 and 1000, inclusive, are divisible by both 5 and 8?

A. 25

B. 76

C. 125

D. 200

16. Victoria and Jerry are running for Student Council. Victoria has 273 votes and Jerry has 289 votes. If the first to reach 350 votes wins, how many more votes does Victoria need than Jerry?

   A. 16

   B. 61

   C. 77

   D. 212

17. Solve. $-12 + 3 \times -7 + |-4 + 6| \times 6 =$

   A. −45

   B. −21

   C. 21

   D. 27

18. What is the product of the least common multiple and greatest common factor of 12, 8, and 6?

   A. 24

   B. 36

   C. 48

   D. 96

19. For the number 63,485, find the product of the value represented by the number 4 and the value represented by the number 3.

   A. 12

   B. 1200

   C. 12,000

   D. 1,200,000

20. The prime factorization of $n = pg^3$, where p and g are different prime numbers. What are all the factors of n?

   A. p, g

   B. 1, 3, p, g, pg^3

   C. 1, p, g, pg, pg^2, pg^3

   D. 1, g, g^2, g^3, p, pg, pg^2, pg^3

1. D Translate the problem from words to numbers. Start with the ages they give you.

The question calls for the "sum of the younger children's ages" and the problem tells you that the "younger children are 1 and 3". Translated: 1 + 3.

The question states that the oldest child is "four times the sum". Translated: 4 x (1 + 3).

Now solve for the oldest child's age.
4 x (1 + 3) = 4 x 4 = 16

2. D To figure out whether or not a number is divisible by 12, you can divide by 12 and see if it goes in evenly. However, the easier way is to check if the number is divisible by both 3 and 4.

To determine divisibility for 3, remember you can add the digits and check if the sum is divisible by 3. 2 + 1 + 9 + 3 + 6 = 21. 21 is divisible by 3, therefore, 21,936 is also divisible by 3.

To determine divisibilty for 4, you can check if the last two digits are divisible by 4. In this case, 36 is divisible by 4, therefore 21,936 is also divisible by 4.

Since, 21,936 is divisible by 3 and 4, it is divisible by 12. I is true.

To determine divisibility by 8, you can check if the last three digits are divisible by 8. In this case, 936 ÷ 8 = 117. Therefore, 21,936 is divisible by 8. II is true.

Since we already determined 21,936 is divisible by 12, we know that it must also be divisible by 6. III is true.

I, II, and III are all true.

3. B If the temperature was originally 3° and then dropped 5 degrees, subtract to find the new temperature.
3° – 5° = –2°
Now, we must factor in the wind chill effect. This would drop the temperature another 10 degrees, so we must subtract.
–2° – 10° = –12°

4. D Integers are numbers that can be positive, negative, or zero, but not including decimals or fractions. Odd integers are not divisible by 2. We want a list of consecutive odd integers, thus each number in the list must be the next biggest odd integer. Let's examine each answer choice:

A: 1, 2, 3, 4 :These are not all odd integers. 2 and 4 are even.

B: 0, 1, 3, 5 :These are not all odd integers. 0 is not odd.

C: –9, –11, –13, –17 :These are all odd integers. However, they are not consecutive. Between –13 and –17 there is another odd integer, –15.

D: –3, –1, 1, 3 :These are consecutive odd integers. Answer D.

5. C The distributive property would be extremely useful in calculating the product.
The property states that a(b+c) = ab + ac.

Let's see how that could be applied in this problem.
The number 100.1 can be broken into the sum of two numbers: 815 x 100.1 = 815 x (100 + .1)

The distributive property could then be used. 815(100+.1) = 815(100) + 815(.1)

Both of these products can be calculated in your head.
815(100) + 815(.1) = 81500 + 81.5 = 81581.5

6. C $-1 \times -1 = 1$. Therefore, -1 times itself an even number of times will always be positive 1. -1 times itself an odd number of times will always be negative.

$(-1)^6 - (-1)^5 - (-1)^4 =$

$1 - (-1) - 1 =$

$1 + 1 - 1 =$

$2 - 1 =$

1

7. A   To determine how many times longer the room is, divide the room length by the length of the bacteria.

$(1.2 \times 10^1) \div (2 \times 10^{-6})$

First, divide the numbers. Then, divide the powers of ten by subtracting the exponents.

$1.2 \div 2 = 0.6$

$10^1 \div 10^{-6} = 10^{1-(-6)} = 10^7$

0.6×10^7

Convert the above into proper scientific notation by converting 0.6 into scientific notation and multiplying by 10^7.

0.6×10^7

$= 6 \times 10^{-1} \times 10^7$

$= 6 \times 10^6$

8. B   To use a number line to solve a problem, start at the first number, in this case -3. Then, the problem asks you to subtract 4. When subtracting, you move to the left on the number line. Therefore, you want to start at -3 and move 4 spaces to the left and then you arrive at -7, which is the answer to $-3 - 4$.

9. A   Whenever you add an even and an odd number you will get an odd number. Here are some examples and then we will prove why this is true.

Examples: $4 + 3 = 7$, $12 + 5 = 17$, $12 + 11 = 23$, $2 + 7 = 9$

An even number is divisible by 2. If you add two even numbers together, you will be adding numbers which are both divisible by 2 and thus the result will also be divisible by 2. Thus, an even plus an even is an even.

An odd number is always 1 bigger than an even number. Therefore, if you add an even and an odd, it is the same as adding an even and an even and 1. Even + even is even. Therefore, it is like adding 1 to an even number, which will always be odd.

Even + Odd = Odd

10. B   You start with an even number. Even.

You add it to an odd number. Even + Odd = Odd

Multiply it by an odd number. Odd x Odd = Odd

Subtract even number. Odd – Even = Odd

Result is odd. Answer B.

You can also try this problem by picking numbers and plugging them in as you go through each step.

11.C   Let's examine each answer choice.

A: $(-2)^0$: Anything to the zero power is equal to 1. Therefore, $(-2)^0 = 1$.

B: $(-2)^7$: This equals -2 times itself 7 times. Since we are multiplying 7 negatives, the answer will be negative. Therefore, this answer is smaller than A. Eliminate B.

C: $(-2)^8$: This equals -2 times itself 8 times. Since we are multiplying 8 negatives, the answer will be positive. Therefore, this equals 2^8.

D: -2^{10}: This equals $-(2^{10})$. Only the 2 is being raised to the 10th power, so the answer will be negative.

Answer C is the largest.

12. B   Let's figure out how to solve each answer choice.

A: You have a string that is 6 feet long and you need pieces that are each 3.5 feet. How many pieces can you make from the string?
This problem would be found by dividing the total amount of string by the length of each piece. $6 \div 3.5$. Eliminate A.

B: There are 6 documentaries whose average length is 3.5 hours. How many total hours of film are there?
The average 3.5 is found by dividing the total by 6. Therefore, you can find the total by finding the product of 3.5 and 6. This is the correct answer.

C: You have $6 and go to a store and buy $3.50 worth of supplies. How much change do you have?
To find the change, subtract what you spent from what you had. $6 - 3.5$. Eliminate C.

D: You are making cookies and put in 6 tablespoons of sugar. The recipe calls for an additional 3.5 tablespoons, how many total tablespoons have you put in?
To find the total amount of sugar you put in, add the 6 tablespoons to the additional 3.5 tablespoons. $6 + 3.5$. Eliminate D.

13. A   This problem tests your understanding of the order of operations, sometimes called PEMDAS.

Let's review the order of operations:
1.   P = parentheses
2.   E = exponents
3.   MD = multiplication and division from left to right
4.   AS = addition and subtraction from left to right

Now, let's solve the problem. First, look for parentheses. Use the order of operations to calculate the terms inside the parentheses. Inside the parentheses, there are no additional parentheses and no exponents, therefore, the next step would be to look for MD, or multiplication and division from left to right.

$14 - 3 \times 5(12 \div 2 \times 3)$

In the parentheses, when looking from left to right, the first operation is $12 \div 2$, so this should be done next.
$14 - 3 \times 5(12 \div 2 \times 3)$ — First, division inside parentheses.
$14 - 3 \times 5(6 \times 3)$ — Next, complete the operations in the parentheses.
$14 - 3 \times 5(18)$ — No more parentheses. No exponents. Next step is multiply/divide left to right.
$14 - 15(18)$ — Since the parentheses here indicate multiplication, multiply the two numbers.
$14 - 270 = -256$ — Final step, is subtract.

Therefore, the student performed the wrong operation at step 1. She should have divided before multiplying. Note, on the actual test, once you noticed that mistake you should move on to the next question and not continue to solve the problem.

14. D   First, change each number from expanded form to standard form.

I. 300,000 + 80,000 = 380,000

II. 30,000 + 9000 + 900 = 39,900

III. 300,000 + 70,000 + 900 + 90 = 370,990

Now, compare the numbers and write them from least to greatest.

39,900 is the smallest

370,990 is next

380,000 is the biggest

II, III, I

15. A   If a number is divisible by both 5 and 8, then it must be divisible by 40. Now, we need to find out how many integers between 1 and 1000 are divisible by 40.

1000/40 = 25. Therefore, there are 25 numbers that are evenly divisible by 1000.

16. A   There are a few steps to this problem. First, determine the number of votes that Victoria needs to win. Next, determine the number of votes that Jerry needs to win. Finally, determine how many additional votes Victoria needs.

Victoria: She has 273 votes and needs 350 votes. Subtract to find the number she needs.

350 − 273 = 77

Jerry: He has 289 votes and needs 350 votes. Subtract to find the number he needs.

350 − 289 = 61

Difference between them:

77 − 61 = 16

Victoria needs 16 more votes than Jerry.

Another way to think of this problem is to see by how much Victoria trails and that will be the number of additional votes she needs to win.

Jerry has 289, Victoria has 273

289 − 273 = 16

16 votes, Answer A

17. B   −12 + 3 x −7 + |−4 + 6| x 6 =

Follow the order of operations. PEMDAS.

P – Parentheses. First, perform what is in the absolute value since the absolute value acts as parentheses.

−12 + 3 x −7 + |−4 + 6| x 6 =

−12 + 3 x −7 + |2| x 6 =

−12 + 3 x −7 + 2 x 6 =

E – No exponents.

MD – Multiplication and Division from left to right.

−12 + 3 x −7 + 2 x 6 =

−12 + −21 + 2 x 6 =

−12 + −21 + 12 =

AS – Addition and subtraction from left to right.

−12 + −21 + 12 =

−33 + 12 = −21

18. C   First, find the LCM of 12, 8, and 6. You can list the multiples until you find a common one.

12: 12, 24

8: 8, 16, 24

6: 6, 12, 18, 24

24 is the least common multiple of the three numbers.

Now, let's find the greatest common factor. List out the factors of each number.

12: 1, 2, 3, 4, 6, 12

8: 1, 2, 4, 8

6: 1, 2, 3

The GCF is 2.

The product of the LCM and the GCF is 2 x 24 = 48.

19. D   The number 63,485 is written in standard decimal notation. Therefore, each digit is multiplied by a power of 10. You can determine the value of each digit by either counting which power of 10 or by figuring out the place value of the digit and multiplying it by the digit. Note that each place value is 10 times larger than the place value to the right.

63,485

5 is in the ones place, the value of this digit is 5 x 1 = 5.

8 is in the tens place, the value of this digit is 8 x 10 = 80.

4 is in the hundreds place, the value of this digit is 4 x 100 = 400.

3 is in the thousands place, the value of this digit is 3 x 1000 = 3000.

6 is in the ten thousands place, the value of this digit is 6 x 10,000 = 60000.

The problem wants you to find the product of the value represented by the number 4 and the value represented by the number 3. So the desired product is 400(3000) or 1,200,000.

20. D   First, let's review the definition of prime factorization: expressing a whole number as a product of factors that are all prime numbers.

If the prime factorization of n is pg^3, that means that n is equal to p x g x g x g.

You could use a trick to find the number of factors. Take the exponents from the prime factorization (in this case, 1 and 3) and add 1 to each and find their product. This would be the number of factors of n.

(1 + 1) x (3 + 1) = 2 x 4 = 8

The only answer with 8 factors is answer D.

Otherwise, not using the trick, to find all the factors of a number, find every possible combination of numbers that divide evenly into n. This can be done by finding all combinations from the prime factorization.

n = p x g x g x g

1 (always a factor of a number)

pg^3 (the original number is also always a factor)

p and g (prime factors are factors)

g^2, g^3 (all combinations with g with no repeats)

pg, pg^2 (all combinations with p with no repeats)

There are 8 total factors: 1, g, g^2, g^3, p, pg, pg^2, pg^3

You could also work backwards and try each number from answer D and see if the number divides evenly into pg^3, and therefore would be a factor of n. This is obviously the case, so answer D is correct.

Finally, you can always try numbers and determine the number of factors. Pick numbers of p and g, such as p=3 and g=2 and solve for n, which equals 24. Then, count the number of factors of 24.

2. Fractions, Decimals, Percents

Fraction Definition

A fraction is simply a number that expresses parts of a whole. The classic way of beginning to work with fractions is to use shapes.

In this example, you see four squares, three of which are shaded. If you think of all four squares as the "whole," then it makes sense to say that three out of four or three fourths of the squares are shaded.

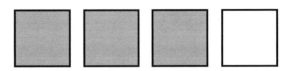

When you write in fractional notation, we use a numerator, the number on top of the bar or division sign (we'll return to the idea of fractions as division later in this lesson), and a denominator, the number on the bottom. Going back to the squares example, you would write three fourths as ¾. The denominator, a 4 in this case, gives the number of parts in the whole. The numerator states the number of parts that satisfy a certain requirement. With regard to the squares, 3 of the 4 total parts meet the requirement of being shaded, so, if asked what fraction of the squares is shaded, you would answer ¾.

Naming Fractions

Now that you understand the parts of a fraction, you need to be able to name them. The system is simple, use the normal word for the number in the numerator and, for the denominator, use the word for describing someone's place in a line. For example, ⅐ is written as one seventh. If the number in the numerator is plural, add –ths to the end of the word for the number in the denominator. For example, $^{82}\!/_{95}$ is written as eighty–two ninety–fifths.

Equivalent Fractions

Since the denominator of a fraction describes the total number of parts in the whole and the numerator states the number of parts that you "have," when does a fraction equal one whole?

In this picture, all of the seven faces are smiling. This fraction is written as 7/7, which equals one. Whenever the numerator of a fraction equals the denominator, the fraction is equal to one. This property of fractions is very useful in mathematics because any number or variable can be multiplied or divided by one, or any fraction that equals one, without changing its value.

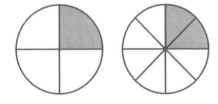

Here's an example of multiplying a fraction by a fraction equal to one without changing its value: ¼ x ²⁄₂ = ²⁄₈

If you look at the shaded areas of the circles to the right, you will see that the fractions ¼ and ²⁄₈ are equal.

Simplifying Fractions

Manipulating numbers by multiplying and dividing by fractions equal to one is necessary to find the simplest form of a fraction. Simplest form is a way of writing a fraction so that the numerator and denominator have no common factors other than one. If asked to put $^{54}\!/_{72}$ into simplest form, you should recognize that 54 and 72 share the factor 9. Divide the numerator by 9, then divide the denominator by 9.

$^{54}\!/_{72} \div ^9\!/_9 = ^6\!/_8$

Now that you have simplified the fraction, see if it can be simplified further. Both 6 and 8 share the factor of 2.

$^6\!/_8 \div ^2\!/_2 = ^3\!/_4$

Since 3 and 4 share no common factors, this fraction is in simplest form. The correct answer to a multiple choice problem will almost always be in simplest form.

Comparing Fractions

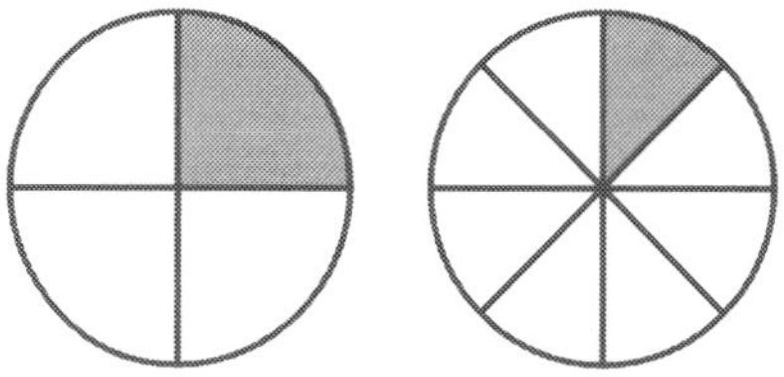

Another time that you will need to manipulate fractions in this way is when you are comparing them. When comparing fractions, remember that the larger the denominator is, the more parts the whole is divided into. Since the whole is split into more parts, the parts are smaller. Look at the figure to the right, which shows that ¼ is greater than ⅛.

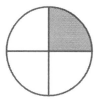

The numerator works in the opposite way. Since the numerator describes the parts of the whole that meet the requirements, a larger numerator includes more parts. Therefore, ⅜ is smaller than ⅞.

One easy way to compare fractions is to manipulate them so that they all have the same denominator. Since you know that you can multiply and divide any number by one, that's easy. Look at the following example:

Put the fractions ¼, ³⁄₃₂, ¹¹⁄₆₄, and ⁹⁄₁₆ in order from least to greatest.

By multiplying by fractions equal to one, all of the numbers can be converted to fractions with a denominator of 64.

¼ x ¹⁶⁄₁₆ = ¹⁶⁄₆₄
³⁄₃₂ x ²⁄₂ = ⁶⁄₆₄
⁹⁄₁₆ x ⁴⁄₄ = ³⁶⁄₆₄

Now the problem is easy, with common denominators, the fractions can be ordered by their numerators from least to greatest: ⁶⁄₆₄ < ¹¹⁄₆₄ < ¹⁶⁄₆₄ < ³⁶⁄₆₄.
Therefore, ³⁄₃₂ < ¹¹⁄₆₄ < ¼ < ⁹⁄₁₆.

While many people find the concept of fractions intimidating, a deep understanding of the subject is necessary for understanding and expressing many concepts, including probabilities, which will be discussed in Lesson 8. Make sure that you are comfortable manipulating fractions before moving on.

Fractions Overview: Practice

1. Write the following words as a mixed number in simplest form. Five and Fifteen Twenty–Fifths

    A. 5 ½

    B. 5 ⅗

    C. 20 ⅗

    D. ⁵¹⁵⁄₂₅

2. What is the denominator of the fraction thirty–five fortieths when put in simplest form?

    A. 7

    B. 8

    C. 35

    D. 40

3. Put ⁴⁰⁰/₆₀₀ into simplest form.

   A. ⁴/₆

   B. ²⁰⁰/₃₀₀

   C. ¹/₂₀₀

   D. ²/₃

4. The shaded triangle is equal to what fraction of the square?

   A. ¼

   B. ½

   C. ¾

   D. ⅛

5. Which is the smallest number of this set: ⁵/₉, ⁹/₁₇, ¹⁰/₂₀, ¹⁴⁰/₃₀₀?

   A. ⁵/₉

   B. ⁹/₁₇

   C. ¹⁰/₂₀

   D. ¹⁴⁰/₃₀₀

6. Charles drew a picture of his family. The picture shows one man, one woman, two boys, and two girls. What fraction of Charles' family is female?

   A. ½

   B. ⅔

   C. ⅓

   D. ³/₇

7. Which of the following fractions represents one whole? ¹⁹/₃₀, ⁵⁰/₅₀, ¹/₀, ⁰/₁

   A. ¹⁹/₃₀

   B. ⁵⁰/₅₀

   C. ¹/₀

   D. ⁰/₁

8. Which of the following fractions is the greatest?

   A. ⅞

   B. ⁸/₉

   C. ⁹/₁₀

   D. ¹⁰/₁₁

Fractions Overview: Answer Explanations

1. B First you must take the words and put them into a fraction, and then reduce.

The whole number will be everything before the "and". In this case, five = 5. Then, for the fraction, first is written the numerator and then the denominator. Fifteen Twenty–Fifths = $^{15}\!/_{25}$

Simplify. Since both the numerator and denominator are divisible by 5, you should reduce. $^{15}\!/_{25} = \frac{3}{5}$
Now put the whole number with the reduced fraction giving you: 5 $\frac{3}{5}$.

2. B The easiest way to answer this question is to first write out the fraction. Remember that the term in the numerator comes first and is the normal word for the number, so 35 is the numerator here. Fortieths is the denominator term for 40. The fraction is 35/40.

Now we must simplify the fraction. 5 divides evenly into both the numerator and denominator.
$^{35}\!/_{40} \div \frac{5}{5} = \frac{7}{8}$
The question asks for the denominator, which is 8.

3. D To simplify a fraction, you must find a number that divides evenly into the numerator and denominator. You could do this in several steps, such as dividing by $\frac{2}{2}$ and then by $^{100}\!/_{100}$.

You could also do it in one step by finding the greatest common factor, which is 200, and dividing the numerator and denominator by that. $^{400}\!/_{600} \div {}^{200}\!/_{200} = \frac{2}{3}$

4. D Approach this question using estimation. The fraction of the square covered by the triangle is clearly smaller than 1/2, so 3/4 can be ruled out as well. That leaves 1/4 and 1/8 as choices. Now it's time to draw on the diagram.

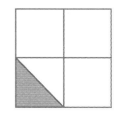

After dividing the square into four parts, it becomes obvious that the triangle is less than 1/4 of the square, so it has to be 1/8, Answer D.

5. D There are many ways to compare fractions. One way is to give them all the same denominator. But in this case, there is no easy common denominator. Here is one solution until you learn more about decimals and other methods. Therefore, let us see if there is a simpler solution. First, look at the third fraction: 10/20. If you reduce this fraction, you get 1/2. Now, let's compare the other fractions to 1/2.

$\frac{5}{9}$ and $\frac{9}{17}$ are both greater than $\frac{1}{2}$. $^{140}\!/_{300}$ is smaller than $\frac{1}{2}$ since $\frac{1}{2}$ of 300 is 150.

6. A There are six people in Charles' family, so the denominator of our fraction is six. Three of the six people are females, making the numerator three. 3/6.
Remember to simplify by dividing the numerator and denominator by 3. $\frac{3}{6} = \frac{1}{2}$

7. B Because the numerator indicates the parts of the whole and the denominator indicates the total number of parts into which the whole has been divided, a fraction is equal to one whole when the numerator and denominator are equal. Therefore, $^{50}\!/_{50}$ is equal to 1.

8. D There are many ways to compare fractions. One way is to find a common denominator for all the fractions and compare the numerators. Another way is to convert all the fractions to decimals and then compare that way. But, in this problem, let us think of what each fraction represents.
The larger the denominator, the greater the number of pieces into which the whole is divided. Since each fraction is missing one piece of the whole, $^{10}\!/_{11}$, the fraction missing the smallest piece, is the greatest.

Process for Adding/Subtracting Fractions

The first step when adding or subtracting fractions is to convert them to a common denominator. To make things simple, use the least common denominator, which is the least common multiple of all of the denominators to be added or subtracted. After all of the fractions have been converted to the same denominator, they can be added and subtracted by adding and subtracting their numerators and keeping the denominator the same. Remember to simplify the result.

Steps for adding or subtracting fractions:

1. Convert all fractions to same denominator
2. Add or subtract numerators, keep denominator the same
3. Simplify result

Example

$9/17 - 17/51 + 6/34$

The least common multiple for 17, 51, and 34 is 102, so that is the least common denominator for the fractions above. Convert each fraction into one with a denominator of 102 by multiplying by a fraction equal to one.

$9/17 \times 6/6 = 54/102$
$17/51 \times 2/2 = 34/102$
$6/34 \times 3/3 = 18/102$

Add and subtract the numerators left to right, then simplify the result.
$54/102 - 34/102 + 18/102$
$= (54-34+18)/102$
$= 38/102$
$= 19/51$

Fractions Adding/Subtracting: Practice

1. $7/34 + 13/34$

    A. $5/17$

    B. $20/68$

    C. $16/34$

    D. $10/17$

2. Robert mowed 1/3 of his lawn and his sister Lisa mowed 1/2 of it. In total, how much of the lawn did they mow?

    A. 5/12

    B. 1/5

    C. 1/6

    D. 5/6

3. Kate is budgeting out her expenses for the next month. She has allotted 2/9 of her salary for food, 1/5 for clothing, 7/18 for rent, and 1/10 for entertainment. Assuming that she sticks to her budget and saves what is left over from her salary, what fraction of her salary will Kate save next month?

  A. 11/42

  B. 4/45

  C. 31/42

  D. 41/45

4. In a bag, 16/30 of the marbles are blue and 4/20 of the marbles are red. What fraction of the marbles are blue or red?

  A. 20/50

  B. 11/15

  C. 12/10

  D. 16/60

5. On her test, Joanne missed 1/9 of the questions. What fraction of the questions did she answer correctly?

  A. 1/9

  B. 8

  C. 8/0

  D. 8/9

6. An elementary school teacher graded 4/7 of her class' test papers before lunch and 2/7 of the papers between lunch and dinner. If she plans to finish her grading by bedtime, what fraction of the papers will she need to grade between dinner and bedtime?

  A. 6/7

  B. 2/0

  C. 1/7

  D. 1/6

7. A couple is flying from Orlando, Florida to Honolulu, Hawaii for a vacation. The first leg of their trip is from Orlando to Atlanta, Georgia and it takes 2 hours. The next leg of their flight is from Atlanta to Los Angeles, California and it lasts 5 hours. If their total flight time is 13 hours, what fraction of their flight time is spent on the last leg, which is from Los Angeles to Honolulu?

  A. 6/13

  B. 6/1

  C. 7/13

  D. 7/1

8. At a county–wide orchestral competition, the only two ratings that earn ribbons are superior and excellent. June has scored a superior on three of her solo violin performances. She has scored an excellent on five performances. If June has given 12 performances, what fraction of her performances have earned ribbons?

    A. 8/24

    B. 2/12

    C. 1/3

    D. 2/3

$$\frac{3}{12} \quad \frac{5}{12} \quad \frac{8}{12} = \frac{4}{6} = \frac{2}{3}$$

Fractions Adding/Subtracting: Answer Explanations

1. D   To add fractions with a common denominator: add the numerators, keep the denominator, and simplify.
$7/34 + {}^{13}\!/_{34} = {}^{20}\!/_{34}$

Then simplify.
${}^{20}\!/_{34} \div {}^{2}\!/_{2} = {}^{10}\!/_{17}$

2. D   Robert and Lisa each mowed part of the lawn, which means that you need to add to find the total amount mowed. Give the fractions a common denominator, in this case 6.
$1/3 = {}^{2}\!/_{6}$
$1/2 = {}^{3}\!/_{6}$

Add the numerators, keep the denominator.
${}^{2}\!/_{6} + {}^{3}\!/_{6} = {}^{5}\!/_{6}$

3. B   In order to find out how much of Kate's salary will go into savings, add up her expenses. First, convert to a common denominator, in this case use 90.
${}^{2}\!/_{9} = {}^{20}\!/_{90}$
${}^{1}\!/_{5} = {}^{18}\!/_{90}$
${}^{7}\!/_{18} = {}^{35}\!/_{90}$
${}^{1}\!/_{10} = {}^{9}\!/_{90}$

Then, add the numerators.
${}^{20}\!/_{90} + {}^{18}\!/_{90} + {}^{35}\!/_{90} + {}^{9}\!/_{90} = {}^{(20+18+35+9)}\!/_{90} = {}^{82}\!/_{90}$

Therefore, she spent ${}^{82}\!/_{90}$. This must be subtracted from what she earned, which is 1 or ${}^{90}\!/_{90}$.
${}^{90}\!/_{90} - {}^{82}\!/_{90} = {}^{8}\!/_{90}$

Simplify
${}^{8}\!/_{90} = {}^{4}\!/_{45}$

4. B   To add fractions, you need to find a common denominator. The least common multiple of 30 and 20 is 60. Convert the fractions so that they have a denominator of 60.
${}^{16}\!/_{30} = {}^{32}\!/_{60}$
${}^{4}\!/_{20} = {}^{12}\!/_{60}$

Add and simplify.
${}^{32}\!/_{60} + {}^{12}\!/_{60} = {}^{44}\!/_{60}$
${}^{44}\!/_{60} = {}^{11}\!/_{15}$

5. D   To find out what fraction of the questions Joanne answered correctly, you need to subtract the fraction she missed from the total. The first step in this problem is to express the total as a fraction. The test is one whole.

$1 - \frac{1}{9}$.

Write 1 as 9/9 so that you can subtract with a common denominator.

$\frac{9}{9} - \frac{1}{9} = \frac{8}{9}$

6. C   To solve this problem, you must understand that the whole, or all of the papers, can be represented as 1 which can also be written as $\frac{7}{7}$. Subtract the completed parts from the whole to find out how much grading the teacher has left to complete.

$\frac{7}{7} - \frac{4}{7} - \frac{2}{7} = \frac{(7 - 4 - 2)}{7} = \frac{1}{7}$

7. A   To solve this problem, you must understand that the whole, or total flight time, can be represented as 1 or $\frac{13}{13}$ hours.

That means that the Orlando to Atlanta leg of the flight is 5 out of the total 13 hours or is $\frac{5}{13}$ of the flight time and the Atlanta to Los Angeles leg is $\frac{2}{13}$ of the trip time. Now this is a simple subtraction problem.

$\frac{13}{13} - \frac{5}{13} - \frac{2}{13} = \frac{(13 - 5 - 2)}{13} = \frac{6}{13}$

8. D   Write the fraction of performances that earned a superior rating, which is 3 out of the 12: $\frac{3}{12}$.

Write the fraction that earned an excellent, which is 5 out of the 12: $\frac{5}{12}$.

Add the two fractions.
$\frac{3}{12} + \frac{5}{12} = \frac{8}{12}$

Simplify.
$\frac{8}{12} = \frac{2}{3}$

Multiplying Fractions

To multiply fractions, simply multiply the numerators to get the new numerator and multiply the denominators to get the new denominator.

¾ x ⁷⁄₉ = ⁽³ ˣ ⁷⁾⁄₍₄ ₓ ₉₎ = ²¹⁄₃₆

Then simplify if applicable. ²¹⁄₃₆ = ⁷⁄₁₂

Often, it is easier to simplify before multiplying. You can simplify when numbers in the numerator and numbers in the denominator share common factors. In the same example from above:
¾ x ⁷⁄₉

There is a 3 in the numerator and a 9 in the denominator. Since 3 divides evenly into both of them, you can simplify those numbers by dividing both by 3. The 3 in the numerator becomes 1 and the 9 in the denominator becomes 3. Now write the simplified problem and multiply.
¼ x ⁷⁄₃ = ⁷⁄₁₂

Dividing Fractions

To divide fractions, invert the divisor and then multiply the fractions. In other words, flip the second fraction and then multiply as described above.

¹⁵⁄₃₂ ÷ ³⁄₂ = ¹⁵⁄₃₂ x ²⁄₃

Now multiply the fractions. Here you see the fractions being simplified before the multiplication, since 15 and 3 are both divisible by 3, and 32 and 2 are both divisible by 2. You could also multiply across and simplify the result.

$$\frac{\overset{5}{\cancel{15}}}{32} \times \frac{2}{\underset{1}{\cancel{3}}} = \frac{5}{32} \times \frac{\overset{1}{\cancel{2}}}{\underset{16}{}} = \frac{5}{16} \times \frac{1}{1} = \frac{5}{16}$$

Fractions Multiplying/Dividing: Practice

1. Solve. ³⁄₅ × ⁸⁄₉ =

    A. ⁸⁄₁₅

    B. ¹¹⁄₁₄

    C. ¹¹⁄₄₅

    D. ²⁴⁄₁₄

2. Solve. ¹⁹⁄₂₀ ÷ ⁴⁄₁₀ ÷ ¹⁹⁄₃₂ =

    A. ⅛

    B. 4

    C. ¼

    D. ⁴²⁄₅₂

3. Solve. $5/7 \div 25/35 \times 4/12 =$

A. $100/588$

B. $25/147$

C. $1/3$

D. $34/54$

4. Solve. $7/9 \times 3/14 \div 8/42 =$

A. $7/8$

B. $2/63$

C. $343/18$

D. $18/65$

5. Juana made two–dozen snowmen this afternoon. One–twelfth of them melted by sunset. How many of Juana's melted by sunset?

A. 2

B. 12

C. 22

D. 24

6. A woman is calculating the dividend she will make from an investment. There are 100 investors, each of whom gets an equal share of the profits. If her share is $80, what were the total profits?

A. $80

B. $0.80

C. $800

D. $8000

$100 \times 80 = $

8000

7. A fifth grade after–school club has 14/16 of an extra large pizza to share. If they divide the pizza equally among the students, each child gets 1/8 of the pizza. How many students are in the club?

A. 7/64

B. 14

C. 8

D. 7

8. Order the following from least to greatest:

I. the number of fourths in ½ · 375

II. 5 x ½ 5.5

III. ½ ÷ 3 4.5

A. I, II, III

B. III, II, I

C. III, I, II

D. II, III, I

Fractions Multiplying/Dividing: Answer Explanations

1. A   *Method 1: Multiply and then Simplify*

Multiply the two numerators to get the new numerator—in this case, 8 x 3 = 24. Then multiply the two denominators to find the new denominator, 5 x 9 = 45. This gives the fraction $^{24}\!/_{45}$, which simplifies to $^8\!/_{15}$.

Method 2: Simplify first

The 3 in the numerator and 9 in the denominator are both divisible by 3. Simplify by dividing both by 3.
$^3\!/_5 \times ^8\!/_9 = ^1\!/_5 \times ^8\!/_3$

Then multiply numerators to get 1 x 8 = 8. Then multiply denominators, 5 x 3 = 15. Giving you: $^8\!/_{15}$.

2. B   Break the problem into multiple steps. Divide the first two fractions, and then take that result and divide it by the last fraction. Remember, to divide fractions, invert the divisor and multiply. The following problem shows the simplification before multiplying.
$^{19}\!/_{20} \div ^4\!/_{10} = ^{19}\!/_{20} \text{ x } ^{10}\!/_4 = ^{19}\!/_2 \text{ x } ^1\!/_4 = ^{19}\!/_8$

Now take the result of that division problem and divide it by the last fraction.
$^{19}\!/_8 \div ^{19}\!/_{32} = ^{19}\!/_8 \text{ x } ^{32}\!/_{19} = ^1\!/_8 \text{ x } ^{32}\!/_1 = ^1\!/_1 \text{ x } ^4\!/_1 = ^4\!/_1 = 4$

3. C   Following order of operations, multiply and divide from left to right. Therefore, do the division problem first, by inverting the divisor, simplifying, and then multiplying:
$^5\!/_7 \div ^{25}\!/_{35} = ^5\!/_7 \text{ x } ^{35}\!/_{25} = ^1\!/_7 \text{ x } ^{35}\!/_5 = ^1\!/_1 \text{ x } ^5\!/_5 = ^5\!/_5 = 1$

Now multiply that result by $^4\!/_{12}$. $1 \text{ x } ^4\!/_{12} = ^4\!/_{12} = ^1\!/_3$

4. A   Following order of operations, multiply and divide from left to right. First multiply: $^7\!/_9$ x $^3\!/_{14}$. Remember, you can simplify the fractions before multiplying. Then, multiply numerators and denominators.
$^7\!/_9 \text{ x } ^3\!/_{14} = ^1\!/_9 \text{ x } ^3\!/_2 = ^1\!/_3 \text{ x } ^1\!/_2 = ^1\!/_6$

Now use the result of the multiplication and divide it by $^8\!/_{42}$.
$^1\!/_6 \div ^8\!/_{42} = ^1\!/_6 \text{ x } ^{42}\!/_8 = ^1\!/_1 \text{ x } ^7\!/_8 = ^7\!/_8$

5. A   The first step in this problem is to write out the information. Juana made two–dozen snowmen, which means she made 24. You also know that 1/12 of the snowmen melted. Multiply the number of snowmen by the fraction that melted to find out how many melted.

$^1\!/_{12} \times 24 = ^1\!/_{12} \text{ x } ^{24}\!/_1 = 2$

Therefore, 2 of the 24 snowmen melted.

6. D   Because the profits will be divided equally among 100 investors, the woman's $80 share of the profits is $^1\!/_{100}$ of the total. To find what the total profits are, divide her share by the fraction of the total.
$\$80 \div ^1\!/_{100} = \$80 \text{ x } ^{100}\!/_1 = \$80 \text{ x } 100 = \$8000$

7. D   To find the number of students in the club, divide the fraction of the pizza that they have to share, 14/16, by the fraction that each child receives, which is 1/8.
$^{14}\!/_{16} \div ^1\!/_8 = ^{14}\!/_{16} \text{ x } ^8\!/_1 = 7 \text{ students}$

8. B   I. The number of fourths in $^3\!/_2$. To calculate this, you want to divide $^3\!/_2$ by $^1\!/_4$. $^3\!/_2 \div ^1\!/_4 = ^3\!/_2 \text{ x } 4 = 6$
II. $5 \text{ x } ^1\!/_2 = ^5\!/_2$
III. $^3\!/_2 \div 3 = ^3\!/_2 \text{ x } ^1\!/_3 = ^1\!/_2$

$^1\!/_2 < ^5\!/_2 < 6$

Mixed Numbers

When a fraction is greater than one, it can be written as a mixed number—a number containing both a fraction and a whole number. In the following example, each square represents 1. We see two whole squares that are shaded, but there is a third square that has been divided into halves. Only one of those parts is shaded. To name the portion of the squares that are shaded, we use the fraction two and one half or $2\frac{1}{2}$.

Mixed numbers can be useful when adding or subtracting fractions and whole numbers, such as $4\frac{1}{2} - 1 = 3\frac{1}{2}$, or fractions with common denominators, such as $5\frac{3}{4} + 4\frac{1}{4} = 9\frac{4}{4} = 9 + 1 = 10$.

Improper Fractions

Mixed numbers can also be written as improper fractions, or fractions with a numerator greater than the denominator. This is useful when multiplying and dividing fractions because improper fractions can be treated the same as proper fractions, those with numerators smaller than their denominators.
$\frac{7}{2} \times \frac{5}{4} = \frac{35}{8}$

Converting from Mixed Number to Improper Fraction

Often you will need to convert mixed numbers into improper fractions. To do this, multiply the whole number by the denominator and then add the numerator to that number. This will give you your new numerator, and the denominator will remain the same. For example:
$5\frac{3}{4} = \frac{(5 \times 4 + 3)}{4} = \frac{23}{4}$

Another way to think of the conversion is that you need to turn the whole number into a fraction with the same denominator as its accompanying fraction and then add the two. To convert $5\frac{3}{4}$, first convert 5 to a fraction with a denominator of 4 and then add that to $\frac{3}{4}$.

$5 \times \frac{4}{4} = \frac{20}{4}$
$5\frac{3}{4} = 5 + \frac{3}{4} = \frac{20}{4} + \frac{3}{4} = \frac{23}{4}$

Converting from an Improper Fraction to a Mixed Number

To convert an improper fraction into a mixed number, divide the numerator by the denominator. The quotient is the whole number and the remainder is the numerator of the fraction.

$\frac{23}{4} = 23 \div 4 = 5 \text{ remainder } 3 = 5\frac{3}{4}$
$\frac{77}{9} = 77 \div 9 = 8 \text{ remainder } 5 = 8\frac{5}{9}$

Remainders as Fractions

When dividing numbers, you can think of the problem as a fraction problem. For instance, $13 \div 5$ is the same as $\frac{13}{5}$, so you can convert the fraction into a mixed number. $\frac{13}{5} = 2\frac{3}{5}$.

Another way to think of this step is to convert the remainder into a fraction. $13 \div 5 = 2$ remainder 3. That means there were only 3 out of the 5 needed to get to the next whole number. Therefore, you can write the remainder as a fraction with the remainder as the numerator and the divisor as the denominator. $13 \div 5 = 2$ remainder $3 = 2\frac{3}{5}$.

Mixed Numbers & Improper Fractions: Practice

1. Jorge is in the middle of doing laundry when a detergent bottle runs out. He needs to pour $1\frac{3}{5}$ cups of detergent into the washing machine for this load, and he poured $1\frac{1}{5}$ cups from the old bottle. How much detergent from the new bottle does Jorge need for washing this load?

    A. $\frac{1}{5}$

    B. $\frac{2}{5}$

    C. $1\frac{2}{5}$

    D. $\frac{4}{5}$

$1\frac{3}{5} - 1\frac{1}{5} = \frac{2}{5}$

2. The Suarez family's pool was finished yesterday, and they started to fill it with water. The pool's capacity is 800 gallons, but they were only able to pump in $400\frac{3}{7}$ gallons. It rained overnight, which added another $3\frac{4}{7}$ gallons to the pool. How many gallons of water will the Suarez family need to finish filling their pool to capacity?

    A. 404 gallons

    B. 399 gallons

    C. 396 gallons

    D. 393 gallons

handwritten: 800 $400\frac{3}{7}$ $\frac{404}{-404}$ 396

3. What improper fraction describes the portion of the circles that is not shaded?

    A. $9\frac{5}{8}$

    B. $\frac{77}{8}$

    C. $\frac{72}{8}$

    D. $\frac{5}{8}$

handwritten: $9\frac{5}{8}$ $\frac{77}{8}$

4. A cake recipe calls for 2 cups of powdered sugar. It says to use $\frac{1}{4}$ of the sugar in the cake batter and the remainder in the frosting. How much sugar, in cups, is needed for the frosting?

    A. $1\frac{1}{2}$

    B. $\frac{3}{4}$

    C. $\frac{3}{8}$

    D. $\frac{1}{2}$

handwritten: $2 - \frac{1}{2}$

5. Solve. $1\frac{3}{9} \times 4\frac{3}{4} =$

    A. $\frac{247}{36}$

    B. $\frac{559}{36}$

    C. $5\frac{1}{12}$

    D. $4\frac{1}{3}$

handwritten: $\frac{13}{9} \times \frac{19}{4} = \frac{247}{36}$

6. Solve. $2\frac{7}{9} - 1\frac{3}{8} + \frac{45}{144} =$

    A. $2\frac{47}{144}$

    B. $1\frac{103}{144}$

    C. $\frac{103}{144}$

    D. 144

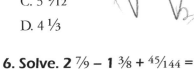

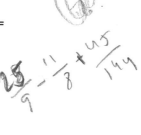

7. Derek ate $1\frac{8}{8}$ of a petite pizza, Cordelia ate $\frac{5}{12}$ of another, and Raul ate $\frac{9}{14}$ of a different pizza. Assuming that the three pizzas were equal in size, how much pizza did all three eat?

A. $\frac{42}{139}$

B. $3\frac{13}{42}$

C. $\frac{32}{34}$

D. $3\frac{1}{2}$

$$\frac{18}{8} \quad \frac{5}{12} \quad \frac{9}{14} = \frac{378}{168} \quad \frac{70}{168} \quad \frac{108}{168}$$

8. What is 27 ÷ 4 ?

A. $3\frac{6}{4}$

B. $7\frac{1}{4}$

C. $6\frac{3}{4}$

D. $6\frac{3}{27}$

$$\frac{556}{168} = \frac{13}{4} \quad 3\frac{1}{2}$$

Mixed Numbers & Improper Fractions: Answer Explanations

1. B   To find the amount that he still needs to pour, subtract what Jorge has already poured into the machine from the total amount needed.

$1\frac{3}{5} - 1\frac{1}{5} = \frac{2}{5}$

2. C   Begin by finding out how much water is in the pool. Do this by adding the volumes of water that were pumped in yesterday and deposited by rain.

$400\frac{3}{7} + 3\frac{4}{7}$

To add mixed numbers, add the whole numbers separately, add the fractions separately and then combine the results.

$400 + 3 = 403$

$\frac{3}{7} + \frac{4}{7} = \frac{7}{7} = 1$

$403 + 1 = 404$ gallons

Now subtract the amount of water in the pool from the pool's capacity of 800 gallons to find out how much more water is needed.

800 gallons – 404 gallons = 396 gallons

3. B   First, look at the circle that is partially shaded and name the fraction of the circle that is not shaded. The circle is divided into 8 parts, 5 of which are not shaded. So the fraction is $\frac{5}{8}$, and there are 9 whole circles that are not shaded. Combining those two gives us the mixed number: $9\frac{5}{8}$.

The question asks for the improper fraction, so we must convert $9\frac{5}{8}$ to an improper fraction. First, take the 9 and give it a common denominator with the fraction.

$9 \times \frac{8}{8} = \frac{72}{8}$

Now add the 9 wholes to the fraction.

$9 + \frac{5}{8} = \frac{72}{8} + \frac{5}{8} = \frac{77}{8}$

Another way to think of converting the mixed number to an improper fraction is to take the whole number, multiply it by the denominator of the fraction, add it to the numerator, and put that all over the denominator of the fraction.

$9\frac{5}{8} = \frac{(9 \times 8 + 5)}{8} = \frac{77}{8}$

4. A To determine how much sugar is needed for the frosting, first figure out the fraction of sugar for the frosting. If $\frac{1}{4}$ is needed for the cake batter, then $\frac{3}{4}$ is needed for the frosting.

Then multiply the fraction that is needed for the frosting by the total amount of sugar the recipe calls for.
$\frac{3}{4} \times 2$ cups $= \frac{3}{4} \times \frac{2}{1} = \frac{6}{4} = \frac{3}{2} = 1\frac{1}{2}$
$1\frac{1}{2}$ cups of sugar for the frosting

5. A To multiply mixed numbers, you must first convert to improper fractions. You can NOT multiply the whole numbers and fractions separately.

First, convert $4\frac{3}{4}$ to an improper fraction.
$4\frac{3}{4} = \frac{19}{4}$

Now, multiply as you would with proper fractions.
$\frac{13}{9} \times \frac{19}{4} = \frac{247}{36}$

6. B First, convert all of the numbers to fractions with a common denominator.
$2\frac{7}{9} = \frac{25}{9} \times \frac{16}{16} = \frac{400}{144}$
$1\frac{3}{8} = \frac{11}{8} \times \frac{18}{18} = \frac{198}{144}$

Then add and subtract from left to right, following order of operations.
$\frac{400}{144} - \frac{198}{144} = \frac{202}{144}$
$\frac{202}{144} + \frac{45}{144} = \frac{247}{144}$

Change from an improper fraction to a mixed number.
$\frac{247}{144} = 1\frac{103}{144}$

7. B To add improper fractions, give them a common denominator, as you would with any fractions.
$\frac{18}{8} \times \frac{21}{21} = \frac{378}{168}$
$\frac{5}{12} \times \frac{14}{14} = \frac{70}{168}$
$\frac{9}{14} \times \frac{12}{12} = \frac{108}{168}$

Then add the fractions by adding the numerators and keeping the denominator. Then, convert the improper fraction to a mixed number.
$\frac{378}{168} + \frac{70}{168} + \frac{108}{168} =$
$\frac{556}{168}$
$= \frac{139}{42}$
$= 3\frac{13}{42}$

8. C Think of $27 \div 4$ as $\frac{27}{4}$. Then convert the improper fraction to a mixed number.
$\frac{27}{4} = 6\frac{3}{4}$

Or divide 4 into 27 and turn the remainder into a fraction.

27 divided by 4 is 6 with a remainder of 3. The remainder is then converted to a fraction by placing the remainder as the numerator and the divisor as the denominator.
$27 \div 4 = 6 \text{ R } 3 = 6\frac{3}{4}$

Fractions with denominators that are powers of 10 (100, 1000, etc.) can also be written as numbers called decimals. In a number with a decimal sign, all of the numbers to the left of the decimal sign are whole numbers, while all of the numbers to the right of it are fractions.

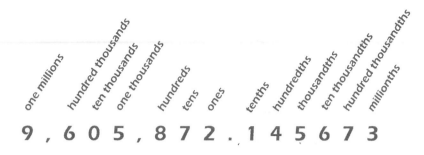

The digit 1 in the tenths place on this place–value chart literally means 1/10. The digit 4 in the hundredths place means $^4/_{100}$ and the 3 in the millionths place symbolizes $^3/_{1000000}$. Here are more examples of decimals written as fractions:

.59 = $^{59}/_{100}$ = fifty–nine hundredths

.2222 = $^{2222}/_{10000}$ = two–thousand two–hundred twenty–two ten–thousandths

.30303 = $^{30303}/_{100000}$ = thirty–thousand three–hundred three one–hundred thousandths

Decimals Overview: Practice

1. Write seven hundred thousand two hundred ninety and four thousand seventy five ten thousandths as a decimal.

A. 7,290.475

B. 700,290.4075

C. 700,294.75

D. 700,294.175

$700,290.40\cancel{75}$

⊗⊗⊙ $700,294.4075$.

2. Which decimal has a 6 in the hundreds place but not in the hundredths place?

A. 632.165

B. 8642.165

C. 64.046

D. 8642.046

3. In words, 637.951 is

A. six hundred thirty–seven and nine hundred fifty one

B. six hundred thirty–seven and nine hundred fifty one hundredths

C. six hundred thirty seven and nine hundred fifty one thousandths ⌐

D. six hundred thirty seven and nine hundred fifty one ten thousandths

4. Write 5.3847 as a mixed number.

A. $^{53847}/_{10000}$

B. $^{53847}/_{100000}$

C. $5\ ^{3847}/_{10000}$

D. $5\ ^{3847}/_{100000}$

5. What number is represented by the letter M on the number line below?

A. 2.40

B. 2.405

C. 2.45

D. 2.50

6. Order the following from greatest to least: 1.389, $^{14}/_3$, 1 $^1/_3$

A. $^{14}/_3$, 1 $^1/_3$, 1.389

B. 1 $^1/_3$, 1.389, $^{14}/_3$

C. $^{14}/_3$, 1.389, 1 $^1/_3$

D. 1.389, $^{14}/_3$, 1 $^1/_3$

7. Four basketball players are comparing their free throw shooting records. These are the fractions of shots made.

> **Player 1:** $^{42}/_{63}$
> **Player 2:** $^{75}/_{94}$
> **Player 3: 0.324**
> **Player 4: 0.846**

Who has the worst free throw shooting record of the four?

A. Player 1

B. Player 2

C. Player 3

D. Player 4

8. Doreen has taken 4 different tests. Each of the tests was scored by a different person. These are the results:

> **Test A:** $^9/_{10}$
> **Test B: .954**
> **Test C: 0.9099**
> **Test D:** $^5/_6$

On which test did Doreen score highest?

A. Test A

B. Test B

C. Test C

D. Test D

1. B   The "and" in a written number always represents a fraction or a decimal sign. Everything to the left of the "and" is a whole number and should be written to the left of the decimal. Seven hundred thousand two hundred ninety is 700,290. Everything to the right of the "and" is a fraction and should be to the right of the decimal. Four thousand seventy five ten thousandths is written: .4075.

2. D   The hundreds place is three to the left of the decimal. Answers A, B, and D each have a six there. The hundredths place is two to the right of the decimal. Answers A and B each have a six in the hundredths place, making D the answer.

3. C   Break the number into two pieces, what is to the left of the decimal point and what is to the right of the decimal point. The two pieces will be joined with "AND".

To the left of the decimal point is 637. This whole number is written as six hundred thirty seven.
To the right of the decimal point is .951. The last digit is in the thousandths place, so the fraction is nine hundred fifty one thousandths.

Now connect the two pieces. six hundred thirty seven AND nine hundred fifty one thousandths. 637.951

4. C   The number to the left of the decimal is a whole number and the digits to the right of the decimal are a fraction. The last digit is in the ten thousandths place.

5. C   On the number line, the letter M is halfway between 2.4 and 2.5. Remembering, adding a zero to the end of a decimal doesn't change the value, therefore we can think of M being halfway between 2.40 and 2.50.

2.40 can be written as $^{240}/_{100}$ 2.50 can be written as $^{250}/_{100}$
It can be seen that the number halfway between those would be $^{245}/_{100}$, which is written as 2.45.

Also, you could just determine that two and 45 hundreds is betwen 2.40 and 2.50.

6. C   You could either convert them all to decimals or convert them all to fractions. In this problem, let's try converting each number to a fraction with the same denominator.

$1.389 = {}^{1389}/_{1000} \times {}^{3}/_{3} = {}^{4167}/_{3000}$
$^{14}/_{3} \times {}^{1000}/_{1000} = {}^{14000}/_{3000}$
$1\,{}^{1}/_{3} = {}^{4}/_{3} \times {}^{1000}/_{1000} = {}^{4000}/_{3000}$

Now we can easily compare the fractions since they have the same denominator. In order from greatest to least, the fractions are: $^{14000}/_{3000}, {}^{4167}/_{3000}, {}^{4000}/_{3000}$.

7. C   Use estimation here. Player 1 has made about 2/3 of his free throws. Player 2 has made approximately 7/8, and Player Four has made about 85/100. These are all significantly greater than 1/2. Player 3, however, has made about 1/3 of his free throws. That's less than half, so Player 3 has the worst record.

8. B   First find the greatest decimal. 0.954 > 0.9099. Eliminate Answer C.

Then find the greatest fraction by giving them the same denominator and comparing.
$^{9}/_{10} = {}^{27}/_{30}$ $^{5}/_{6} = {}^{25}/_{30}$ $^{27}/_{30} > {}^{25}/_{30}$ Eliminate Answer D.

Finally, compare the greatest fraction, 9/10, with the greatest decimal, 0.954, to find the highest test score.
$0.954 = {}^{954}/_{1000}$ $^{9}/_{10} = {}^{900}/_{1000}$ $^{954}/_{1000} > {}^{900}/_{1000}$ Answer B, 0.954

Adding and Subtracting Decimals

Adding or subtracting decimal numbers is very similar to adding and subtracting whole numbers. The key is to line up the decimal points in a column. Even if the two numbers have a different number of digits after the decimal point, as long as the decimal places are lined up, you can add as you normally would.

$$
\begin{array}{r}
3.425 \\
+\,12.2 \\
\hline
15.625
\end{array}
$$

↑
└──Line up the decimal places

Remember, if you are adding or subtracting a number with no decimal point, the decimal goes after the number.

Placeholder Zeros

People often find it easier to add and subtract decimals by putting in placeholder zeros. This can be seen in the following problem.

$$
\begin{array}{r}
7.243 \\
+\,11.1 \\
3 \\
8.53 \\
\hline
\end{array}
\qquad
\begin{array}{r}
7.243 \\
+\,11.100 \\
3.000 \\
8.530 \\
\hline
29.873
\end{array}
$$

←──Add placeholder zeros.

↑
└──Line up the decimal places.

Decimals Adding/Subtracting: Practice

1. You open a bank account and deposit $150. Over the next month you withdraw $12.50, $17, and $45.23. How much money is left in the account?

   A. $74.27

   B. $75.27

   C. $76.73

   D. $92.10

2. Jake stayed home from school because he had a fever. In the morning, his temperature was 100.8 degrees. By the afternoon, it was 103.4 degrees. How many degrees had his temperature gone up?

   A. 3.6 degrees

   B. 2.4 degrees

   C. 2.6 degrees

   D. 3.4 degrees

3. Solve. 0.695 – 0.0021 =

   A. 0.6939

   B. 0.6829

   C. 0.6929

   D. 0.6839

4. Solve. 49.627 + 321.395 – 10.001 =

   A. 371.022

   B. 371.021

   C. 361.021

   D. 361.022

5. A woman has seven ten dollar bills, two nickels, seven quarters, and six pennies in her purse. How much will she have after buying groceries for $25.72 and lunch for $4.90?

   A. $40.39

   B. $41.29

   C. $71.91

   D. $30.62

6. Chris needs a plant to grow 12 inches before he can put it in his shop window. The first month it grew 5.47 inches, the next month it grow 3.94 inches, and in the last two weeks it has grown 1.13 inches. How many inches are left for it to grow before it can be displayed?

   A. 2.35

   B. 1.79

   C. 1.46

   D. 10.54

7. Three students are competing. In the first phase of the competition, Julie scored 93.67 points, Sophia scored 75.12, and Travis earned 82.53. In the second phase, Julie and Sophia each scored 58.34 points. How many points must Travis score in the second phase to tie with Julie?

   A. 144.6

   B. 101.08

   C. 70

   D. 69.48

8. Frank deposits all of his extra income into savings. He earned $762.97 last week, $832.64 the week before, and $1000.74 this week. If Frank took a vacation for the rest of the month and his total expenses for the month were $2235.52, how much will he be able to save this month?

   A. $360.83

   B. $36.83

   C. $2596.35

   D. $258.64

Decimals Adding/Subtracting: Answer Explanations

1. B To figure out how much money is left in the account, first find the total amount that was withdrawn. Then, subtract that from the original deposit.

The withdrawal amounts are $12.50, $17, and $45.23. To add, line up the decimal places and add as normal. For $17, put the decimal point after the number and use placeholder zeros so everything lines up.

$$
\begin{array}{r}
\$12.50 \\
+ \ \$17.00 \\
\underline{\$45.23} \\
\$74.73
\end{array}
$$

Now, we must subtract the withdrawals from the original deposit.

$$
\begin{array}{r}
\$150.00 \\
- \ \underline{\$74.73} \\
\$75.27
\end{array}
$$

2. C To subtract decimals, make sure to line up the decimal places. Then subtract as you normally would.

$$
\begin{array}{r}
103.4 \\
- \ \underline{100.8} \\
2.6
\end{array}
$$

3. C To subtract decimals, line up the decimal points, add placeholder zeros, and subtract.

$$
\begin{array}{r}
0.6950 \\
- \ \underline{0.0021} \\
0.6929
\end{array}
$$

4. C Split it into two problems. First, line up the decimal places and add 49.627 and 321.395.

$$
\begin{array}{r}
49.627 \\
+ \ \underline{321.395} \\
371.022
\end{array}
$$

Now, subtract 10.001 from that sum.

$$
\begin{array}{r}
371.022 \\
- \ \underline{10.001} \\
361.021
\end{array}
$$

5. B Seven ten dollar bills is $70, two nickels is $0.10, seven quarters is $1.75, and six pennies can be written $0.06. Add them together to find out how much money she started with.

$$
\begin{array}{r}
70.00 \\
0.10 \\
+ \ 1.75 \\
\underline{0.06} \\
71.91
\end{array}
$$

Calculate the total amount that she spent.

$$
\begin{array}{r}
25.72 \\
+\ \ 4.90 \\
\hline
30.62
\end{array}
$$

Subtract the amount she spent from what she started with.

$$
\begin{array}{r}
71.91 \\
-\ 30.62 \\
\hline
41.29
\end{array}
$$

6. C   Add up the amount that the plant has grown until now and subtract that from 12 to find how much is left to grow.

$$
\begin{array}{r}
5.47 \\
+\ 3.94 \\
1.13 \\
\hline
10.54
\end{array}
$$

Now subtract the height it grew from the total that Chris needs.

$$
\begin{array}{r}
12.00 \\
-\ 10.54 \\
\hline
1.46
\end{array}
$$

7. D   Since Julie and Sophia scored the same number of points in the second phase and Julie scored more in the first phase, Travis will need to beat Julie. Calculate Julie's point total.

$$
\begin{array}{r}
93.67 \\
+\ 58.34 \\
\hline
152.01
\end{array}
$$

Then subtract Travis' first round points from her total.

$$
\begin{array}{r}
152.01 \\
-\ 82.53 \\
\hline
69.48
\end{array}
$$

8. A   First, add up Frank's earnings.

$$
\begin{array}{r}
1000.74 \\
+\ 762.97 \\
832.64 \\
\hline
2596.35
\end{array}
$$

Next, subtract his expenses.

$$
\begin{array}{r}
2596.35 \\
-\ 2235.52 \\
\hline
360.83
\end{array}
$$

Multiplying Decimals

Like adding and subtracting decimals, multiplying decimals is similar to multiplying whole numbers. Simply multiply the digits as you would with whole numbers, and then count the digits to the right of the decimal in all of the multipliers. Place the decimal point so that the product has an equal number of digits to the right of the decimal point.

```
    6  2
  49.83        ← two digits to the right of the decimal sign
x    5.7        ← one digit to the right of the decimal sign
  34881
+ 249150
  284.031      ← three digits to the right of the decimal sign
```

Dividing Decimals

To divide a decimal by a whole number, simply transfer the decimal sign to the quotient directly above its position in the dividend; then divide as usual.

```
      7.05      The divisor has no decimal places,
  7│49.35       so divide as you normally would.
        ̭         But in this case, bring the decimal point
       035      from the dividend up to the answer.
```

To divide any number by a decimal, multiply the divisor and the dividend by the power of ten necessary to turn the divisor into a whole number. Then divide as usual.

```
             First multiply the divisor by a power of ten
             necessary to make it a whole number,
0.3│9.42     in this case, 10.

       31.4  Multiply the dividend by the same.
  3│94.2
             Then divide as normally would, bringing the
             decimal point up to the quotient.
```

Decimals Multiplying/Dividing: Practice

1. A restaurant uses 1.5 pounds of flour every hour that it is open. It is open for 5.75 hours per day, 6 days per week. How many pounds of flour does the restaurant use each week?

A. 5.175

B. 13.25

C. 45.75

D. 51.75

2. What is one millionth of 12.97?

A. 12,970,000

B. 12.97

C. 0.000001297

D. 0.00001297

3. Sandra got up early and ran 7.8 km. Debra had more energy, and ran 1.5 times the distance that Sandra did. How far did Debra run?

   A. 9.3 km

   B. 10.6 km

   C. 11.3 km

   D. 11.7 km

4. Average 0.7, 0.11, and 0.75.

   A. 0.52

   B. 1.56

   C. 156/100

   D. 156/3

5. Adam is 3.5 times the age of his son. If Adam is 42, how old is his son?

   A. 7

   B. 12

   C. 14

   D. 21

6. Solve. 72.4 ÷ 0.004 =

   A. .0181

   B. 1.81

   C. 1810

   D. 18100

7. Solve. 0.003 x 1.24 ÷ 0.05 =

   A. 0.00744

   B. 0.0744

   C. 0.744

   D. 7.44

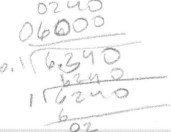

8. Solve. 0.2 x 3.12 ÷ 0.1 =

   A. 0.00624

   B. 0.0624

   C. 0.624

   D. 6.24

Decimals Multiplying/Dividing: Answer Explanations

1. D   First, calculate the number of hours the restaurant is open per week and then multiply that by the amount of flour used each hour.

   To calculate the number of hours it is open, multiply the hours per day by the days per week.

   5.75 x 6 = 34.50 = 34.5

   Now, multiply that result by the amount of flour used per hour.

   34.5 x 1.5 = 51.75, 51.75 pounds

2. D   Write one millionth as a decimal and then multiply the numbers. Remember, "of" means multiply.

$$12.97 \quad \leftarrow \text{two digits to the right of the decimal sign}$$
$$\times \quad .000001 \quad \leftarrow \text{six digits to the right of the decimal sign}$$
$$\overline{0.00001297} \quad \leftarrow \text{eight digits to the right of the decimal sign}$$

3. D   To find out how far Debra ran, multiply Sandra's distance by 1.5. Notice that 7.8 has one digit to the right of the decimal and 1.5 also has one digit, thus the product will have two digits to the right of decimal.

$$7.8$$
$$\times \quad 1.5$$
$$\overline{390}$$
$$+ \quad 780$$
$$\overline{11.70}$$

4. A   To average three numbers, add them up and divide by 3.

First, line the decimals up and add them.

$$0.70$$
$$0.11$$
$$+ \quad 0.75$$
$$\overline{1.56}$$

Now, divide their sum by 3. $1.56 \div 3 = 0.52$

5. B   Since Adam is 3.5 times the age of his son, if we know Adams age we divide to find his son's age.

Adam's age divided by 3.5 = Son's Age

$42 \div 3.5 = 420 \div 35 = 12$, Adam's son is 12. Answer B.

You can also work backwards in problems like this. Take each answer choice and multiply it by 3.5 to see which one gets you to 42.

6. D $0.004\overline{)72.4}$ $4\overline{)72400}$ = 18100   To divide decimals, you need to move the decimal points and then divide as normal. 18100, Answer D

Move the decimal point 3 places.

7. B   Following order of operations, multiply and divide from left to right. First, multiply 0.003 by 1.24 and then take that product and divide it by 0.05.

0.003 x 1.24 = 0.00372

Since there were 3 digits to the right of the decimal point in 0.003 and 2 digits to the right of the decimal point in 1.24, you multiply the numbers and then move the decimal point 5 places.

Now, take the result and divide it by 0.05.

$0.00372 \div 0.05 = 0.372 \div 5 = 0.0744$

8. D   First, multiply 0.2 x 3.12. Multiply the numbers as if there were no decimals, and then move the decimal point 3 places to left since there are 3 digits after the decimal place in the original question.

0.2 x 3.12 = 0.624

Now, divide 0.624 by 0.1. Move the decimal point the same number of times in both the dividend and divisor, in this case move it once.

$0.624 \div 0.1 = 6.24 \div 1 = 6.24$

Percent Definition

Percents are a way of expressing fractions, where the "whole" is 100%. Therefore, 1 is the same as 100%. If you have a fraction with a denominator of 100, then the numerator of that fraction is equal to the percent and vice versa.

$3/100 = 3\%$

$17\% = 17/100$

$50\% = 50/100 = \frac{1}{2}$

Finding Percents

To find the percent when given a fraction, convert the fraction to an equivalent fraction with a denominator of 100, then the numerator of that fraction is the percent.

$7/25 = 28/100 = 28\%$

$1/20 = 5/100 = 5\%$

Solving Percent Problems

Generally, convert the percent to a fraction or a decimal and then solve as you normally would.

What is 20% of 30?

$= 20\% \times 30$

$= 20/100 \times 30$

$= \frac{1}{5} \times 30$

$= 6$

Percents: Practice

1. In how many of the categories in the figure is the annual budget allotment less than $8,000?

    A. One

    B. Two

    C. Three

    D. Four

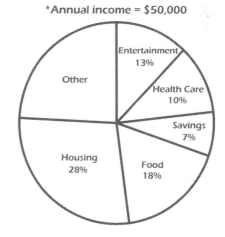

Family annual budget by percents of annual income *

*Annual income = $50,000

Entertainment 13%

Other

Health Care 10%

Savings 7%

Housing 28%

Food 18%

2. If a bear that weighs 962 pounds in the autumn loses 20% of its weight while hibernating, what will the bear weigh in the spring?

    A. 769.6

    B. 76.96

    C. 192.4

    D. 942

3. A group of 7 women bought a lottery ticket. If they win 84% of the million dollar jackpot and share their winnings equally, how much, will each woman receive?

    A. $120

    B. $1,200

    C. $12,000

    D. $120,000

4. What is 29% of 13%?

    A. $37 \frac{7}{10}$

    B. $\frac{377}{1000}$

    C. $\frac{377}{10000}$

    D. $\frac{377}{100000}$

5. If a > b, what would replace the question mark?

              a% of b   ?   b% of a

    A. >

    B. <

    C. =

    D. Not enough information

6. Two trees were hit by lightning. The sycamore is now 57% of its original 58 foot height. The elm is now 34% of its original 79 foot height. Which tree is taller now?

    A. The sycamore is taller.

    B. The elm is taller.

    C. They are equal.

    D. Not enough information.

7. Choose the best answer to replace the question mark:

              20% of 97   ?   97% of 20

    A. >

    B. <

    C. =

    D. ≤

8. Order the following from least to greatest: 40% of 70, 45% of 70%, 70% of 60.

    A. 40% of 70, 45% of 70%, 70% of 60

    B. 40% of 70, 70% of 60, 45% of 70%

    C. 45% of 70%, 40% of 70, 70% of 60

    D. 45% of 70%, 70% of 60, 40% of 70

Percents: Answer Explanations

1. C   To determine how many categories are less than $8,000, we must first figure out the value of each category. To do this, we convert the percent to a fraction and multiply that by the annual budget of $50,000.

Entertainment: 13% = 13/100
13/100 x $50,000 = $6500
Since Entertainment was 13% and that was below $8000, we know that Health Care and Savings will also be under $8000.

Food: 18% = 18/100
18/100 x $50,000 = $9000
This is too high.

Housing will also be too high since it is 28% and Food was only 18%.

The percent for the Other category wasn't listed. Therefore, it must be calculated. All the percents will add up to 100%, so add up the other categories and subtract the sum from 100.
13% + 10% + 7% + 18% + 28% = 76%
100% − 76% = 24%
The other category will also be more than $8000.

The only categories less than $8,000 are Entertainment, Health Care, and Savings.

2. A   There are two ways to solve this problem.
Option 1:
If the bear loses 20% of its bodyweight, then it keeps 80% of it. Multiply the original weight by 80% to find what it will weigh in spring.
962 x 80% = 962 x $^{80}/_{100}$ = $^{76960}/_{100}$ = 769.6 pounds

Option 2:
Calculate the amount of weight the bear will lose and subtract that amount from the original weight.
962 x 20% = 962 x $^{20}/_{100}$ = $^{19240}/_{100}$ = 192.4 pounds
962 − 192.4 = 769.6 pounds

3. D   To find the amount that each woman receives, you need to calculate the amount that the entire group won and divide that amount by 7.
84% x $1,000,000 = $^{84}/_{100}$ x $1,000,000 = $840,000
$840,000 ÷ 7 = $120,000

4. C   Convert each percent to a fraction and then multiply.
29% = $^{29}/_{100}$
13% = $^{13}/_{100}$
$^{29}/_{100}$ x $^{13}/_{100}$ = $^{377}/_{10000}$

5. C   Let's examine each side of the question mark.
a% of b = a/100 x b = ab/100
b% of a = b/100 x a = ba/100
It doesn't matter whether a is bigger than b, both sides of the question mark are equal.

6. A To calculate their new heights, convert the percents to fractions and multiply their original heights by those fractions.

Sycamore: 57% of 58 feet

57% x 58 = $\frac{57}{100}$ x 58 = $\frac{3306}{100}$

Elm: 34% of 79 feet

34% x 79 = $\frac{34}{100}$ x 79 = $\frac{2686}{100}$

The sycamore is taller.

7. C Convert the percents to fractions and then multiply to compare.

20% of 97 =

20% x 97 =

$\frac{20}{100}$ x 97 =

$\frac{1940}{100}$

97% of 20 =

97% x 20 =

$\frac{97}{100}$ x 20 =

$\frac{1940}{100}$

They are equal.

8. C Let's examine each of the three expressions. Remember, that "of" means multiply and a percent could be made into a fraction with a denominator of 100.

40% of 70 = $\frac{40}{100}$ x 70 = 28

45% of 70% = $\frac{45}{100}$ x $\frac{70}{100}$ = $\frac{3150}{10000}$

70% of 60 = $\frac{70}{100}$ x 60 = 42

Therefore, ordering from least to greatest: 45% of 70%, 40% of 70, 70% of 60.

Decimals to Fractions

To convert a fraction to a decimal, simply write out the decimal as a fraction with a denominator that is a power of ten. Look at the place value of the last digit to determine what power of ten to use as the denominator. Then simplify.

$0.125 = {}^{125}\!/_{1000} = {}^{1}\!/_{8}$

Fractions to Decimals

Remember that the / in a fraction is actually a division sign. To convert a fraction to a decimal, simply divide the numerator by the denominator.

${}^{855}\!/_{4} = 855 \div 4 = 213.75$

Decimals to Percents

To convert a decimal to a percent, multiply the decimal by 100%. Another way to think about this process, is move the decimal point two places to the right and add a percent sign.

$0.7345 = 0.7345 \times 100\% = 73.45\%$

Percents to Decimals

To convert a percent to a decimal, divide the percent by 100%. Another way to think about it, is move the decimal point two places to the left and remove the percent sign.

$154.9\% = 154.9\% \div 100\% = 1.549$

Fractions to Percents

To convert a fraction to a percent, first convert the fraction to a decimal and then multiply the decimal by 100%.

${}^{3}\!/_{4} = .75 = 75\%$

Percents to Fractions

To convert a percent to a fraction, convert the percent to a decimal by dividing by 100% and then write the decimal as a fraction with a denominator that is a power of 10. If possible, simplify the fraction.

$40\% = 0.40 = {}^{40}\!/_{100} = {}^{2}\!/_{5}$

Conversions: Practice

1. Write the following words as a decimal.
Eighteen and Thirty One Fiftieths

   A. 18.31

   B. 18.62

   C. 18.3150

   D. 49.50

$18.\frac{31}{50}$

2. Write 504.30% as a fraction.

   A. 504 $\frac{3}{10}$

   B. 5 $\frac{43}{1000}$

   C. $\frac{5043}{100}$

   D. 50 $\frac{43}{100}$

3. Express 0.0375 as a fraction.

   A. $\frac{375}{1000}$

   B. $\frac{3}{80}$

   C. 3 $\frac{75}{100}$

   D. $\frac{3}{8}$

4. For an internet startup, sales increased this quarter by 716%. If their sales last quarter totaled $10,000, what was the sales total for this quarter?

   A. $10,716

   B. $17,160

   C. $71,600

   D. $81,600

5. Which answer choice has the largest value?

   A. 28% of 75

   B. product of 0.75 and 28

   C. ($\frac{3}{4}$)(28)

   D. All of the above are equal.

6. Two teenagers go to a batting cage. One of them bats .287 and the other bats .345. If the decimal represents the fraction of balls thrown that each of them hit, what is the average percent of balls that the two players hit?

   A. 0.316%

   B. 0.632%

   C. 31.6%

   D. 63.2%

7. Drew answered all of the questions on a test correctly, and he also answered one extra credit question. If each of the test questions were counted equally, including the extra credit and his score was 112.5%, how many questions were on the test, including the extra credit?

   A. 8

   B. 9

   C. 10

   D. 12.5

8. Darlene washed 7 ²⁄₅ loads of laundry, what percent of a full load did she wash?

A. 37%

B. 74%

C. 370%

D. 740%

Conversions: Answer Explanations

1. B   It is easiest to first take the words and make them into a mixed number.

Eighteen and Thirty One Fiftieths
Eighteen is the whole number, and Thirty One Fiftieths is the fraction.
18 ³¹⁄₅₀

Now we must take this fraction and convert it to a decimal. There are multiple ways to do this.

Method 1: Divide 31 by 50 and get a decimal and then put the whole number in front. 31 divided by 50 is 0.62. Therefore, the answer would be 18.62.

Method 2: Find an equivalent fraction whose denominator is a multiple of 10. In this case, ³¹⁄₅₀ can easily be converted to a fraction whose denominator is 100. Multiply numerator and denominator by 2, giving you ⁶²⁄₁₀₀. Therefore, the equivalent mixed number is 18 ⁶²⁄₁₀₀, which is 18 and 62 hundredths, which is written as 18.62

2. B   First convert the percent to a decimal and then convert the decimal to a fraction.

To convert a percent to a decimal, divide by 100%.
504.30% ÷ 100% = 5.043

To convert a decimal to a fraction, look at the place value of the last digit, and put the number over that power of 10. In this case, the 3 is in the thousandths place so put the number over 1000.
5.043 = ⁵⁰⁴³⁄₁₀₀₀

Now make the fraction a mixed number and reduce if possible.
⁵⁰⁴³⁄₁₀₀₀ = 5 ⁴³⁄₁₀₀₀

3. B   To convert a decimal to a fraction, look at the place value of the last digit and make the denominator a power of 10 corresponding to that place.

In 0.0375, the last digit is in the ten thousandths place. Therefore, 0.0375 = ³⁷⁵⁄₁₀₀₀₀.

Now simplify. ³⁷⁵⁄₁₀₀₀₀ ÷ ¹²⁵⁄₁₂₅ = ³⁄₈₀

4. D   Convert the percent to a decimal.
716% ÷ 100% = 7.16

Multiply the decimal by which the sales have increased by the sales total from last quarter.
7.16 x $10,000 = $71,600

Therefore, the sales have increased by $71,600. Add this to the sales total from last quarter to find out the sales total for this quarter.
$71,600 + $10,000 = $81,600

5. D   Let's examine each answer choice.

A: 28% of 75
= 28% x 75
= $\frac{28}{100}$ x 75
= $\frac{7}{25}$ x 75
= 21

B: product of 0.75 and 28
= 0.75 x 28
= $\frac{75}{100}$ x 28
= ¾ x 28
= 21

C: (¾)(28)
= ¾ x 28
= 21

All of the above are equal.

6. C   Average the decimals by adding them and dividing by two.

0.287 + 0.345 = 0.632
0.632 ÷ 2 = 0.316

Convert the decimal to a percent by multiplying by 100%.
0.316 x 100% = 31.6%

7. B   Answering the regular questions correctly earned Drew 100%. Subtract 100% from his total score to calculate the value of the extra credit question.
112.5% – 100% = 12.5%

Since the extra credit counted equally with a regular test question, convert the percent of the test that consists of extra credit to a fraction with one in the numerator to find the number of regular test questions.

Begin by converting the percent to a decimal.
12.5% ÷ 100% = 0.125

Convert the decimal to a fraction.
0.125 = $\frac{125}{1000}$ = ⅛

There were 8 regular test questions, plus 1 extra credit, so there were 9 questions total.

8. D   Write the mixed number of loads that she washed as an improper fraction.
7 ⅖ = $\frac{37}{5}$

Convert the fraction of loads to a decimal.
$\frac{37}{5}$ = 37 ÷ 5 = 7.4

Now, convert the decimal to a percent.
7.4 x 100 % = 740%

1. Order the numbers from least to greatest: 0.81, $\frac{9}{100}$, 0.819, $\frac{4}{5}$.

   A. $\frac{9}{100}$, $\frac{4}{5}$, 0.81, 0.819

   B. 0.81, $\frac{4}{5}$, $\frac{9}{100}$, 0.819

   C. $\frac{9}{100}$, 0.819, 0.81, $\frac{4}{5}$

   D. $\frac{4}{5}$, 0.81, 0.819, $\frac{9}{100}$

2. A company's sales revenue was \$1,000,000 last year. This year its expected revenue is \$25,000,000. What percentage of last year's sales revenue is this year's projected revenue?

   A. 2.5%

   B. 25%

   C. 250%

   D. 2500%

3. Doug worked 3 ½ hours on Monday and 1 ¾ hours on Tuesday. If Susanna worked 4 hours on Monday and 2 $\frac{3}{7}$ hours on Tuesday. How many more hours did Susanna work than Doug on those two days?

   A. 1 $\frac{2}{3}$

   B. 1 $\frac{5}{28}$

   C. 2 ¼

   D. 2 $\frac{2}{5}$

4. Aaron works 7.5 hours per day, 6 days per week. If he makes \$9.35 per hour, how much does he make each week?

   A. \$42.75

   B. \$70.13

   C. \$374

   D. \$420.75

5. My cat eats $\frac{3}{5}$ cups of food every day. How many cups of food does she eat in two weeks?

   A. $2\frac{1}{5}$ cups

   B. 8 $\frac{2}{5}$ cups

   C. 10 cups

   D. 10 $\frac{2}{5}$ cups

6. Steven owns 17,000 shares of stock in a company with 51,000 equal shares. If the annual profits for the company are \$270,000 and each stockholder gets a share proportionate to the amount of stock he or she owns, how much should Steven get for the year?

   A. \$90,000

   B. \$180,000

   C. \$200,000

   D. \$287,000

7. In a speed–eating contest, Bart ate ¾ of a pizza and Darlene ate ⅞ of another the same size. Who won, and how much more pizza did he or she eat?

A. Darlene won by ⁴⁄₄ of a pizza.

B. Bart won by ⁴⁄₄ of a pizza.

C. Darlene won by ⅛ of a pizza.

D. Bart won by ⅛ of a pizza.

8. Solve. ⁶⁄₉ − ²⁄₄ − ¹⁄₇ =

A. ¹²⁄₂₅₂

B. ³⁄₂

C. ¹⁄₄₂

D. ³⁄₂₀

9. Carol bought 6 books for $6.95 each. She was charged an additional $3.34 total on her purchases. She was left with $5.96. How much money did Carol start with?

A. $39.08

B. $50.00

C. $51.00

D. $67.70

10. The electronics store is holding a sale where everything in the store is 20% off. If the sale price of the stereo is $47.00, what was the original price?

A. $37.60

B. $47.20

C. $56.40

D. $58.75

11. Hannah's cat eats pet food that is 2.9% protein. What fraction of her cat's food is not protein?

A. ⁹⁷¹⁄₁₀₀₀

B. ⁹⁹⁷¹⁄₁₀₀₀₀

C. 97 ¹⁄₁₀

D. ⁷¹⁄₁₀₀

12. A yardwork company cut down a tree that was 98 ¼ feet tall. They must divide the tree into segments no larger than ¹³⁄₁₆ feet for disposal. What is the minimum number of segments into which they can cut the tree for disposal?

A. 119

B. 120

C. 121

D. 122

13. Convert $^{5692}/_{10}$ **to a decimal.**

A. 569.2

B. 56.92

C. 5.692

D. 0.5692

14. Debra worked 4.25 hours on Monday, 5.6 hours on Tuesday, 8 hours on Wednesday, and she took off both Thursday and Friday. What was the average number of hours she worked over the 5 days?

A. 3.462 hours

B. 3.57 hours

C. 5.95 hours

D. 6.85 hours

15. One liter of a solution is .723 water and .178 hydrochloric acid. What part of the solution's composition is unstated?

A. 0.901

B. 9.01

C. 0.99

D. 0.099

16. Susanna runs her own jewelery shop. For each necklace, it costs her $2.21 for materials, $1.24 for overhead, and $0.47 for marketing. She charges $19.60 per necklace. What percentage of the selling price of the necklace is Susanna's profit? (hint: Profit = Revenue – Cost)

A. 16%

B. 20%

$19.60 = R - 3.92$

C. 80%

12.98

D. 83%

17. The average precipitation for the first 3 months of the year was 12.5mm. If the precipitation for each month had been 1.5mm greater, what would the average have been?

A.13mm

B.14mm

C.17mm

D.39mm

18. Which answer choice is the smallest?

A. 2 ⅕

B. 215%

C. 2.5

D. ¹²⁄₅

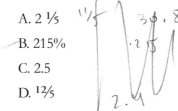

19. Matthew was offered 2 possible salaries for the month. Option 1: $10,000 plus 10% of whatever he sold. Option 2: $8,000 plus 15% of whatever he sold. If Matthew sold $35,000 worth of goods, which option should he choose?

A. Option 1

B. Option 2

C. Either, they are the same

D. Not enough information.

20. What is equal to the following expression?

$3/1000 + 1/10 + 1/2000 + 6/500$

A. 0.011

B. 0.1128

C. 0.1155

D. 0.0165

Fractions, Decimals, Percents: Chapter Review Answer Explanations

1. A   The easiest way to compare numbers is to make them all decimals. So, convert 9/100 and 4/5 to decimals.

$9/100$ = nine hundredths = 0.09

$4/5 = 8/10$ = eight tenths = 0.8

Now your task is to order: 0.81, 0.09, .819, 0.8

There are two methods for ordering decimals.

Method 1: Line up the decimal places and compare one digit at a time.

        0.81
        0.09
        0.819
        0.8

So, comparing the first digit of each of those numbers, you see 8, 0, 8, 8. The smallest is 0, so that number (0.09) is the smallest. Now compare the next digit for the remaining numbers (0.81, 0.819, 0.8). The next digit is 1, 1, and no digit, which can be thought of as 0. Thus, the 0 is the smallest and 0.8 is the next smallest number. Then compare the third digit, nothing (or zero) and 9. The smallest is again 0, so that is the next smallest number.

Final order: 0.09, 0.8, 0.81, 0.819

Method 2: You can also add zeros so that every number has the same number of decimal places, which may make it easier to compare.

Add zeros so each has 3 decimal places: 0.810, 0.090, 0.819, 0.800

Now order by comparing the numbers after the decimal place. From smallest to biggest: 90, 800, 810, 819. Therefore, the decimal order is 0.090, 0.800, 0.810, 0.819

2. D   This year's projected revenue is $25,000,000, which is 25 times last year's revenue. Multiply by 100% to find its percent of last year's revenue.

25 x 100% = 2500%

Another way to think about this word problem is to take the words and translate them into an equation. "What percentage of last year's sales revenue is this year's projected revenue?"

"What percentage" = n %, "of" = multiplication, "last year's sales revenue" = $1,000,000, "is" = equals, "this year's projected revenue" = $25,000,000

$n\% \times \$1,000,000 = \$25,000,000$
$n\% = 25$
$n = 2500$

3. B   We first should find Doug's total, then Susanna's total, and then find the difference.
Doug's Total: $3\frac{1}{2} + 1\frac{3}{4}$

You can convert the mixed numbers to improper fractions, give them the same denominator, and then add.
$3\frac{1}{2} = \frac{7}{2} = \frac{14}{4}$
$1\frac{3}{4} = \frac{7}{4}$
$\frac{14}{4} + \frac{7}{4} = \frac{21}{4}$

Find Susanna's total: $4 + 2\frac{3}{7}$. You can add the whole numbers and fractions separately. Therefore, Susanna's total = $6\frac{3}{7}$.

Now, we must find the difference. $6\frac{3}{7} - \frac{21}{4}$

Give the fractions the same denominator.
$6\frac{3}{7} = \frac{45}{7} = \frac{180}{28}$
$\frac{21}{4} = \frac{147}{28}$
$\frac{180}{28} - \frac{147}{28} = \frac{33}{28} = 1\frac{5}{28}$

4. D   To calculate how much Aaron makes per week, multiply the dollars per hour by the number of hours per day by the days per week.

$\$9.35 \times 7.5 = 70.125$
$70.125 \times 6 = \$420.75$

5. B   There are 14 days in two weeks (7 days per week times 2 weeks).

Multiply the amount she eats each day by the total number of days to find out the total amount of food the cat eats.

$\frac{3}{5}$ cups per day x 14 days = $\frac{42}{5}$ cups = $8\frac{2}{5}$ cups

6. A   Break the problem into multiple steps. First determine what fraction of the total shares Steven owns. Then determine how much Steven should get.

Steven owns 17,000 shares out of a total of 51,000 shares. Therefore, Steven owns: $\frac{17000}{51000}$ which equals $\frac{1}{3}$ of the shares.

To find out how much Steven should get, multiply the fraction he owns by the total annual profits.
$\frac{1}{3} \times \$270,000 = \$90,000$

7. C   This problem includes two tasks. The first thing you must do is compare the fractions to find the one that is greater. This can be accomplished by converting to a common denominator. The least common multiple of 4 and 8 is 8.

¾ = ⁶⁄₈

Now compare the fractions.

⅞ > ⁶⁄₈

Therefore, Darlene won the contest. Now subtract the lesser number from the greater.

⅞ − ⁶⁄₈ = ⅛

8. C   Before subtracting fractions, you must give them a common denominator. The least common multiple (See Numbers and Properties: Factors, Multiples, and Divisibility for help) of 9, 4, and 7 is 252. You must convert each fraction so that it has a denominator of 252.

⁶⁄₉ × ²⁸⁄₂₈ = ¹⁶⁸⁄₂₅₂
²⁄₄ × ⁶³⁄₆₃ = ¹²⁶⁄₂₅₂
¹⁄₇ × ³⁶⁄₃₆ = ³⁶⁄₂₅₂

Subtract the numerators. ⁽¹⁶⁸₋¹²⁶₋³⁶⁾⁄₂₅₂ = ⁶⁄₂₅₂
Simplify. ⁶⁄₂₅₂ ÷ ⁶⁄₆ = ¹⁄₄₂

9. C   Break the problem into steps. First, figure out the total cost of the books.
Books: 6 books x $6.95 each = $41.70

Now, add the sales tax. $41.70 + $3.34 = $45.04

Then, if Carol left with $4.96, add that back to the $45.04 to see how much she started with.
$45.04 + $5.96 = $51.00

10. D   There are two ways to approach this problem, either solve or work backwards using the answer choices.

Method 1: To solve the equation, we must first take the word problem and translate it into an equation. If $47.00 is 20% off the original price, that means that $47 is 80% of the original price.

$47 = 80% x P	translate into an equation with P as the original price
$47 = 0.80 x P	convert percent to decimal, 80% is the same as 0.80
$47/0.80=0.80xP/0.80	divide both sides by 0.80
$58.75 = P	

Method 2: Work backwards. Try each answer choice and take 20% of each of them and subtract it from the price to see which gives you $47.00.

$58.75 * 20% =	Try answer choice D.
$58.75 * 0.20 =	convert from percent to a decimal
$11.75	this was the savings
$58.75 – $11.75	subtract the savings from the price
$47.00	this would give you the correct sale price
Answer D. $58.75	

11. A   Convert the percent that is protein to a decimal and then to a fraction. To convert to a decimal, divide by 100%. To convert to a fraction, look at the place value of the last digit and make a denominator that is a power of 10.

$2.9\% \div 100\% = 0.029 = {}^{29}\!/_{1000}$

Subtract the fraction of her cat's food that is protein from 1 (use ${}^{1000}\!/_{1000}$ to give the two fractions a common denominator).
${}^{1000}\!/_{1000} - {}^{29}\!/_{1000} = {}^{971}\!/_{1000}$

12. C   Convert the tree height into an improper fraction so that it can be divided by the maximum segment length.
$98 \, \tfrac{1}{4} = {}^{393}\!/_{4}$ feet

Now, divide the total tree height by the length of each segment.
${}^{393}\!/_{4} \div {}^{13}\!/_{16} = {}^{393}\!/_{4} \times {}^{16}\!/_{13} = {}^{393}\!/_{1} \times {}^{4}\!/_{13} = {}^{1572}\!/_{13} = 120 \, {}^{12}\!/_{13}$

That means 120 segments with 12/13 of a segment left over. Round up to the nearest whole to find the minimum number of segments the yardwork company will need to cut.

13. A   The fraction is over 10, so the last digit of the numerator should be in the tenths place. Remember that the tenths place is the first place after the decimal point. Therefore the answer is 569.2.

14. B   To find the average, add up all the numbers and divide by the total number of numbers.

When adding, line up the decimal places.

$$
\begin{array}{r}
4.25 \\
+ \quad 5.6 \\
\underline{8} \\
17.85
\end{array}
$$

Now, divide by 5 to find the average.
$17.85 \div 5 = 3.57$
3.57 hours

15. D   Add the known or stated fractions of the solution.

$$
\begin{array}{r}
0.723 \\
+ \; 0.178 \\
\hline
0.901
\end{array}
$$

Then subtract the fraction of the solution that is known from the total.

$$
\begin{array}{r}
1.000 \\
- \; 0.901 \\
\hline
0.099
\end{array}
$$

16. C You must first determine Susanna's profit. This can be found by adding her costs and subtracting that from her revenue or what she charges. Remember, when adding or subtracting decimals, make sure to line up the decimal places.

$$\begin{array}{r} 2.21 \\ 1.24 \\ +\ 0.47 \\ \hline 3.92 \end{array}$$

Total costs = $3.92

Profit = Revenue – Costs = 19.6 – 3.92

$$\begin{array}{r} 19.60 \\ -\ \ 3.92 \\ \hline 15.68 \end{array}$$

Profit = $15.68

To find out what percentage of the selling price Susanna's profit was, you divide the profit by the selling price: $15.68/19.60$.

You can get rid of the decimal places in both the dividend and divisor by multiplying each of them by 100. This will move the decimal place to the right for both values: $1568/1960$.

Then divide as you normally would, and your answer = 0.80.

To convert from a decimal to a percent, you move the decimal point two places to the right. 0.80 = 80%

17. B There are two ways to approach this problem.

Method 1: Convert to totals.

Instead of dealing with averages, deal with total amount of precipitation. If the average as 12.5mm for 3 months, the total precipitation during those 3 months can be found by multiplying average by number of months.

Total Precipitation = 12.5 x 3 = 37.5mm

If the precipitation increased by 1.5mm each month, multiply by 3 to find total precipitation increase.
Precipitation increase = 1.5 x 3 = 4.5mm

New total prec. = 37.5mm + 4.5mm = 42mm

To find new average, divide new total by 3 months.
Average = 42mm ÷ 3 = 14mm

Method 2: Keep everything in averages.

If the average was 12.5mm, you can think of each month as having 12.5mm of precipitation. If each month it increased by 1.5mm, you can add 1.5mm to each month to figure out new amount of precipitation.

12.5mm + 1.5mm = 14mm

If you think of each month as 14mm, then the average across all 3 months is 14mm.

18. B Convert each answer choice to a decimal and compare.

A: $2\frac{1}{5} = 2\frac{20}{100} = 2.20$

B: $215\% = 2.15$

C: 2.5

D: $\frac{12}{5} = 2\frac{2}{5} = 2\frac{40}{100} = 2.40$

The smallest is 2.15, answer choice B.

19. A Option 1: $10,000 plus 10% of what he sold.

Matthew sold $35,000, so find 10% of that.

$35,000 x 10% =

$35,000 x 0.10 =

$3,500

Option 1: $10,000 + $3,500 = $13,500

Option 2: $8,000 plus 15% of what he sold.

$35,000 x 15% =

$35,000 x 0.15 =

$5,250

Option 2: $8,000 + $5,250 = $13,250

Option 1 will give Matthew more money.

20. C First, scan your answers. Note that all the answers are in decimal form. Therefore, you can either add the fractions first and then convert the result to a decimal, or you could convert all the fractions to decimals and then add. Either are acceptable, just depends on your preference.

$\frac{3}{1000} + \frac{1}{10} + \frac{1}{2000} + \frac{6}{500}$

Method 1: Add Fractions then Convert to Decimal

To add fractions, first give them all the same denominators. The least common denominator is 2000.

$\frac{3}{1000} = \frac{6}{2000}$

$\frac{1}{10} = \frac{200}{2000}$

$\frac{1}{2000} = \frac{1}{2000}$

$\frac{6}{500} = \frac{24}{2000}$

Now, add.

$\frac{6}{2000} + \frac{200}{2000} + \frac{1}{2000} + \frac{24}{2000} = \frac{231}{2000}$

Next, you must convert to a decimal. You can either put the fraction over an exact power of ten or divide.

$\frac{231}{2000} = \frac{1155}{10000} = 0.1155$

$231 \div 2000 = 0.1155$

Method 2: Convert to Decimals and then Add

To convert each fraction to a decimal, convert the denominator to an exact power of ten and then move the decimal place accordingly. Otherwise, you can divide the numerator by the denominator.

$\frac{3}{1000} = 0.003$

$\frac{1}{10} = 0.1$

$\frac{1}{2000} = \frac{5}{10000} = 0.0005$

$\frac{6}{500} = \frac{12}{1000} = 0.012$

When adding decimals, be sure to line up the decimal places. Often people find it easier to add placeholder zeros after the decimal so every number has the same number of places.

$0.003 + 0.1 + 0.0005 + 0.012 = 0.0030 + 0.1000 + 0.0005 + 0.0120 = 0.1155$

3. Algebra

Variables

A variable is a letter that represents a value. If you are solving a problem and you have an unknown value, you could use a variable to represent that value. For example, if you knew that Sam was 5 years older than Andrew, but you were unsure of how old Andrew was, you could use a variable to represent Andrew's age, let's use "a" and then Sam's age could be expressed as: a + 5.

Once the value for the variable is determined, it can replace the variable in an expression. For instance, in the above expression, we know that Sam's age is a + 5, where a represents Andrew's age. If we found out that Andrew was 10, then we could substitute 10 in for a, and solve for Sam's age.

a + 5 = 10 + 5 = 15. Therefore, if we knew that Andrew was 10, we would know that Sam was 15.

Algebraic Expressions

An algebraic expression is a phrase (no equality sign) that contains terms with numbers or variables and one or more operations. For example, 4 + y is an algebraic expression. When expressing relationships between numbers or variables, algebraic expressions are used. For example, above we used the algebraic expression a + 5 to represent Sam's age. Algebraic expressions are also conveniently a shorter way to write a long statement.

Add three to a number and then multiply the sum by six and take the result and subtract seven = 6(n+3) – 7

Patterns

A pattern is a predictable set of elements. The two basic types of patterns are those that repeat and those that are generated based on a model. We will briefly examine repeating patterns, but the focus of the lesson is on the second type of pattern, which is one of the more basic forms of algebra. Algebraic expressions are used to represent these patterns.

Repeating Patterns

A repeating pattern is one in which a sequence of elements, called a core, is repeated two or more times. The elements can be anything from shapes to letters to numbers. These patterns show several examples of repeated cores which are underlined.

Patterns based on models

The second type of pattern is a much broader category, but it is one that is vital to mathematics. A non–repeating pattern is any predictable set of elements, so anything that uses a template or model to create output for a given input generates a pattern. For mathematical purposes, the input is generally the element number (1st, 2nd, 3rd, 4th, etc) and the output is the element itself.

Example: 3, 6, 9, 12, 15, ...

For the input 1, there is an output of 3. For the input 2, there is an output of 6. This data is exhibiting a pattern y=3x, where x is the input, and y is the output.

On a multiple choice test, determining which pattern is exhibited by a set of data is often as simple as plugging in element numbers into the answer choices to find the expression that generates the appropriate outputs.

Example: Which pattern is exhibited by the data? –2, –4, –8, –16, –32, –64, –128, ...

      A. y = 2x   B. y = –2x   C. y = x – 3   D. y = 4x

You can see in the pattern that the 1st input gives you a value of –2. Let's plug in 1 for x in each of the answer choices to see which gives a –2. Only answer choices B and C work, eliminate A and D. Now, try plugging in a 2 for x in the remaining equations to see which outputs a 4.

Answer choice C: y = x – 3, when x = 2, y = 2 – 3 = –1. This does not work.

Answer choice B: y = –2x, when x = 2, y = –2(2) = –4. This works. This is your answer.

Patterns & Variables: Practice

1. What is the next element in the pattern? −125, 25, −5, 1, ... ?

    A. 0.5

    B. −0.5

    C. $\frac{1}{5}$

    D. $-\frac{1}{5}$

2. Roger's age is 2 less than 5 times Luke's age. If Luke's age equals n, what expression represents Roger's age?

    A. $2 - 5n$

    B. $5n \div 2$

    C. $3n$

    D. $5n - 2$

$5x - 2$

3. Which of the following expressions has the largest value when x = 10?

    A. $x + 10{,}000$

    B. $x^5 + 100x^4$

    C. 10^x

    D. $1000x$

4. If the pattern below continues, how many shaded triangles will be in the fourth figure?

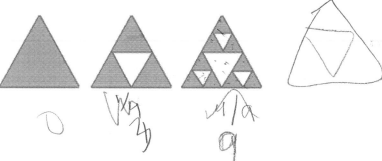

    A. 12

    B. 18

    C. 27

    D. 81

5. Write "the product of 6 and the sum of 3 and a number n" as an expression.

    A. $6 + 3n$

    B. $6(3n)$

    C. $6(3 + n)$

    D. $6 + 3 + n$

$6 + (3 + n)$

6. If each diamond has a value of ¾, what is the value of the expression below?

A. ¼

B. 2 ¼

C. 3 ¾

D. 4

7. Patricia makes $200 more per month than Mike. If Mike makes m dollars per month, how much does Patricia make in a year?

A. m + 200

B. 12m + 200

C. m + 2400

D. 12m + 2400

8. Identify the pattern exhibited by: 10.5, 20.5, 30.5, 40.5, ...

A. 10.5x

B. 10x + 0.5

C. 0.5x + 10

D. x + 10.5

Patterns & Variables: Answer Explanations

1. D   −125, 25, −5, 1, ...

In the above pattern, to get from one element to the next divide by −5. Therefore, the next number will be 1 divided by −5, which is −⅕.

2. D   Take the words and translate them into an expression.

Roger's age is 2 less than 5 times Luke's age

Roger's age = 2 less than 5 times Luke's age

Roger's age = 2 less than 5 times n

Roger's age = 2 less than 5n

Roger's age = 5n − 2

3. C   For each answer choice, plug in x = 10.

A: $x + 10{,}000 = 10 + 10{,}000 = 10{,}010$

B: $x^5 + 100x^4 = 10^5 + 100(10^4) = 100{,}000 + 100(10{,}000) = 100{,}000 + 1{,}000{,}000 = 1{,}100{,}000$

C: $10^x = 10^{10} = 10{,}000{,}000{,}000$

D: $1000x = 1000(10) = 10{,}000$

Answer C has the largest value. Exponential equations will increase faster than linear equations.

4. C There are a couple ways to approach this problem. Here are a few methods:

Method 1: Draw the fourth figure
Following the same pattern, let's draw the next figure and count the number of shaded triangles. The pattern involves taking each shaded triangle and creating four triangles by cutting each side of the shaded triangle in half. Then, out of the new triangles, the three outside triangles are shaded.

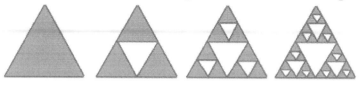

Okay, now all we have to do is carefully count the number of shaded triangles in the fourth figure. There are 27 shaded triangles.

Method 2: Determine pattern from figure to figure
Let's look from figure to figure to see what is happening. In the first figure we have one shaded triangle. To get to the second figure, that triangle makes three shaded triangles and one white triangle.

Now, let's see what happens to each of the shaded triangles from figure 2 to figure 3. Each of the shaded triangles in figure 2 creates three shaded triangles in figure 3.

Okay, this is a consistent pattern. If you have a shaded triangle in one figure, in the next figure it will create three more. So, in figure 1 we had one shaded triangle, this created 3 shaded triangles in the second figure. Then, each of these 3 shaded triangles created 3 more, totaling 9 shaded triangles in the next figure.

Therefore, to get to the next figure, we multiply the number of shaded triangles by another 3, so 9 x 3 = 27.

Method 3: Identify a pattern in the total number
In figure 1, there is 1 shaded triangle.
In figure 2, there are 3 shaded triangles.
In figure 3, there are 9 shaded triangles.

Let's look for a pattern in the numbers: 1, 3, 9...

We note that the difference between each number is not the same, as it is growing much faster than just adding. Therefore, let's think of multiplication or powers. Each number is being multiplied by 3 or is the next power of 3.

1, 1 x 3, 1 x 3 x 3, so the next number would be 1 x 3 x 3 x 3 = 27
or if you think in terms of exponents: $3^0, 3^1, 3^2$, so the next number would be 3^3 or 27.

5. C A product is the result of a multiplication problem. A sum is the result of an addition problem.

The problem states: the product of 6 and the sum of 3 and a number. Break it into two parts. The product of "6" and "the sum of 3 and a number" is the same as 6 multiplied by the "sum of 3 and a number."

Let's translate: "the sum of 3 and a number" into an expression.
Since we don't know the number, we are using n to represent it.
3 + n

Now, going back to the product:
6 multiplied by "the sum of 3 and a number" equals 6 multiplied by (3 + n), or 6(3 + n).

6. B   In problems with shapes, treat the unknown as a variable if that is easier to conceptualize. In this case, let's represent each diamond with the variable d.

Therefore, we know that $d = \frac{3}{4}$ and the equation we are solving for is:

$d + d + d$

$= 3d$

$= 3(\frac{3}{4})$

$= \frac{9}{4}$

$= 2\frac{1}{4}$

7. D   Be careful and note that the question is asking about how much Patricia makes in a year, not just a month.

Let's start by examining how much Patricia makes in a month, since that was the information provided in the question stem. We are told that Patricia makes $200 more than Mike does per month and that Mike makes m dollars per month. Therefore, we can quickly see that each month Patricia makes:

$m + 200$

Now, the question is asking about how much does she make a year and we know that there are 12 months. Therefore, multiply the amount she makes per month by 12.

$12(m + 200)$

$= 12m + 2400$

8. B   Solve this problem by plugging in the element number for x into each equation. 10.5, 20.5, 30.5, 40.5, ...

A: 10.5x
$10.5(1) = 10.5$
$10.5(2) = 21$
This works for the first element but not the other elements. Eliminate A.

B: 10x + 0.5
$10(1) + 0.5 = 10.5$
$10(2) + 0.5 = 20.5$
$10(3) + 0.5 = 30.5$
$10(4) + 0.5 = 40.5$
This works for all elements and shows the pattern exhibited.

C: 0.5x + 10
$0.5(1) + 10 = 10.5$
$0.5(2) + 10 = 11$
This only works for the first element. Eliminate C.

D: x + 10.5
$1 + 10.5 = 11.5$
This doesn't work for any elements. Eliminate D.

Solving for a Variable

Solving an equation means finding the set of values for the variable in the equation that makes the equation true. For example: $x^2 = 25$ is true when $x = 5$ or $x = -5$.

Plugging In

You can see if a number is a solution to an equation by plugging in the value for the variable and seeing if the equation is true. For example, to check if $x = 5$ is a solution to $x^2 = 25$, plug in 5 for x: $5^2 = 25$. This is true, thus 5 is a solution.

Isolate the Variable

To solve for a variable in an equation, you need to isolate the variable on one side of the equal sign, with all of the numbers on the other side. This can be done by performing the inverse of whatever operations are performed on the variable on both sides of the equation. In the example above, x was squared in the equation. Taking the square root of both sides gives the two possible x values of 5 and –5.

Let's go through a few examples to illustrate how to solve for a variable.

$y + 5 = 12$

You want the y to be alone, so perform the inverse to both sides of what is happening to the y. Since 5 is being added to the y, subtract 5 from both sides.

$y + 5 - 5 = 12 - 5$

Now simplify.

$y = 7$

$\frac{n}{6} = 10$

You want the n to be alone, so perform the inverse operation to both sides of the equation. Since n is being divided by 6, multiply both sides of the equation by 6.

$\frac{n}{6} \times 6 = 10 \times 6$

Now simplify.

$n = 60$

You must perform the inverse operations in the reverse of the order of operations.

Example: $6x - 12 = 24$

Perform the inverse operation of the subtraction of 12. Therefore, add 12 to both sides.

$6x - 12 + 12 = 24 + 12$

$6x = 36$

Perform the inverse operation of the multiplication of 6. Therefore, divide by 6 on both sides.

$6x \div 6 = 36 \div 6$

$x = 6$

One–variable Equations: Practice

1. If you subtract 6 from a number and then multiply the difference by 8, how can you manipulate the result to return to the original number?

    A. Add 6. Then, divide by 8.

    B. Subtract 6. Multiply by 8.

    C. Divide by 8. Then, add 6.

    D. Multiply by 8. Subtract 6.

(handwritten: $n - 6 = m + 8$, $20 - 6 = 14$, $2 - 6 = $)

2. What is the value of n in the following equation? $-3n + 6 = 12$

    A. -6

    B. -2

    C. 2

    D. 4

3. What would you do to both sides of the following equation to solve for y? $-\frac{3}{4}y = 12$

    A. Add ¾

    B. Multiply by $-\frac{3}{4}$

    C. Multiply by $-\frac{4}{3}$

    D. Divide by $\frac{4}{3}$

(handwritten: $-\frac{3}{4}y = 12 \cdot \frac{4}{3}$)

4. Solve for y. $14y + 27 = 6$

    A. $\frac{33}{14}$

    B. $-\frac{3}{2}$

    C. 3

    D. $26\frac{4}{7}$

(handwritten: $14 \times -\frac{3}{2}$)

5. What would you do to both sides of the following equation to solve for m? $\frac{m}{4} - 6 = 10$

    A. Add 6. Then, divide by 4.

    B. Subtract 6. Then, divide by 4.

    C. Multiply by 4. Then, add 6.

    D. Add 6. Then, multiply by 4.

(handwritten: $\frac{m}{4} - 6 = 10$, $\frac{m}{4} = 16$)

6. What is the value of the hexagon in the following equation?

    A. -4

    B. -8

    C. $\frac{8}{3}$

    D. Not enough information.

7. Solve for n in the following equation: 3n + 4 = 5n + 8

    A. –2

    B. $\frac{4}{3}$

    C. 2

    D. –4

$$3n + 4 = 5n + 8$$
$$-4$$
$$\overline{}$$
$$-2n + 4 =$$
$$n = -2$$

8. What is the value of m in the following equation? $(6m + 3)/3 = 11$

    A. $\frac{5}{3}$

    B. 4

    C. 5

    D. 6

One–variable Equations: Answer Explanations

1. C   To "undo" an operation, apply its inverse. Addition is the inverse of subtraction. Multiplication is the inverse of division.

Since multiplication was the last operation performed, you must first undo this operation. The inverse of multiply by 8 is divide by 8.

The next operation to undo is subtracting 6, so you must add 6.

Divide by 8. Then, add 6.

2. B   Isolate the variable by performing inverse operations to both sides of the equation.

–3n + 6 = 12

First subtract 6 from both sides.

–3n + 6 – 6 = 12 – 6

–3n = 6

Next, divide both sides by –3

–3n ÷ –3 = 6 ÷ –3

n = –2

3. C   To solve for a variable, you must get that variable alone. In this case, you are multiplying the variable y by –3/4. Therefore, you must perform the inverse operation to get y alone. The inverse operation of multiplying by –¾ is dividing by –¾. Since this isn't one of the answer choices, we have to determine if there is another way that this operation can be written.

Dividing by –¾ is the same as multiplying by its reciprocal.
Therefore, multiplying both sides by –⁴⁄₃ will solve for y.

–¾ y = 12

(–¾y)(–⁴⁄₃) = 12(–⁴⁄₃)

y = –16

4. B   To isolate the variable, first subtract 27 from both sides and then divide by 14.

14y + 27 = 6

14y + 27 – 27 = 6 – 27

14y = –21

14y ÷ 14 = –21 ÷ 14

y = –²¹⁄₁₄ = –³⁄₂

5. D To solve for m, you must isolate the variable. $m/4 - 6 = 10$

Addition is the inverse of subtraction; add 6 to both sides of the equation.

$m/4 - 6 = 10$

$m/4 - 6 + 6 = 10 + 6$

$m/4 = 16$

Multiplication is the inverse of division; multiply both sides of the equation by 4.

$m/4 = 16$

$m/4 \times 4 = 16 \times 4$

$m = 64$

Add 6. Then, multiply by 4.

6. B A variable is a letter used to represent an unknown value in an equation. Sometimes, symbols or shapes are used to represent unknown values. When presented with problems of this type, it is easiest if you assign a variable to the unknown symbol and then solve for the variable.

In this case, since it is a hexagon, let's assign the variable h to the hexagon. Then, the equation becomes: h + h + 8 = h

Now, solve for h.

$h + h + 8 = h$

$2h + 8 = h$

$2h + 8 - 2h = h - 2h$

$8 = -h$

$-8 = h$

You can verify your answer by plugging in −8 for the hexagon.

7. A In this case, there are variables on both sides of the equation. Move all terms with the variable to one side of the equation, and then isolate n.

$3n + 4 = 5n + 8$ Subtract 3n from both sides.

$3n + 4 - 3n = 5n + 8 - 3n$

$4 = 2n + 8$ Subtract 8 from both sides to isolate n.

$4 - 8 = 2n + 8 - 8$

$-4 = 2n$ Divide both sides by 2.

$-4 \div 2 = 2n \div 2$

$-2 = n$

8. C Isolate the variable by performing inverse operations to both sides of the equation.

$(6m + 3)/3 = 11$ Multiply both sides by 3.

$(6m + 3)/3 \times 3 = 11 \times 3$

$6m + 3 = 33$ Subtract 3 from both sides.

$6m + 3 - 3 = 33 - 3$

$6m = 30$ Divide both sides by 6.

$6m \div 6 = 30 \div 6$

$m = 5$

Relations

A relation is simply a patterned relationship between two variables: by applying an independent variable to a model, it is possible to generate the corresponding dependent variable. Relations are often shown in t–charts, with the input listed in a column on the left side of the "t" and the corresponding output listed on the right.

x	y
2	5
3	7
4	9
5	?
?	15

From a set of data you might be asked to derive the relationship. In the relation on the right, $y = 2x + 1$.

You might also be asked to use the relationship to fill in missing information. To find the y value that corresponds with x = 5, plug 5 into the equation:

$y = 2x + 1$

$y = 2(5) + 1 = 11$

To find the x–value that pairs with y=15, plug 15 into the equation for y, solve for x:

$y = 2x + 1$

$15 = 2x + 1$

$14 = 2x$

$x = 7$

Solving for a variable

If you are presented an equation with two unknowns or variables, you can solve for one variable in terms of the other. You would follow all the same steps you learned in the previous lesson to isolate the variable that you want to solve for.

For example, solve for c in the following equation:

$3c - 12 + d = 9d - c$	Initial equation
$3c - 12 + d + c = 9d - c + c$	Move all c's to one side by adding c to both sides.
$4c - 12 + d = 9d$	Simplify both sides by combining like terms.
$4c - 12 = 8d$	Start to isolate c by subtracting d from both sides.
$4c = 8d + 12$	Continue to isolate c by adding 12 to both sides.
$c = 2d + 3$	Isolate c by dividing both sides by 4.

Systems of Equations

A system of equations is a set of equations that can be used to find possible values for multiple variables. Generally, you will be given two equations with two unknowns, and you will solve for the values that make both equations true. Systems of equations can be solved in four ways.

1. Graphing

To find the possible values of a set of variable for two equations, find the point or points where the graphs of the equations intersect. A graph of an equation represents all the points that make the equation true. Therefore, the point where two graphs intersect is the point that makes both equations true.

For example, if you were asked to solve the following system of equations: $y = 2x + 2$ and $y = -3x - 3$, you could graph both equations. The point where they intersect, $(-1, 0)$, represents the solution (x = –1, and y = 0).

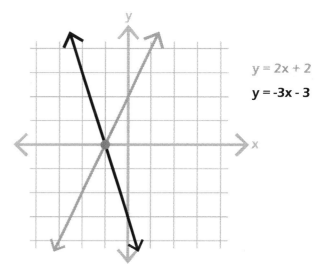

$y = 2x + 2$

$y = -3x - 3$

2. Substitution

Another way to solve a system of equations is by substitution. This involves isolating a variable in one equation, and then substituting the value of that variable into the other equation.

Example: $3x + y = -5$, $2x + 3y = -1$

Using the first equation, solve for y:
$3x + y = -5$, $y = -5 - 3x$

Now, plug that value for y into the second equation:

$$2x + 3y = -1$$
$$2x + 3(-5 - 3x) = -1$$
$$2x - 15 - 9x = -1$$
$$-7x = 14$$
$$x = -2$$

Now, plug the value of x back into any equation to solve for y:
$y = -5 - 3x = -5 - 3(-2) = 1$

Solution: $x = -2$, $y = 1$

3. Elimination

You can also solve a system of equations with elimination. Manipulate the equations so that you can add them to eliminate all but one variable. After solving for that variable, plug it into one of the original equations to solve for the other variable.

Example: $3x + y = -5$, $2x + 3y = -1$.

Choose which variable to eliminate – in this case, let's choose y.
Multiply the first equation by -3:
$-9x - 3y = 15$

Now, add the two equations:

$$-9x - 3y = 15$$
$$+ \quad 2x + 3y = -1$$
$$-7x = 14$$
$$x = -2$$

Now, plug in $x = -2$ to solve for y:
$y = -5 - 3x = -5 - 3(-2) = 1$

Solution: $x = -2$, $y = 1$

4. Plugging In

The final option works when you are given a multiple–choice question with a set of possible answers. You can plug each set into the original equations and see which solution makes both equations true.

Two–variable Equations: Practice

1. Which equation is exhibited by the data in the table below?

A. $x = y^3$

B. $y = x^3$

C. $y = x \div 4$

D. $x = y^2 + 4$

x	y
1	1
8	2
27	3
125	5

2. What is the sum of the two missing values in the table below?

A. 31

B. 32

C. 33

D. 34

x	y
5	8
7	10
10	13
12	15
17	20
21	24

3. Each shape represents the length of an object in inches. If the square equals 3 inches, what is the value of each circle?

A. 1.5 inches

B. 2 inches

C. 4.5 inches

D. 7 inches

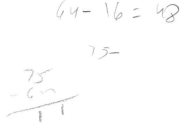

4. Solve for b in the following equation. 3a – 2b = 12

A. $b = 6a + 24$

B. $b = 6 - (\frac{3}{2})a$

C. $b = 14 - 3a$

D. $b = (\frac{3}{2})a - 6$

$-2b = -3a + 12$

5. In the equation, $y = x^3 - x^2$, what is the change in the y value when x increases from 4 to 5?

A. 0

B. 52

C. 70

D. 148

$64 - 16 = 48$

6. Which equation represents the relationship between a and b in the table below?

A. $b = a - 1$

B. $b = 2a - 3$

C. $b = -3a + 7$

D. $b = -4a + 7$

a	b
2	1
5	-8
7	-14
12	-29

7. Which of the following are solutions to the system of equations, $y = x^2$ and $y = 2x^2 - 1$? They are both graphed below.

    I. $(-1,-1)$
    II. $(-1, 1)$
    III. $(1,1)$

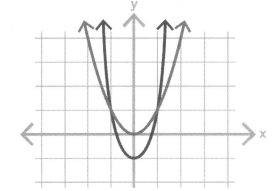

    A. I and II

    B. III only

    C. II and III

    D. I, II, and III

8. Use the table below to answer the question that follows.

Plan	Line fee	Cost per minute
A	$20	$0.05
B	$10	$0.10

How many minutes of talking in one month would cost the same on either phone plan?

    A. 10 minutes

    B. 20 minutes

    C. 100 minutes

    D. 200 minutes

Two–variable Equations: Answer Explanations

1. A   Plug in the values in the table into each equation and see which equation is true for every set of values.

$$x = y^3$$

This is true for all the data in the table. Answer A is correct.

Answer B switches x and y.
Answer C only works for one set of values.
Answer D only works for one set of values.

2. D   First, figure out the pattern between x and y. Then, determine the missing values, and find their sum.

The y value is always 3 greater than the x value; you can write this as: $y = x + 3$.

The first question mark represents 3 less than 13, which is 10.
The second question mark represents 3 more than 21, which is 24.

Sum = 10 + 24 = 34

3. C   To find the value of the circle, plug in the value for each square and solve. It is probably easiest to represent each circle with a variable. Let's choose c.

3 inches + 3 inches + 3 inches = c + c
9 inches = 2c
4.5 inches = c

Each circle, c, is equal to 4.5 inches.

4. D   To solve for b, you must isolate b on one side of the equation. To get the variable b by itself, you must perform the inverse operation to move every other term to the other side of the equation.

First, let's move the term 3a to the other side. Since the term 3a is being added to the left hand side of the equation, we can subtract 3a to remove it from that side.

$3a - 2b = 12$

$3a - 2b - 3a = 12 - 3a$

$-2b = 12 - 3a$

Now, we want to continue to isolate b. Since b is multiplied by -2, we must divide by -2 to isolate b.

$-2b = 12 - 3a$

$-2b \div -2 = (12 - 3a) \div -2$

Note, that we have to make sure to divide the entire right hand side of the equation by -2. To divide the entire side by -2, we can divide each term.

$-2b \div -2 = (12 - 3a) \div -2$

$b = (12 \div -2) - (3a \div -2)$

$b = -6 - 3a/-2$

$b = -6 - (-\frac{3}{2})a$

$b = -6 + (\frac{3}{2})a$

You can rearrange the right hand side to get: $b = (\frac{3}{2})a - 6$

5. B   Plug in $x = 4$ into the equation and $x = 5$ into the equation and calculate the difference in the outputs.

$x = 4: \quad y = x^3 - x^2 = 4^3 - 4^2 = 64 - 16 = 48$

$x = 5: \quad y = x^3 - x^2 = 5^3 - 5^2 = 125 - 25 = 100$

Difference in y–values: $100 - 48 = 52$

6. C   The easiest way to solve this problem is to try each answer choice to see which makes all the equations true. A only works for the first pair of values. B also works for just the first pair of values. D does not work for any pair. C works for everything. $b = -3a + 7$

$a = 2, b = 1: 1 = -3(2) + 7 = -6 + 7 = 1$

$a = 5, b = -8: -8 = -3(5) + 7 = -15 + 7 = -8$

$a = 7, b = -14: -14 = -3(7) + 7 = -21 + 7 = -14$

$a = 12, b = -29: -29 = -3(12) + 7 = -36 + 7 = -29$

7. C   When solving a system of equations using graphs, the points of intersection are the solutions. In this case, the lines cross twice, once at $(-1, 1)$ and another time at $(1,1)$.

You could also plug in each set of points into both equations and see which solutions make them both true.

8. D   Set up a system of equations to solve this word problem. If m equals minutes talked, then the amount paid using each plan can be represented as follows:

Plan A: Cost = $20 + 0.05m$

Plan B: Cost = $10 + 0.10m$

To find the number of minutes that would cost the same, set the two equations equal.

$20 + 0.05m = 10 + 0.10m$

$0.05m = 10$

$m = 200$

This problem also could have been solved by working backwards and plugging in each answer choice into each plan until you found an answer where the plans were equal.

Written Forms of Ratios

A ratio is a means of comparing one expression containing numbers or variables to another. In words, ratios are written using "to". For example, in a group of animals containing 3 fish and 2 parakeets, the ratio of fish to parakeets is 3 to 2. This same ratio can be written as 3:2 or $\frac{3}{2}$. Mathematically, the most useful expression of a ratio is a fraction.

Ratios as rates of change

In most practical applications, ratios are used to indicate rates of change – the rate at which one variable changes with respect to another. For example, if a student reads 2 pages per minute, then every minute that goes by will increase the number of pages by 2. This can be written: $\frac{2 \text{ pages}}{1 \text{ min}}$.

Directly Proportional

If two variables are directly proportional, when one goes up the other goes up. In direct proportionality, the value of a variable is equal to a constant multipled by another variable.

variable 1 = constant x variable 2

In the previous example, a student was reading 2 pages per minute. In other words,
number of pages = 2 x number of minutes

Therefore, as the number of minutes increases, the number of pages will go up by a factor of 2.

Inversely Proportional

If two variables are inversely proportional, when one goes up the other goes down.

variable 1 = constant/variable 2

For example, volume and pressure vary indirectly for a gas. What happens to the pressure of gas when you double its volume?
pressure = constant/volume
P = constant/V
If you double the volume: constant/2V = P/2 the pressure is halved.

Proportionality

Generally, a proportion is two equal ratios. For example, if the ratio of red to blue marbles in a bag is 3/5 and the bag has 20 blue marbles, you can determine the number of red marbles.

$$\frac{\text{red}}{\text{blue}} = \frac{3}{5} = \frac{x}{20}$$

x must equal 12 for the ratios to be equal, therefore there are 12 red marbles.

Cross Multiplication

You can use cross–multiplication to easily solve for variables.

$$\frac{a}{b} = \frac{c}{d}$$

$$\frac{a}{b} \diagdown \frac{c}{d}$$

$$ad = bc$$

In the above example, $\frac{3}{5} = \frac{x}{20}$, you can cross multiply and get: 3(20) = 5x, 60 = 5x, 12 = x.

Ratios & Proportions: Practice

1. A bag contains only red and blue marbles and the ratio of red marbles to blue marbles is 3 to 5. What fraction of the bag is blue marbles?

    A. 3/5

    B. 5/3

    C. 5/8

    D. 3/8

2. If Georgia bakes 8 cakes for every 4 hour shift she works, how many hours will it take her to bake 96 cakes?

    A. 24 hours

    B. 48 hours

    C. 96 hours

    D. 192 hours

3. Two thirds of the students at Sequoia Junior High are female. If 200 students are male, how many females attend Sequoia Junior High?

    A. 100

    B. 200

    C. 400

    D. 600

4. If the height of plant A is always 4/3 the height of plant B, how tall is plant A when plant B is 9 feet tall?

    A. $27/4$ feet

    B. 9 feet

    C. 10 feet

    D. 12 feet

5. For every 25 pairs of shoes he has, Gary has 60 complete outfits. Assuming this proportion stays the same, how many outfits could he make with only 10 pairs of shoes?

    A. 18

    B. 20

    C. 22

    D. 24

6. If Anita needs 24 lbs of mix for every 120 gallons of concrete she mixes, how many pounds of mix will she need for a driveway that will require 35 gallons of concrete?

A. 5

B. 7

C. 131

D. 175

$$\frac{24}{120} = \frac{n}{35} = 7$$

7. If y is directly proportional to x, and is y is 20 when x is 10, what is x when y is 5?

A. 2.5

B. 10

C. 20

D. 40

$$\frac{y\ 20}{x\ 10} = \frac{5}{x} = \frac{50}{20} = 2.5$$

8. An old machine can put 240 caps on bottles every 2 minutes. If the newer model can work at twice the rate of the old machine, how long will it take the new machine to cap 72000 bottles?

A. 2.5 hours

B. 5 hours

C. 10 hours

D. 20 hours

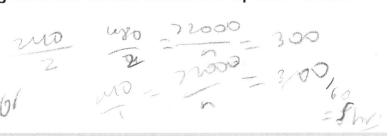

Ratios & Proportions: Answer Explanations

1. C If the ratio of red to blue is 3 to 5, that means for every 3 red in the bag there are 5 blue, making a total of 8 marbles for each of those groups. Therefore, the ratio of blue to total is 5 to 8. So, the fraction of blue marbles in the bag is: 5/8.

2. B Set up the ratio between cakes and hours it takes to build.

$$\frac{8 \text{ cakes}}{4 \text{ hours}} = \frac{96 \text{ cakes}}{n \text{ hours}}$$

Cross multiply to solve for n

8n = 96(4)

n = 48

48 hours to make 96 cakes.

3. C If ⅔ of the students are female, then subtract ⅔ from 1 to determine the fraction of males.

1 − ⅔ = ⅓

Therefore, ⅓ of the students are males.

Thus, if ⅓ are males and ⅔ are females, there are twice as many females as males. Therefore, if 200 are male, then 400 are female.

Another way to think of the problem, is that if ⅓ of the students are male and that is 200 students, then the total number of students must be 600. Therefore, subtract the number of males from total to find number of females. 600 − 200 = 400. 400 females.

4. D   This is a case of direct proportionality with a proportionality constant of 4/3.

Plant A's height = ⅘ x Plant B's height

If plant B is 9 feet, plug it into above formula to find plant A's height.
Plant A = ⅘ x 9 feet = 12 feet

5. D   Set up a proportion between pairs of shoes and complete outfits.

$$\frac{25 \text{ pairs}}{60 \text{ outfits}} = \frac{10 \text{ pairs}}{n \text{ outfits}}$$

Cross multiply and then solve.
$25n = 60(10)$
$n = 600/25 = 24$ outfits

6. B   Set up the proportion between mix and concrete.

$$\frac{24 \text{ lbs mix}}{120 \text{ gal concrete}} = \frac{n \text{ lbs}}{35 \text{ gal}}$$

Cross multiply and then solve for n.
$120n = 24(35)$
$120n = 840$
$n = 7$

7 pounds of mix

7. A   Set up an equation between x and y. If y is directly proportional to x, the equation can be written:
$y = kx$, where k is the proportionality constant

Given the fact that y is 20 when x is 10, let's solve for k. Plug in x and y into the equation.

$20 = 10k$
$k = 2$

Now, plug in y = 5, to solve for x.
$y = 2x$
$5 = 2x$
$x = 2.5$

8. B   The rate of the old machine is 240 caps per 2 minutes, which reduces to 120 caps per minute.

The newer model works at twice the rate of the old machine. Therefore, the newer model can cap 240 caps per minute.

If the newer machine can cap 240 caps per minute and there are 72000 bottles to cap, divide 72000 by 240 to figure out how long it will take this machine.

$72000 \div 240 = 300$
300 minutes

All the answers are in hours, so convert 300 minutes to hours.
$300 \text{ minutes} \times \frac{1 \text{ hour}}{60 \text{ mins}} = 5 \text{ hours}$

Definition of Inequalities

An inequality is a statement about the relationship between two values. The greater than >, the less than <, the greater than or equal to ≥, and less than or equal to ≤ signs are used to define the relationship in an inequality. For example, $y \geq 2$ means that the value of y is greater than or equal to 2.

Simplifying Inequalities

It is possible to solve for variables in inequalities in a way that is similar to solving for variables in an equation. Essentially, it is possible to simplify an inequality to generate a range of possible values for a variable. Simplify the inequality in the same way that you would approach an equation. You want to isolate the variable on one side of the inequality symbol.

Example: $3x - 6 > 12$
$3x - 6 + 6 > 12 + 6$
$3x > 18$
$x > 6$

Some inequalities are compound, or contain two separate statements. To solve these, follow the same steps of isolating the variable, but make sure to perform the operations on all sides of the inequalities.

Example: $-4 \leq x + 8 < 3$
$-4 - 8 \leq x + 8 - 8 < 3 - 8$
$-12 \leq x < -5$

Multiplying/Dividing by Negative Numbers

When multiplying or dividing an inequality by a negative number, switch the signs. Therefore, < becomes > and ≤ becomes ≥.

Example: $-2x > 8$, divide both sides by −2 and flip the sign
$x < -4$

Example: $12 \geq -2x + 4 > -2$
$8 \geq -2x > -6$
$-4 \leq x < 3$

Graphing Inequalities

The range of values for x can be shown graphically.

$-4 \leq X < 3$

A closed circle is used to represent ≤ or ≥ to show that the end value is included, and an open circle is used for > or < to show that the value is not included.

1. Simplify the inequality $3r + 4 > 19$.

   A. $r < 5$

   B. $r < 3$

   C. $r > 3$

   D. $r > 5$

handwritten: $3r+4>19$ $-4\ -4$ $\dfrac{15}{3}$ $r=5$ $r>5$

2. Which answer shows $x \le 90$ on a number line?

   A.

   B.

   C.

   D.

3. Solve the inequality: $16 < -2w$

   A. $w > -32$

   B. $w < -8$

   C. $w > -8$

   D. $w < 8$

handwritten: $\dfrac{-2w}{-2} > \dfrac{16}{-2}$ $w < -8$

4. Solve for n in the following inequality. $-\tfrac{3}{5} n + 2 \le 11$

   A. $n \ge -15$

   B. $n \ge -\tfrac{27}{5}$

   C. $n \le -\tfrac{27}{5}$

   D. $n \le -15$

handwritten: $-\tfrac{3}{5}n \le 9 \cdot \tfrac{5}{3}$ $n \ge -15$

5. Solve for x in the following inequality. $-4 \le -3x + 2 < 11$

   A. $-3 < x \le 2$

   B. $-3 \le x < 2$

   C. $-2 < x \le 3$

   D. $2 \le x < -3$

handwritten: $\dfrac{-6}{-3} \le \dfrac{x}{} < \dfrac{9}{-3}$ $2 \ge x > -3$

6. Give a range of possible values for n if: $1 + 9n > 100$ and $210 > (\tfrac{1}{2})n$.

   A. $100 < n < 210$

   B. $11 > n > 420$

   C. $11 < n < 105$

   D. $11 < n < 420$

handwritten: $1 + 9n > 100$

7. If the sum of seven and the product of three and the opposite of a number is less than 25 and greater than –2, what are all the possible values for the number?

    A. $-6 < n < 3$

    B. $-3 < n < 6$

    C. $-2.5 < n < 0.2$

    D. $-6 > n > 3$

(handwritten work):
$-2 < 7 - 3n < 25$
$\quad -7 \qquad \mathbb{B}$
$-9 < -3n < \dfrac{18}{-3}$
$\qquad \overline{-3}$
$3 > n > -6$

$n < 25$
$n > 2$

8. What is the range of possible values for m if $-14 \le 2(-3m + 5) < 28$?

    A. $-3 < m \le 4$

    B. $-3 > m \ge 4$

    C. $3 \le m < -4$

    D. $-3 \ge m > 4$

(handwritten work):
$-14 \le -6m + 10 < 28$
$\qquad\quad -10 \quad -10$
$-24 \le -6m < 18$
$\overline{-6} \quad \overline{-6} \quad \overline{-6}$
$4 \ge m > -3$

Inequalities: Answer Explanations

1. D $3r + 4 > 19$

To isolate the variable, the first step is to subtract 4 from all sides.
$3r + 4 - 4 > 19 - 4$
$3r > 15$

Then, divide both sides by 3 to solve for r.
$3r > 15$
$3r \div 3 > 15 \div 3$
$r > 5$

2. A   If x is less than or equal to 90, you need to include 90 (by using a closed circle) and an arrow pointing left towards all smaller numbers.

3. B   You need to get w by itself. You must remember that when dividing or multiplying sides of an inequality by a negative, then the inequality sign must be flipped.

From the original equation: $16 < -2w$, you need to divide both sides by –2 and thus flip the inequality sign:
$16/(-2) > -2w/(-2)$
$-8 > w$
Rearranging, $w < -8$.

4. A   Isolate the variable, just as you would if the equation was an equality.
$-\tfrac{3}{5}n + 2 \le 11$

Subtract 2 from both sides.
$-\tfrac{3}{5}n + 2 - 2 \le 11 - 2$
$-\tfrac{3}{5}n \le 9$

Now, multiply both sides by –5/3. When you multiply both sides of an inequality by a negative, you must flip the inequality sign.
$-\tfrac{3}{5}n \le 9$
$(-\tfrac{3}{5}n)(-\tfrac{5}{3}) \ge 9(-\tfrac{5}{3})$
$n \ge -15$

5. A   Isolate the variable. Ensure that what you do to one side of the inequality, you do to all sides.

$-4 \leq -3x + 2 < 11$ Subtract 2.

$-4 - 2 \leq -3x + 2 - 2 < 11 - 2$

$-6 \leq -3x < 9$ Divide by -3. When dividing by a negative, flip the inequality signs.

$-6 \div -3 \geq -3x \div -3 > 9 \div -3$

$2 \geq x > -3$ Rearrange the inequality statement.

$-3 < x \leq 2$

6. D   Solve both inequalities and then combine them.

$1 + 9n > 100$

$9n > 99$

$n > 11$

$210 > (\frac{1}{2}) n$

$420 > n$

Now we must combine the two inequalities. The first one, $n > 11$, states that n is greater than 11. The second one, $420 > n$, states that n is less than 420. We can combine this into one statement.

$11 < n < 420$

7. A   If there is an unknown, the first step is always to assign a variable to the unknown. A quick scan of the answers shows that the variable in the choices is n, so let's also use n to represent the unknown number.

Next, let's translate the words into an inequality. Take each phrase and represent it in terms of operations with the variable.

"sum of seven and the product of three and the opposite of a number"
Sum is the result of an additional problem. Product is the result of a multiplication problem. The opposite of a number is $-n$. The product of three and the opposite of a number is $-3n$.

This phrase is equivalent to: $7 + (-3n)$ which simplifies to $7 - 3n$.

The rest of the words: "is less than 25 and greater than -2" means $7 - 3n < 25$ and $7 - 3n > -2$ or $-2 < 7 - 3n$. Simplifying this compound inequality statement into one inequality gives. $-2 < 7 - 3n < 25$.

$-2 < 7 - 3n < 25$

Now, time to solve. To isolate the variable, first subtract 7 from all sides of the inequality.

$-2 - 7 < 7 + -3n - 7 < 25 - 7$

$-9 < -3n < 18$

Next, divide all sides of the inequality by -3. Remember, when dividing an inequality by a negative number, you must reverse (flip) the inequality to make it a true statement.

$-9/-3 > -3n/-3 > 18/-3$

$3 > n > -6$

Rearrange the inequality. $-6 < n < 3$

8. A   Isolate the variable by performing inverse operations to all sides of the inequality.

$-14 \leq 2(-3m + 5) < 28$ Distribute

$-14 \leq -6m + 10 < 28$ Subtract 10 from all sides

$-24 \leq -6m < 18$ Divide all sides by -6. When dividing by a negative, flip the inequality signs.

$4 \geq m > -3$ Rearrange

$-3 < m \leq 4$

Translating Word Problems into Equations

Algebraic word problems are similar to the word problems you encountered involving basic operations, and the same strategies are applicable. However, they require you to form an equation containing a variable, and that adds a level of difficulty.

Let's begin with a simple example of translating a given situation into a mathematical equation:

> Nadine has only red shirts and blue shirts. She has 29 red shirts and 43 shirts total. How many blue shirts does she have?

Use key words such as "total" to determine the function that needs to be performed. Then, use a variable to represent any unknown quantities.

> Red shirts + Blue shirts = Total shirts
> 29 + b = 43

> In the equation above, b represents the number of blue shirts Nadine has. Solve for the variable b by subtracting 29 from both sides:
> 29 + b − 29 = 43 − 29
> b = 14
> Nadine has 14 blue shirts.

The most complex algebra word problems involve multiple unknown quantities. Whenever possible, represent all unknown quantities in terms of a single variable. This is easy to do when a specific relationship is given for two or more unknowns.

> Example: Colleen bought twice as many oranges as apples at the grocery store. If she bought 45 apples and oranges, how many apples did Colleen buy? $2x + x = 45$

Choose as the variable the quantity the question asks you to find, then define the relationship between that variable and any other unknown quantities.

> Let x represent the number of apples Colleen buys.
> Therefore, the number of oranges is 2x.

> Then, write and solve an equation using only 1 variable:
> Apples + Oranges = 45
> x + 2x = 45
> 3x = 45
> x = 15
> Colleen buys 15 apples.

Algebra Word Problems: Practice

1. Andrew has pennies, dimes and quarters. He has a total of $8.70. There are two times as many pennies as quarters. There are six times as many dimes as quarters. How many dimes does he have?

$2x + 6q = 8.70$

   A. 6

   B. 10

   C. 60

   D. 87

2. Find three consecutive odd integers, such that the sum of the third and twice the first is 7 more than twice the third. What is the largest number?

    A. 7

    B. 11

    C. 13

    D. 15

3. A toy store purchased the latest remote controlled car from a manufacturer at a cost of 30% more than it cost the manufacturer to make it. The toy store then sold the car at a price that was 20% higher than the price they they paid for it. If it cost the manufacturer n dollars to make the car, how much did the toy store sell the car for?

    A. 0.5n

    B. 1.5n

    C. 1.56n

    D. 50n

4. Two trains, A & B, are 540 km apart and travel toward each other on parallel tracks. Train A travels 40 km per hour and train B, 10 km per hour faster than A. In how many hours will they meet?

    A. 6 hours

    B. 7 hours

    C. 8 hours

    D. 9 hours

5. At Fred's Furniture, the owner purchased new sanding equipment for his chair production line at a cost of $48,000. The equipment depreciates at a constant rate of $1,500 per year. If Fred wants to replace the equipment when the value of the equipment is $30,000, how many years will it be before he has to replace the equipment?

    A. 6

    B. 10

    C. 12

    D. 20

6. You have 10L of a 40% saline solution. Which equation would help you calculate how much pure saline (100% saline) you need to add to create a 60% solution?

    A. $40\% (10) + X = 60\% (10 + X)$

    B. $40\% (10 + X) = 60\%(X)$

    C. $40\%X = 60\% (10 + X)$

    D. $40\% (10 + X) = 60\%$

7. Admission to a game is $2 for general admission and $3.50 for reserved seats. If 12,500 people paid a total of $36,250 to attend the game, how many general admission tickets were sold?

   A. 3500

   B. 5000

   C. 7250

   D. 18125

8. A jet flies from Hong Kong to Mumbai in 4 hours and from Mumbai to Hong Kong in 3 hours 45 minutes. The wind velocity is 14 mph and decreases the plane's speed on the journey from Hong Kong to Mumbai and increases the plane's speed from Mumbai to Hong Kong. If rate x time = distance, which of the following equations could be used to find the average speed s of the jet?

   A. $0.25(s - 14) = s$

   B. $(4 + 3.75) = (s+14) + (s-14)$

   C. $(s - 14)4 = (s + 14)3.75$

   D. $4(3.75) = (s + 14)(s - 14)$

Algebra Word Problems: Answer Explanations

1. C   You need to assign a variable to one of your unknowns. In this case, let's choose the number of quarters and set that equal to q. Now, relate all the unknowns in terms of that variable:

Number of quarters: q

Number of pennies: 2q

Number of dimes: 6q

Now, you must make an equation. Since you know the total amount of money and the value of each coin, you can write the following equation:

(0.25)(Number of Quarters)+(0.10)(Number of dimes)+(0.01)(Number of pennies)=$8.70

$(0.25)(q) + (0.10)(6q) + (0.01)(2q) = \$8.70$

$0.25q + 0.6q + 0.02q = \$8.70$

$0.87q = 8.70$

$q = 10$

The number of dimes is $6q = 6(10) = 60$

2. D   For algebra word problems, you need to assign a variable to the unknown. You could set the smallest integer to x. Then, we can find out what the other two numbers are in terms of x. Since we are dealing with consecutive odd integers, the second number will be two more than the first, and the third number will be two more than the second. Therefore, the three unknowns are: x, x+2, and x+4.

Now, we must set up an equation by taking each word and translating it into an equation.

The sum of the third and twice the first is 7 more than twice the third.

Sum = addition, third = x+4, twice = multiply by 2, first = x, more = add

$(x + 4) + 2(x) = 7 + 2(x + 4)$	Translate words into equation
$x + 4 + 2x = 7 + 2x + 8$	Distribute
$3x + 4 = 15 + 2x$	Combine like terms on each side
$3x = 11 + 2x$	Subtract 4 from each side
$x = 11$	Subtract 2x from each side

Integers: 11, 13, 15. You solved for x, the first. You can easily find the other integers. The largest is 15.

3. C   Let's step carefully through this problem. If it cost the manufacturer n dollars to make the car, let's determine the price at which the toy store purchased it. We know they purchased it at a cost of 30% more than n. Let's multiply the percent by the price.

$30\% \times n = 0.30 \times n = 0.3n$

So, the toy store purchased the car for 0.3n more than the n that it cost to make it. Therefore, the toy store purchased it for: $0.3n + n = 1.3n$.

Now, on to the price that the toy store sold it for. 20% higher than the price they paid for it. Again, multiply. $20\% \times 1.3n = 0.2 \times 1.3n = 0.26n$

So, they sold it for 0.26n higher than 1.3n or they sold it for $1.3n + 0.26n = 1.56n$.

4. A   When solving a traveling problem, keep in mind the three aspects: rate, time, and distance, where rate x time = distance.

Rate:
Train A: 40 km per hour
Train B: 10 km per hour faster than Train A = 50 km per hour

Time:
This is unknown, but is the same for both trains, so let's create a variable to represent the time, t.

Distance:
The total distance they travel is 540 km.
Train A travels: 40 km per hour x t hours = 40t
Train B travels: 50 km per hour x t hours = 50t

Set up an equation to relate the distances.
$40t + 50t = 540$
$90t = 540$
$t = 6$
6 hours

5. C   This problem describes a linear relationship between the value of the sanding equipment and time. We know the starting point value and how fast it will depreciate; therefore we can set up the linear equation to represent the change in value over time. Let V be the value of the equipment, in dollars and t be the time in years in our linear equation.

We know the original value of the equipment when we start to depreciate the equipment, when time, t equals 0 is $48,000. As time goes on, the equipment depreciates in value at a constant rate of $1500 each year. This –$1500/year is the slope of the graph line associated with the linear equation describing the change in value over time and $48,000 is the vertical axis intercept.

Therefore, we know the y–intercept and slope and can write this as an equation: $V = 48,000 - 1500t$

Now that we know the equation, we substitute $30,000 for the value of the equipment and find the time t.
$30,000 = 48,000 - 1500t$
$1500t = 48000 - 30000$
$1500t = 18000$
$t = 12$

After 12 years, the value of the equipment will be $30,000.

6. A   Let X represent the unknown, which is the amount of pure saline that must be added.

Now, set up an equation relating the amount of saline in the solutions. Remember, the amount of saline will be the percentage of saline in each solution multiplied by the total amount of that solution. For example, the amount of saline in the 40% solution is equal to 40% times the total amount of that solution = 40% (10L)

amount of saline in 40% soln + amount of added saline = amount of saline in 60% soln

40% (10) + 100%(X) = 60% (10 + X)

40% (10) + X = 60% (10 + X)

7. B   Create a variable for each unknown.

g for the number of general admission tickets sold

r for the number of reserved seat tickets sold

Now, set up equations.

12,500 paid = therefore, 12,500 total tickets were sold.

g + r = 12,500

$36,250 was brought in, $2 for general admission and $3.50 for reserved seats

The amount of money generated for the general admission tickets is: 2g

Amount of money for reserved tickets: 3.50r

2g + 3.5r = 36,250

Now solve the system of equations.

g + r = 12500

2g + 3.5r = 36250

You can use any method, let's try substitution in this case.

Take the first equation and solve for r.

g + r = 12500, r = 12500 − g

Substitute r into the second equation.

2g + 3.5r = 36250

2g + 3.5(12500 − g) = 36250

2g + 43750 − 3.5g = 36250

−1.5g = −7500

g = 5000

5000 general admission tickets were sold

8. C   Set up two distance equations, with d as the distance between Hong Kong and Mumbai.

Rate x time = distance

When the plane is flying against the wind, the speed of the wind is subtracted from the plane's speed to get the overall rate.

Rate of plane = s − 14

(s − 14)4=d

When the plane is flying with the wind, the speed of the wind is added to the plane's speed to get the rate.

Rate of plane = s + 14

(s + 14) 3.75=d

Set the equations equal: (s − 14)4=(s + 14)3.75

1. If $\frac{2n}{3} - 6 = 12$, then what is the value of n?

  A. 9

  B. 12

  C. 24

  D. 27

2. A tree that is 18 feet tall casts a shadow that is 8 feet long. If the height of an object and the length of its shadow is proportionate, how long of a shadow will a man that is 6 feet tall cast?

  A. 2 ft

  B. 2 $\frac{1}{3}$ ft

  C. 2 $\frac{2}{3}$ ft

  D. 3 ft

3. The average number of points you scored in the first 9 basketball games of the season was 23. What do you need in the 10th game to get your average to n?

  A. n – 23

  B. 10n – 207

  C. 9n – 23

  D. 207 – 9n

4. Solve for m. 3m + 2a = 5(m – 4)

  A. a – 1/2

  B. –a + 2

  C. –2/3 a – 1/3

  D. a + 10

5. Doug is twice as tall as Sandra, who is 5 inches shorter than Melissa. If Melissa's height is m inches, what expression represent Doug's height?

  A. 2m – 5

  B. 2m – 10

  C. 2(m + 5)

  D. m – 10

6. Give a range of possible values for d if –48 < –3(12d – 4) < 48.

  A. –1 < d < 1

  B. $-\frac{5}{3}$ < d < $\frac{5}{3}$

  C. $\frac{5}{3}$ < d < –1

  D. –1 < d < $\frac{5}{3}$

7. In the local college, the ratio of engineering majors to non–engineering majors is 2 to 7. If there are 1260 students in the whole school and all students fall under one of those categories, how many non–engineering majors are at the school?

    A. 140

    B. 180

    C. 630

    D. 980

8. You have 16 coins in your pocket that are all pennies and nickels. If the coins are worth 32 cents, how many pennies do you have?

    A. 4

    B. 8

    C. 10

    D. 12

9. Given the following equations, what is the sum of one square and one circle?

    A. 3

    B. 4.5

    C. 9

    D. 21

$$\square + \square + \square + 6 = \bigcirc$$

$$\bigcirc + \bigcirc + \bigcirc - \square = 15$$

10. Jennifer types at an average rate of 12 pages per hour. At that rate, how long will it take Jennifer to type 100 pages?

    A. 8 hours and 3 minutes

    B. 8 hours and 4 minutes

    C. 8 hours and 20 minutes

    D. 8 hours and 33 ⅓ minutes

11. The price of a camera was first increased by $17 and then decreased by 38%. If the final price of the camera was y, what was the original price?

    A. y/0.62 – $17

    B. 0.62(y + $17)

    C. $17 + (1.38)y

    D. 0.38(y + $17)

12. A woman on a bike and a man in a car leave a restaurant at the same time. The woman heads due East and the man goes due West. If the woman is biking at 15 mph, and the car is traveling at 35 mph, in how many hours will they be 300 miles apart?

    A. 2

    B. 4

    C. 6

    D. 8

13. Which of the following patterns does the following data fit? 1, 4, 9, ...

   A. $y = 2x$

   B. $y = x^2$

   C. $y = x + 3$

   D. $y = 3x - 2$

14. Solve for y. (y+3)/5 = (y+2)/6

   A. 8

   B. 5

   C. –1

   D. –8

15. Carol is looking to buy a machine for her workshop. Machine Y costs $500 and needs $40 in maintenance and supplies each year. Machine Z costs $400 but needs $50 in maintenance and supplies each year. After how many years will the cost of Machine Y be the same as the cost for Machine Z?

   A. 4 years

   B. 5 years

   C. 9 years

   D. 10 years

16. Find three consecutive odd integers, such that three times the second is 9 more than twice the third. What is the smallest number?

   A. 9

   B. 11

   C. 12

   D. 15

17. Belmont Middle School is headed on a field trip to the museum. Adult tickets are $5 and student tickets are $3. If there are 50 people total who go to the museum and they pay a total of $162, how many adults are on the trip?

   A. 10

   B. 8

   C. 6

   D. 4

18. Identify the pattern shown by the following numbers: –2.1, –3.2, –4.3, –5.4, –6.5

   A. $y = 0.1x - 2$

   B. $y = -2.1x + 1$

   C. $y = -x^2 - 1.1$

   D. $y = -1.1x - 1$

19. A farmer decided to go outside and check on his animals. He passed by the chickens and counted their feet and then he passed by the pigs and counted their feet. He got a total of 100 feet. He knew he had 8 more chickens than pigs, so he knew the animals were okay. How many chickens did he have?

 A. 14

 B. 22

 C. 23

 D. 44

20. Solve for y in the following equations:

$$2y - 3x = 8$$
$$x = 3y + 2$$

 A. –4

 B. –2

 C. 3

 D. 6

Algebra: Chapter Review Answer Explanations

1. D   To solve equations, you must isolate the variable.

$2n/3 - 6 = 12$

First, since 6 is subtracted from the left side, you must do the opposite, so add 6 to both sides.

$2n/3 - 6 + 6 = 12 + 6$

$2n/3 = 18$

Since you are dividing n by 3, perform the opposite operation. Multiply both sides by 3.

$2n/3 \times 3 = 18 \times 3$

$2n = 54$

Since you are multiplying n by 2, you must divide both sides by 2 to get n alone.

$2n = 54$

$2n \div 2 = 54 \div 2$

$n = 27$

You can plug the 27 back into the original equation to make sure that it works.

2. C   Draw a picture to help you understand the problem.

The sun shines on both the tree and the man at the same angle. This means that the triangles formed by the tree, the shadow, and the light will be similar to the triangle formed with the man, his shadow, and the light.

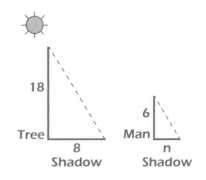

Use a proportion to solve for the shadow length.

$6/18 = n/8$

Cross multiply to solve.

$18n = 6(8)$

$n = 48/18$

$n = 2\frac{2}{3}$ feet

3. B If the average on the first 9 games was a 23, then the total number of points you scored in those games was 9 x 23 = 207.

If the average on all 10 games is n, then the total number of points scored in all 10 games must be 10 x n = 10n.

To find what you need to get in the 10th game, subtract the total number of points in the first 9 games from the total number of points in all 10 games.
10n – 207 is what is needed in the 10th game.

4. D Follow the order of operations and isolate m.

3m + 2a = 5(m – 4)	Distributive Property on right hand side of equation
3m + 2a = 5m – 20	Subtract 3m from both sides
2a = 2m – 20	Add 20 to both sides
2a + 20 = 2m	Divide by 2 on both sides
a + 10 = m	Rearrange equation
m = a + 10	

5. B This question asks you to translate the words into an expression. In this case, the unknown quantity, Melissa's height is represented with the variable m. Now, take the rest of the words to write an expression.

Let's start with Sandra's height. We know that she is 5 inches shorter than Melissa. Therefore, subtract 5 from Melissa's height to get Sandra's.

Sandra's height = Melissa's height – 5
Sandra's height = m – 5

We know that Doug is twice Sandra's height. Therefore, multiply Sandra's height by 2 to get Doug's height.
Doug's height = 2 (Sandra's height)
Doug's height = 2(m – 5)

Use the distributive property.
Doug's height = 2m – 10

6. D Solve for d by isolating the variable. Make sure what is done to the middle is done to all three sides of the inequality. Also, remember that when you multiply or divide by a negative, all signs flip.

–48 < –3(12d – 4) < 48	divide all sides by –3 and flip the signs
16 > 12d – 4 > –16	add 4 to all sides
20 > 12d > –12	divide by 12 on all sides
$20/12$ > d > –1	reduce the fraction and rearrange the inequality
–1 < d < 5/3	

7. D The ratio of engineering majors to non-engineering majors is 2 to 7. Therefore, the ratio of engineering to non-engineering to total students is 2 to 7 to 9. Thus, the ratio of non–engineering to total students is 7 to 9.

If there are 1260 students in the school, set up a proportion with n representing the number of non–engineering majors at the school.

non–eng majors to total = 7 to 9 = n to 1260
$7/9 = n/1260$
Cross multiply to solve.
1260(7) = 9n
8820 = 9n
n = 980

8. D   There are two unknowns in this equation, set up a variable for each.

p = number of pennies

n = number of nickels

Now, set up equations.

"You have 16 coins" – Therefore, the total number of pennies and nickels will equal 16.

p + n = 16

"the coins are worth 32 cents" – Therefore, the total value of the pennies plus the total value of the nickels is worth 32.

1p + 5n = 32

Now, solve the system. Use substitution and isolate a variable in the first equation.

p + n = 16

n = 16 – p

Plug in the value for n into the second equation.

1p + 5n = 32

1p + 5(16 – p) = 32

p + 80 – 5p = 32

–4p + 80 = 32

–4p = –48

p = 12

9. B   When dealing with problems with shapes, it is often easiest to use variables to represent the shapes. In this case, let's use s to represent each square and c to represent each circle.

3s + 6 = c

3c – s = 15

Next, it is often a good idea to try adding the equations to form a new equation to help solve the problem.

$$\begin{array}{rl} 3s + 6 & = c \\ 3c - s & = 15 \\ \hline 3s + 3c + 6 - s & = c + 15 \end{array}$$

Now, simplify each side and combine like terms. Bring all variables to one side and all numbers to the other.

3s + 3c + 6 – s = c + 15

2s + 3c + 6 = c + 15

2s + 3c = c + 9

2s + 2c = 9

The question asks you to find s + c, therefore divide both sides of the equation by 2.

s + c = 4.5

10. C   If Jennifer types 12 pages per hour, set up a proportion to find how long it will take her to type 100 pages.

12 pages/1 hour = 100 pages/y hours

Now, cross multiply to solve this proportion.

12y = 100

y = 100/12 = 8⅓

8⅓ hours

All the answer choices have minutes, so let's convert the ⅓ hour to minutes.

⅓ hour x 60 minutes/1 hour = 20 minutes

8 hours 20 minutes

11. A   Let the original price equal p. The price was first increased by $17.

p+17

This was decreased by 38%.

$(100\% - 38\%)(p + 17)$

Now, set this price equal to y and rearrange to isolate the original price p.

$(100\% - 38\%)(p + 17) = y$

$(62\%)(p + 17) = y$

$p + 17 = y/0.62$

$p = y/0.62 - 17$

12. C   Since the man and woman are traveling in exactly opposite directions, the distances they travel can be added together to find out how far apart they are at a given time. The distance a person or thing has traveled can be calculated by multiplying the rate of travel by the time traveled. You know the rate and the total distance that the man and woman need to have traveled, so use a variable such as t to represent the time they have traveled. Since they have both traveled for the same amount of time, you can use one variable for both people.

15 (the speed of the woman on the bike) x t + 35 (the speed of the man on the bike) x t = 300 (the total distance they have gone in opposite directions)

Then solve for time.

$15t + 35t = 300$

$50t = 300$

$t = 6$ hours

13. B   1, 4, 9, ...

To determine which of the patterns does the data fit, try each answer.

A: $y = 2x$

The first input of 1 should give you a 1 as a result. $2(1) = 2$. This does not work.

B: $y = x^2$

An input of 1 should give you a 1. $1^2 = 1$

An input of 2 should give you a 4. $2^2 = 4$

An input of 3 should give you a 9. $3^2 = 9$

All those are true for the equation $y = x^2$.

C: $y = x+3$

An input of 1 should give you a 1. $1 + 3 = 4$. This does not work.

D: $y = 3x - 2$

An input of 1 should give you a 1. $3(1) - 2 = 3 - 2 = 1$. That works.

An input of 2 should output a 4. $3(2) - 2 = 6 - 2 = 4$. That works.

An input of 3 should output a 9. $3(3) - 2 = 9 - 2 = 7$. This does not work.

14. D

$(y+3)/5 = (y+2)/6$	First, cross–multiply to remove the fractions.
$5(y+2) = 6(y+3)$	Use distributive property.
$5y + 10 = 6y + 18$	Bring all the variables to one side. Subtract 5y from both sides.
$10 = y + 18$	Isolate y by subtracting 18 from both sides.
$-8 = y$	
$y = -8$	

15. D   Set up equations to represent the cost of each machine. Let t represent the unknown value, which is in this case is the number of years.

Machine Y costs $500 and needs $40 in maintenance and supplies each year.
Cost of Machine Y = 500 + 40t

Machine Z costs $400 but needs $50 in maintenance and supplies each year.
Cost of Machine Z = 400 + 50t

Now, set the two costs equal to find after how many years the cost will be the same. Then solve for t.
500 + 40t = 400 + 50t
100 = 10t
t = 10
After 10 years.

16. B   Use variables to represent the unknown quantities. Let the smallest number = n. Then, the second number would be n+2. The next number would be n+4.

n, n + 2, and n + 4

Now, set up an equation and solve for n.

Three times the second is 9 more than twice the third.
3(n + 2) = 9 + 2(n + 4)
3n + 6 = 9 + 2n + 8
3n + 6 = 2n + 17
n + 6 = 17
n = 11

17. C   Use variables to represent the unknowns:
a = number of adult tickets
s = number of student tickets

Now, set up equations with the variables.
"50 people total who go to the museum"
a + s = 50

"they pay a total of $162"
5a + 3s = 162

Now, solve the system of equations. In this case, let's use elimination. Multiply the first by –3, so that the s's will cancel.

a + s = 50
–3a – 3s = –150

Now, add the two equations.

$$
\begin{array}{r}
-3a - 3s = -150 \\
5a + 3s = 162 \\
\hline
2a = 12
\end{array}
$$

a = 6
6 adult tickets were sold

18. D Plug in values for each answer choice, and see which exhibits the pattern: –2.1, –3.2, –4.3, –5.4, –6.5

For x=1, y=–2.1; For x=2, y=–3.2; etc.

A: $y = 0.1x - 2$

$x = 1$, $y = 0.1(1) - 2 = -1.9$ Not true.

B: $y = -2.1x + 1$

$x = 1$, $y = -2.1(1) + 1 = -3.1$ Not true.

C: $y = -x^2 - 1.1$

$x = 1$, $y = -1^2 - 1.1 = -2.1$

$x = 2$, $y = -2^2 - 1.1 = -5.1$ Not true.

D: $y = -1.1x - 1$

$x = 1$, $y = -1.1(1) - 1 = -2.1$

You can try more values for x, but it is the only answer remaining.

19. B For algebra word problems, you should assign variables to the unknowns. In this case, there are two unknowns: the number of chickens and the number of pigs.

Let c = number of chickens

Let p = number of pigs

Then set up equations by using information in the problem.

We know that the farmer had 8 more chickens than pigs.

$c = p + 8$

We know that the total number of feet is 100 and that each chicken has 2 feet and each pig has 4.

$2c + 4p = 100$

Now, solve this system of equations.

$c = p + 8$

$2c + 4p = 100$

You can use the substitution method by substituting for c in the second equation what c equals in the first equation.

$2c + 4p = 100$	Second Equation
$2(p + 8) + 4p = 100$	Substitute first equation for c
$2p + 16 + 4p = 100$	Distribute
$6p + 16 = 100$	Combine like terms
$6p = 84$	Subtract 16 from both sides
$p = 14$	Divide both sides by 6 to solve for p
$c = p + 8$	Use first equation to solve for c
$c = 14 + 8 = 22$	Plug in value for p, and solve for c

20. B Use substitution to solve this system of equations. Plug the value for x from the second equation into the first equation:

$2y - 3x = 8$

$2y - 3(3y + 2) = 8$

$2y - 9y - 6 = 8$

$-7y - 6 = 8$

$-7y = 14$

$y = -2$

4. Graphing

Number Line

When studying the fundamental concepts of math, particularly signed numbers, you were introduced to the concept of the number line, a straight line used for representing positive and negative numbers.

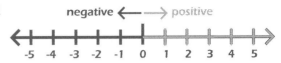

x–axis and y–axis

Graphs are useful for showing the relationships between variables. The coordinate plane on which graphs are shown is simply a two–dimensional variation of the number line.

The horizontal number line, labeled the x–axis, represents all possible values of the x variable. The vertical number line, called the y–axis, serves the same function for the y values. Any pair of possible x and y coordinates is called a coordinate pair (also know as an ordered pair). Coordinate pairs are always written in the order (x, y). The point at which the x–axis and y–axis intersect (0,0) is called the origin.

Quadrants

The Roman numerals on the graph show the four quadrants of the coordinate plane.

Quadrant I: all x and y values are positive

Quadrant II: x is negative, y is positive

Quadrant III: x and y are negative

Quadrant IV: x is positive, y is negative

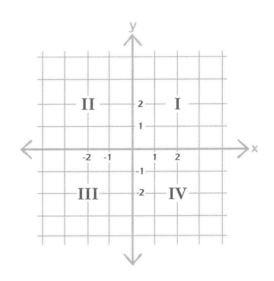

Plotting Coordinate Pairs

The graph below shows a few points and their coordinate pairs. The coordinate pair for point A is (1,2). To plot point A, you start at the origin (0,0) and move 1 space to the right along the x–axis. From there, move 2 spaces upwards along the y–axis.

Now check to see that you understand how to plot the rest of the coordinate pairs shown.

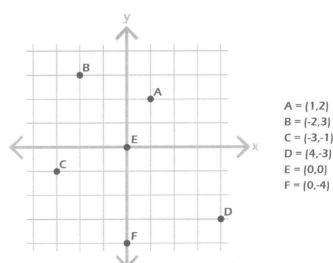

A = (1,2)
B = (-2,3)
C = (-3,-1)
D = (4,-3)
E = (0,0)
F = (0,-4)

Number Line & Coordinate Plane: Practice

1. What is the distance between points A and B on the number line below?

A. –6

B. 5

C. 6

D. 7

2. Name the coordinate pair which represents the point on the graph.

A. (–3, 1)

B. (1, –3)

C. (1, –4)

D. (–1, –3)

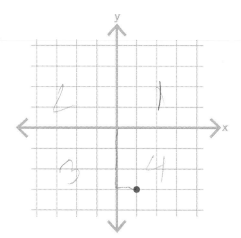

3. All of the points in quadrant III:
   I. Have negative x–values.
   II. Have negative y–values.
   III. Can be described by a coordinate pair.

A. I and III

B. I and II

C. II and III

D. I, II, and III

4. If the graph below shows a circle with center at the origin, and the coordinates of the point shown is (3,0) , what are the coordinates of point A?

A. (–3, 0)

B. (0, –3)

C. (0, 3)

D. (3, 0)

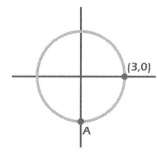

5. Point M is the midpoint of the line PQ. If the coordinates of P are (9, 11) and M is at (4, 7.5), find the coordinates of Q.

A. (–1, 4)

B. (5, 3.5)

C. (6.5, 9)

D. (–1, 3)

6. What is the distance between point A and point B in the graph?

    A. 3

    B. 4

    C. 5

    D. 6

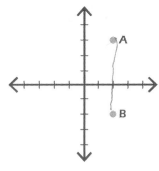

7. What is the coordinate pair for the last corner of a rectangle if the first 3 corners are at (−2, −3), (−2, 4), and (4, 4)?

    A. (−2, −2)

    B. (−2, 3)

    C. (4, −3)

    D. (−4, −3)

8. What values does the number line represent?

    A. whole numbers

    B. real numbers greater than −1

    C. positive integers

    D. integers greater than −2

Number Line & Coordinate Plane: Answer Explanations

1. D   Point B is at 6, point A is at −1. Find the difference between them to find the distance. 6 − (−1) = 6 + 1 = 7.

2. B   When naming a coordinate pair, the x value is always first. The x values are horizontal and this point is 1 away in the positive horizontal direction.

    The y–value is second. The y–values are vertical and this point is 3 points below the y–axis, therefore, the y–value is −3.

    Coordinate pair = (1, −3)

3. D   Any point in the coordinate plane can be described by a coordinate pair, therefore III is true.

    Any point in quadrant III will have negative x and y values. Therefore, I and II are also true.

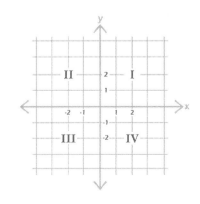

4. B   All points on a circle are the same distance from the center, therefore each point is 3 away from the origin. In a coordinate pair, the first element listed is the x–coordinate. In this case, point A is on the y–axis and did not move horizontally at all. Therefore, the x–coordinate is 0.

    The y–coordinate of point A is −3 since it is 3 away from the origin in the negative direction. (0, −3)

5. A   To find the coordinates of a midpoint, you find the average of the x coordinates of the endpoints and the average of the y coordinates of the endpoints.

In this problem, they have given you the midpoint and you need to find the other endpoint. Let's first look at the x–coordinates. The x coordinate of the end point is 9 and the x coordinate of the midpoint is 4. Therefore, 4 equals the average of 9 and Q's x coordinate.

$4 = (9 + x)/2$
$8 = 9 + x$
$-1 = x$

Now, do the same thing for the y coordinate.
$7.5 = (11 + y)/2$
$15 = 11 + y$
$4 = y$

Therefore, the coordinates of Q are $(-1, 4)$.

6. C   Points A and B have the same x coordinate, they only differ in y coordinates.
Point A is 3 units above the x axis, and Point B is 2 units below. That makes a total of 5 units separating the two points.

You could also do this by determining the coordinate pair of each point and then subtracting. Point A = (2, 3) and Point B = (2, –2). Therefore, the difference between the y coordinates is $3 - (-2) = 3 + 2 = 5$.

7. C   Graphing the coordinate pairs will help you find the last corner of the rectangle.

The coordinates: $(-2, -3)$, $(-2, 4)$, and $(4, 4)$ are graphed, and the last corner to complete the rectangle has been included in the bottom right corner.

The last corner is at $(4, -3)$.

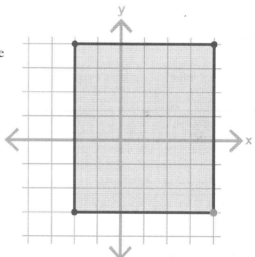

8. D   As you can see in the number line, only the values greater than –2 are marked. In addition, only the integers are marked, all the fractions or decimals in between are not highlighted. Therefore, the number line only represents integers.

Answer D: integers greater than –2

Rate of Change

In the previous chapter you learned to set up proportions based on the concept of equivalent ratios or rates of change – the relative change in one variable with respect to another. You were able to use the fact that two variables (such as number of pages read by a student and time) interacted in a predictable way to determine what the value of one variable would be for a given value of the other.

Example: How many pages has a student read in one hour if she reads 2 pages per minute?

This information can easily be represented graphically, and the rate of change will be the slope of that graph. 2 pages/1 min

For every minute that she reads, the numbers of pages she has read will increase by 2. The rate of change is 2 pages per minute.

Calculating Slope

The slope of a line is the change in the y coordinate divided by the change in the x coordinate. This often referred to as "rise over run". Slope = rise/run = change in y / change in x

If you have two points on a graph (x_1, y_1) and (x_2, y_2) then you can use the following formula to find the slope of the straight line that connects them:

$$\text{Slope} = (y_2 - y_1) \div (x_2 - x_1)$$

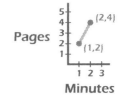

The slope between (1,2) and (2,4) is = $(4 - 2)/(2 - 1)$ = 2/1 To travel between these two points, a line must rise 2 units and run 1 unit to the right.

Negative Slope

The slope of a line is negative if its y–coordinate decreases as you move to the right. In other words, the slope is negative if the rise is negative as the run stays positive. For example, the graph to the left has a slope of –3/5.

Zero Slope

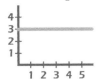

A horizontal line has a slope of 0. There is no rise as you move to the right.

Undefined Slope

A vertical line's slope cannot be defined. It continually rises but has a run of zero, and it is not possible to divide a number by zero.

Slope & Rate of Change: Practice

1. What is the slope of the line that passes through points A and B in the figure?

    A. –³⁄₅

    B. –⁵⁄₃

    C. ³⁄₅

    D. ⁵⁄₃

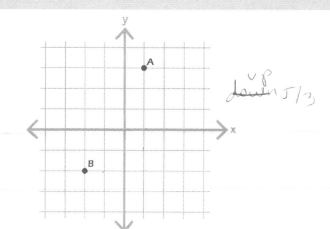

2. What is the slope of the line in the graph below?

    A. 3

    B. –3

    C. 1

    D. ⅓

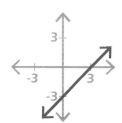

3. What is the slope of the line that passes through the origin and (–3, –4)?

    A. ⁴⁄₃

    B. ¾

    C. –¾

    D. –⁴⁄₃

4. Choose the best answer to replace the question mark.
The slope from point A to point B   ?   The slope from point B to point C.

    A. >

    B. <

    C. =

    D. One slope is undefined, so it can't be determined

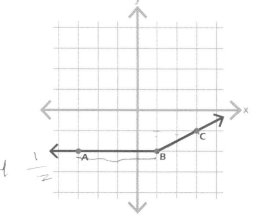

5. If Melissa can type 80 words for every 3 minutes and she needs to finish typing 6 pages with 1000 words on each page, how long will it take her?

    A. 37.5 mins

    B. 1 hour, 15 mins

    C. 3 hours, 45 mins

    D. 4 hours

6. A line with a slope of −12 that passes through the origin has what y value when x is 5?

A. 60

B. −60

C. −7

D. 17

7. Which of the following lines has an undefined slope?

A.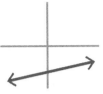

B.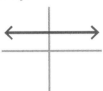

C.

D.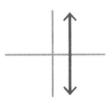

8. What is the slope of the line that passes through (−2, 4) and (5, 3)?

A. −1/7

B. 3/7

C. −7

D. −5/6

$$\frac{3-4}{5+2} = \frac{-1}{7}$$

Slope & Rate of Change: Answer Explanations

1. D   Slope is rise over run. From point B to point A, the rise is 5 and the run is 3. Therefore, the slope of that line is 5/3.

2. C   To determine slope, figure out how much the line rises over how much it runs. In other words, find the change in the y coordinates and divide by the change in the x coordinates.

For this line, let us start at (0, −3) and go to (3,0). From the first point to the second point, the line rises 3 and goes across 3. Therefore, the slope is equal to 3/3 = 1.

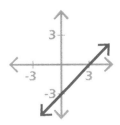

3. A   The slope is the rise over run. Therefore, the slope is the change in the y coordinates over the change in the x coordinates. Thus, find the change between the following 2 coordinate pairs (0,0) and (−3,−4).
Slope = (−4 − 0)/(−3 − 0) = −4/−3 = 4/3

4. B The slope from point A to point B is zero since it is a horizontal line. The slope from point B to point C is positive since the line is increasing.

Therefore, the slope from point A to B is less than the slope from B to C.

Answer B: <

5. C The rate for Melissa is 80 words for 3 minutes. She needs to type 6 pages with 1000 words each, a total of 6000 words. Since we assume that Melissa's rate remains the same, set up a ratio between words and minutes.

80 words/3 mins = 6000 words/y mins

$80/3 = 6000/y$

Cross multiply and solve.

80y = 6000(3)

80y = 18000

y = 225

225 minutes

The answers are in terms of hours and minutes, so convert 225 minutes to hours and minutes.

225 minutes x ^{1} hour/60 mins = $^{225}/_{60}$ hours = 3 $^{45}/_{60}$ hours = 3 hours 45 mins

6. B The formula to find slope is:

Slope = change in y/change in x

Plug in the values you know and solve for y.

Slope = change in y/change in x = (y − 0)/(5 − 0) = −12

y/5 = −12

y = −60

7. D Answer choice A has a positive slope since the line is increasing.

Answer B has a slope of zero since it is a horizontal line.

Answer C has a slope that keeps changing, but it is always defined.

Answer D has an undefined slope since it is a vertical line.

8. A The slope of a line is the rise over the run. Therefore, slope is the change in y over the change in x.

The two points are: (−2, 4) and (5, 3).

The change in y value is 4 − 3 = 1

The change in x value is −2 − 5 = −7

Slope = change in y/change in x

= 1/−7

= −1/7

Often, it is possible to gather information about an equation or real–life situation by looking at a graph that represents it. When interpreting graphs, notice the slope at various points and any x and y–intercepts.

Slope

When using the slope of a graph to gain information about a situation keep a few things in mind:

1: Is the slope positive or negative? – For example, if given the scenario that sales of a computer have increased significantly, you should pick out the graph with a positive slope. The one circled below.

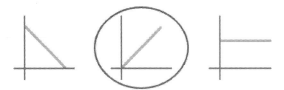

2: What is the rate of change? – You should use information about variations in slope to your advantage. For example, if asked which graph represents the temperature for a month that warmed up for the first two weeks and then remained steady for the rest of the month, you should recognize that the circled graph follows this pattern.

Intercepts

The x and y intercepts of word problems can have many different meanings depending on how the problem is set up. You should practice identifying the meaning of intercepts in graphs of real–world situations. Here's an example:

The graph to the right shows the profits on t–shirt sales. As can be seen, the y–intercept is the point at which x = 0, or 0 t–shirts are sold. The y–intercept is –$500. Therefore, before any t–shirts are sold, the profit is –$500, which means that the costs are $500. The x–intercept in this case is at 25, so the breakeven point is when 25 t–shirts are sold.

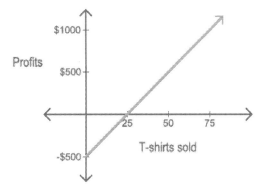

1. Which graph best represents the growth of a plant that took 2 weeks to begin growing and then grew at a steady rate?

A.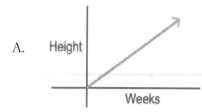

B.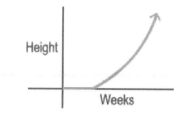

C.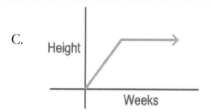

D.

2. Which graph shows only a positive slope?

A.

B.

C.

D.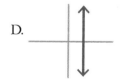

3. What is the initial cost of the candy bars?

A. $0

B. $1

C. $10

D. –$10

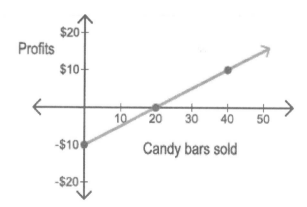

4. How much is being charged per candy bar?

A. 25 cents

B. 50 cents

C. 75 cents

D. $1

5. How many candy bars must be sold to break even?

A. 0

B. 10

C. 20

D. 30

6. In the graph below, where is the slope of the line negative?

A. before 2006

B. for part of 2006

C. after 2007

D. up to 2007

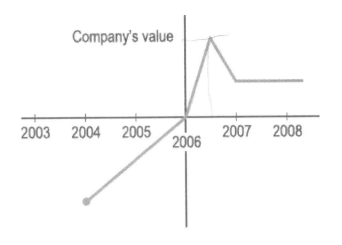

7. When did the value of the company peak?

A. In 2005

B. In 2006

C. In 2007

D. In 2008

8. Based on the information in the graph, which is true?

A. The company was started in 2006.

B. It took 2 years for the company to break even.

C. The company's value has increased steadily since it began.

D. The company's value decreased overall between 2006 and 2007.

Qualitative Graphing: Answer Explanations

1. D   Since the plant did not begin growing for 2 weeks, there should be a straight line along the x–axis until week 2. Then, the plant grew at a steady rate which would be represented by a straight line with a positive slope. This is seen in the graph on the right.

2. A   Graphs with positive slope increase as you look at them from left to right. The graph in answer A does that.

3. C   The initial cost of the candy bars can be seen at the y–intercept. Where the line crosses the y–axis, means that the number of candy bars sold is 0, so we are dealing with initial costs.

The y–intercept is at –$10, but the y–axis shows profit. Therefore, if the profit is –$10, that means that the initial cost was $10.

4. B   The amount being charged per candy bar is the slope of the line. Slope is rise over run. In this case that would be the profit divided by the number of candy bars sold, which is the price of a candy bar.

Use any two coordinate pairs to help you find slope. In the graph, you can see the following coordinate pairs, (20 candy bars, $0) and (40 candy bars, $10). Now find the slope:

Slope = ($10 – $0)/(40 – 20 bars) = $10/20 bars = $0.50 per candy bar

50 cents

5. C   The break even point is when the costs = revenue, which means that the profit = $0. The profit is $0 on this graph at the x–intercept. You can see that the line crosses the x–axis at 20 candy bars.

20 candy bars

6. B   A negative slope occurs when a line goes down. Slope is rise over run, so a negative slope means that the rise is negative as you move along in the x–direction.

In the graph, there is only one section of the line with a negative slope, and that occurs towards the end of 2006. Therefore, answer B is correct.

Do not be confused by the time before 2006. Even though the company's value is negative, the value is increasing, so the slope is positive.

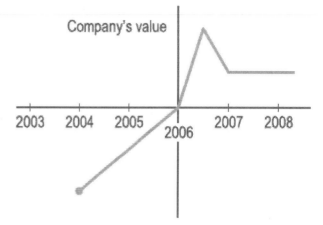

7. B   The point with the highest company value is the point with the greatest y–coordinate. This occurs in 2006.

8. B   Let's examine each answer choice.

A. The company was started in 2006.
This is not true. In the graph you can see that the company started in 2004.

B. It took 2 years for the company to break even.
This is true. The company started in 2004 and then in 2006 the company's value was at $0, which means the company broke even. This is 2 years.

C. The company's value has increased steadily since it began.
This is not true. The company's value decreased in 2006.

D. The company's value decreased overall between 2006 and 2007.
This is not true. Even though the value of the company decreased for part of 2006, when 2007 began the company's value was higher than it was when 2006 began.

Linear Equations

A linear equation is one that results in a straight line when graphed. The equation of a straight line typically takes the form:

$y = mx + b$

In this equation, m is the slope and b is the y–intercept. The y–intercept is the point at which the line crosses the y–axis; in other words, the y–value when x = 0. The x and y represent the x– and y– values of any coordinate pair on the line.

Let's graph the following linear equation: $y = \frac{3}{2}x - 2$

You can see from the equation that the y–intercept is –2. This point is plotted on the graph as (0, –2). The equation also tells us that the slope is 3/2. Starting at (0, –2), draw a second point up 3 and 2 to the right. Now, connect those points to create the graph of the line:

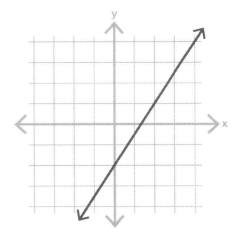

Determining Equations

If you are given two coordinate pairs, you can calculate the slope using the formula you learned in the lesson "Slope & Rate of Change". Once you have the slope, plug in either pair to solve for the y–intercept.

Example: Find the equation for the line through the two pairs of points (–4, 6) and (–2, –8).
Slope = (–8 – 6)/(–2 – –4) = –14/2 = –7

Use the slope and one point to calculate the y–intercept:
$y = mx + b$
$y = -7x + b$
$6 = -7(-4) + b$
$6 = 28 + b$
$-22 = b$

$y = -7x - 22$

Graphing Equations: Practice

1. What is the equation of the line in the graph below?

A. $y = \frac{1}{2}x + 1$

B. $y = x$

C. $y = x + 1$

D. $\frac{1}{2}y = x + 1$

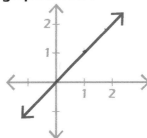

2. What is the slope of the line represented by this equation?   1 – ¾ y = ⅓ x – 2

   A. ¾

   B. ⅓

   C. –2

   D. –⁴⁄₉

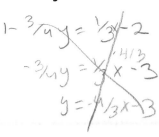

3. What is the y–intercept of the line represented by: –7x + 14 = 2y – 19 ?

   A. –19

   B. 14

   C. 33

   D. 16 ½

4. What is the equation of the line that passes through the points (4, –3) and (2, 7)?

   A. y = 6x + 4

   B. y = –5x + 17

   C. y = –⅕ x – 3

   D. y = –5x + 4

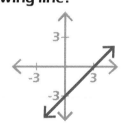

5. What is the y–intercept of the following line?

   A. 3

   B. –3

   C. 1

   D. –⅓

6. What is the equation of the line that passes through (12, 16) and (–4, 8)?

   A. y = –½ x + 22

   B. y = –2x + 40

   C. y = 2x – 8

   D. y = ½ x + 10

7. What is the equation of the line in the graph?

   A. y = –2x – 1

   B. y = 2x – 1

   C. y = ½ x – 1

   D. y = –2x + 1

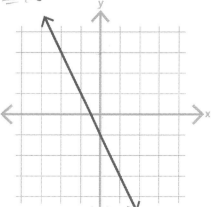

8. Which of the following equations has a slope of ⅗ and y–intercept of 2?

A. $-3x + 5y = 10$

B. $3x + 5y = 2$

C. $5x + 3y = 2$

D. $-5x - 3y = 10$

$5y = \dfrac{3x}{5} + \dfrac{10}{5}$ $3+8=8$

Graphing Equations: Answer Explanations

1. B Use the following format of an equation: $y = mx + b$, where m is the slope and b is the y–intercept. The y–intercept is where the line crosses the y–axis. In this case, the line crosses at 0. Therefore, $b = 0$. The slope is the rise over the run. In this case, the line goes up 1 every time it goes across 1. Therefore, slope is 1.

$y = mx + b$
$y = 1(x) + 0$
$y = x$

2. D Manipulate the equation to isolate y and get the equation in the form: $y = mx + b$. Once it is in that form, you can see the coefficient in front of the x, represented by m, will be the slope.

$1 - \frac{3}{4}\, y = \frac{1}{3}\, x - 2$
$-\frac{3}{4}\, y = \frac{1}{3}\, x - 3$
$(-\frac{4}{3})(-\frac{3}{4})y = (-\frac{4}{3})(\frac{1}{3}\, x - 3)$
$y = -\frac{4}{9}\, x + 4$
Slope is $-\frac{4}{9}$

3. D Manipulate the equation to isolate y and get the equation in the form: $y = mx + b$, where the b will represent the y–intercept.
$-7x + 14 = 2y - 19$
$-7x + 33 = 2y$
$-\frac{7}{2}\, x + \frac{33}{2} = y$
$y = -\frac{7}{2}\, x + \frac{33}{2}$
The y–intercept is $\frac{33}{2} = 16\,\frac{1}{2}$

4. B Find equation between: $(4, -3)$ and $(2, 7)$.
The form of the equation is $y=mx+b$, where m is the slope and b is the y–intercept. First, find the slope of the line between the points. Slope is rise over run, or the change in y over the change in x.
Slope $= (-3 - 7)/(4 - 2) = -\frac{10}{2} = -5$
$y = -5x + b$

Now, find the y–intercept. Plug in either point into the equation and solve for b. Let's use the point $(4, -3)$.
$y = -5x + b$
$-3 = -5(4) + b$
$-3 = -20 + b$
$b = 17$

Equation: $y = -5x + 17$

5. B The y–intercept is where the line crosses the y–axis at $x=0$. In the graph, you can see that the line crosses at –3. The y–intercept is at –3.

6. D To find the equation of the line through the two coordinate pairs, first find the slope. The slope is rise over run, so find the difference in y coordinates and divide by the difference in x coordinates.

(12, 16) and (–4, 8)
slope = (8 – 16)/(–4 – 12) = –8/–16 = 1/2

Therefore, the equation, y = mx + b, now is $y = \frac{1}{2}x + b$

Plug in either coordinate pair to solve for b.

$y = \frac{1}{2}x + b$
$16 = \frac{1}{2}(12) + b$
$16 = 6 + b$
$b = 10$
$y = \frac{1}{2}x + 10$

7. A When finding the equation of a line, find the slope and intercept, and put in the form y = mx + b.

This line crosses the y–axis at –1. Therefore, b = –1.
The slope is rise over run, pick any two points on the line and then figure out how much from one point to the next the line rises and runs. This line goes down 2 for every 1 across. Slope = –2/1 = –2.
y = –2x – 1

8. A There are two methods to solving this problem. The first method involves rewriting the answer choices in slope–intercept form (y = mx+b). The second method involves writing the problem in slope–intercept form and then rearranging that equation to match the form of the answer choices.

Method 1: Rearrange each answer choice so that the equations are in slope–intercept form.
A: –3x + 5y = 10
5y = 3x + 10
$y = \frac{3}{5}x + 2$
Slope = $\frac{3}{5}$, y–intercept = 2

B: 3x + 5y = 2
5y = –3x + 2
$y = -\frac{3}{5}x + \frac{2}{5}$
Slope = $-\frac{3}{5}$, y–intercept = $\frac{2}{5}$

C: 5x + 3y = 2
3y = –5x + 2
$y = -\frac{5}{3}x + \frac{2}{3}$
Slope = $-\frac{5}{3}$, y–intercept = $\frac{2}{3}$

D: –5x – 3y = 10
–3y = 5x + 10
$y = -\frac{5}{3}x - \frac{10}{3}$
Slope = $-\frac{5}{3}$, y–intercept = $-\frac{10}{3}$

Method 2: First, write the equation in slope, intercept form: y = mx + b. Then, you can rearrange the equation to standard form: ax + by = c. In this case, the problem states both the slope and y–intercept. Therefore, immediately plug them into the equation. y = mx + b

$y = \frac{3}{5}x + 2$	Now, rearrange the equation. First, multiply everything by 5 to get rid of the fraction.
5y = 3x + 10	Now, bring the x's and y's to the same side of the equation.
–3x + 5y = 10	Rearrange to standard form.

Graphing Inequalities

You've seen inequalities graphed on a number line, but how would you visually represent an inequality with multiple variables? If you have an inequality with two variables, you can graph it on a coordinate plane.

First, you determine the boundary line and graph it. Then, you shade one side of the line.

Boundary Line

To determine the boundary line, treat the inequality as if it were an equation. For example, to graph $y > x + 2$, the boundary line would be the graph of $y = x + 2$. Graph how you would like. One way is to plug some values for x into the equation, and use the resulting coordinate pairs to plot your line. For example, let's plug in the values 2 and 4 for x:

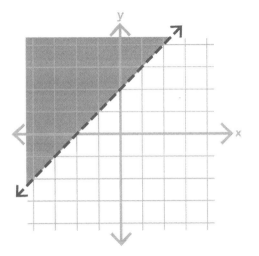

When x = 2: $y = 2 + 2 = 4$
When x = 4: $y = 4 + 2 = 6$

Now, we have two pairs to plot the line with: (2,4) and (4,6).

If the inequality contains the symbols $\geq$ or $\leq$, the boundary line should be included as part of the inequality. This is indicated by drawing a solid line. If the inequality contains the symbols $>$ or $<$. the boundary line is not included and so should be drawn as a dashed line.

Shading

Now you need to shade one side of the line or the other, to represent the range of values that correspond to the inequality. In this case, we want to graph $y > x + 2$, so we shade the part above the boundary line. As you can see, the shaded part of the graph shows all values for y that are greater than $x + 2$.

A good way to determine what side of the line to shade is to test a point. Pick any point that is not on the line, usually the origin is the easiest. Then, test that point in the equation. If it holds true, shade the side of the graph that includes that point. If it is not true in the equation, then shade the opposite side of the line.

For example, in the equation above $y > x + 2$, we can plug in the origin (0, 0). $0 > 0 + 2$ is not true. Therefore, we shade the side of the line that does not contain the origin.

Multiple Inequalities

You may be asked to graph a system of inequalities on the same graph. If so, follow the same steps you would for each inequality, but plot the results on the same coordinate plane. If the system has an "or," then leave everything shaded. If the system of inequalities has an "and," then only shade the region of overlap.

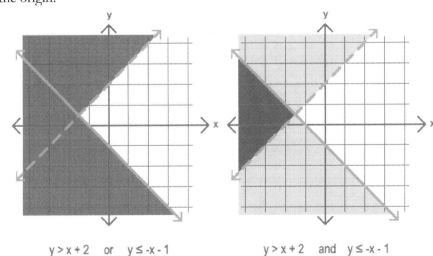

$y > x + 2$ or $y \leq -x - 1$

The entire shaded region is the solution to this set of inequalities.

$y > x + 2$ and $y \leq -x - 1$

The overlapped darker region is the solution to this set of inequalities.

Graphing Inequalities: Practice

1. y < 2x would be graphed as:

A. 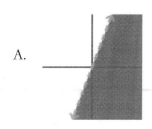 B. 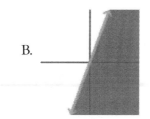 C. 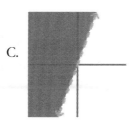 D.

2. Which represents the graph of –x – 19 ≤ y ?

A. 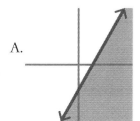 B. 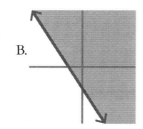 C. 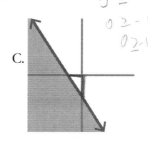 D.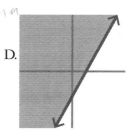

y ≥ –x – 19

0 ≥ –0 – 19

0 ≥ 19

3. The following is the graph of which inequalities?

A. y ≤ –2x or y ≥ 4x

B. y ≤ –2x and y ≥ 4x

C. y ≥ –2x or y ≤ 4x

D. y ≥ –2x and y ≤ 4x

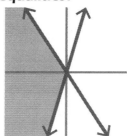

4. Which inequalities would represent a graph with just quadrant II shaded?

A. x ≤ 0 or y ≥ 0

B. x ≤ 0 and y ≤ 0

C. x ≥ 0 or y ≤ 0

D. x ≤ 0 and y ≥ 0

5. The following graph can be represented by what set of expressions?

A. y < 5 and y > –5

B. y < 5 or y > –5

C. y ≤ 5 and y ≥ –5

D. y > 5 or y < –5

y = 5

y = -5

6. Which of the following graphs represents the inequality: −3n + 5 < −4

A.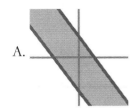

B.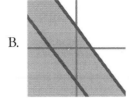

$-3n < -9$

$n > 3$

C.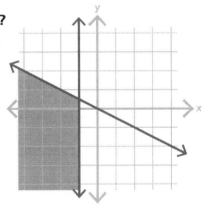

D.

7. How would you graph   y ≤ −x + 2   OR   y ≤ −x − 3 ?

A.   B.   C.   D.

8. The shaded region in the graph represents what set of inequalities?

A. $y \leq -1$ or $y \leq -\frac{1}{2}x$

B. $y \leq -1$ and $y \leq \frac{1}{2}x$

C. $x \leq -1$ and $y \leq -\frac{1}{2}x$

D. $x \leq -1$ and $y \leq -2x$

Graphing Inequalities: Answer Explanations

1. A   The inequality would be graphed as the area below the dotted line y=2x. The line would be dotted rather than solid to show that the values on the line y=2x do not fulfill the inequality.

You can also try a point, such as (3, 0) to see if it makes the statement true.
y < 2x , 0 < 2(3), 0 < 6, True. Therefore, the point (3, 0) must be shaded which it is in answer A.

2. B   First, rewrite the inequality with the y on the left side, since that is the form you are used to seeing.
−x − 19 ≤ y
y ≥ −x − 19

The line should be solid since it is ≥ and not just >. Then graph the line y = −x − 19, and then decide which side of the line to shade.

The graph of the line y = −x − 19 has a negative slope, which only happens in answer choices B and C.

Then, you must determine which side of the graph needs to be shaded. You want to graph y ≥ −x − 19, you can try plugging in a point and in this case you want to graph above the line.

3. B   Let's start by looking at the line y = −2x. This is the line with the negative slope. The section of the graph that is shaded represents all y values less than −2x. Therefore, we want the line y ≤ −2x, which is in answer choices A and B.

The next thing to look at is whether you want "and" or "or". If you are graphing with "and" then you want just the area of overlap, but, if you are graphing two inequalities with "or" then you want to include all values that both satisfy. In this case, it is clear that only the overlap has been graphed, so look for "and".

$y \leq -2x$ and $y \geq 4x$

4. D As can be seen in the graph to the right, quadrant II is in the top left corner.

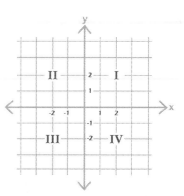

The x–value of any point in quadrant II are negative. Therefore, x is less than or equal to 0.

$x \leq 0$

The y–values of any point in quadrant II are positive. Therefore, y is greater than or equal to 0.

$y \geq 0$

Since only quadrant II is shaded, we want to use AND to restrict the area to just the overlap of the two inequalities.

$x \leq 0$ and $y \geq 0$

5. A The area represented on the graph is the set of y values between –5 and 5. The graph does not include $y = 5$ or $y = -5$, so you want to use > or <, not $\geq$ or $\leq$.

The graph represents the values greater than –5 and less than 5 at the same time, so you want to use "and" not "or".

$y < 5$ and $y > -5$

6. A $-3n + 5 < -4$
Subtract 5 from both sides.
$-3n < -9$
Divide by –3. When dividing by a negative, flip the inequality sign.
$n > 3$

To determine which graph correctly represents the equation, note that the inequality is >, so the circle on the 3 should be open. Also, n is greater than 3, so all values that are larger than 3 should be shaded.

7. B When graphing inequalities with an OR, you want to shade anything that satisfies either expression. Graph both inequalities, and keep all parts that are shaded for either of them.

The values that satisfy $y \leq -x - 3$ are already included in the graph of the values that satisfy $y \leq -x + 2$. Therefore, answer B shows both lines graphed and the parts below each line shaded in.

8. C Let's first determine the equation of each line.
The vertical line: The equation for the vertical line is $x = -1$. In this case, the values that are less than –1 are shaded. Therefore, the inequality that represents this is $x \leq -1$.

The diagonal line: The diagonal line has a y–intercept of 0 and a slope of $-\frac{1}{2}$. Therefore, the equation of the line is $y = -\frac{1}{2}x$. The region below this line is shaded. The inequality that represents this is $y \leq -\frac{1}{2}x$.

Only the overlapped region of the two inequalities is shaded, which is only the areas that make both inequalities true. "AND" is used to represent only areas that satisfy the first inequality and the second inequality.

$x \leq -1$ and $y \leq -\frac{1}{2}x$

1. A scientist is growing bacteria in a petri dish. Every minute, the scientist measures how many bacteria are in the dish. He starts with 20, by the end of the first minute there are 60, and at the end of the second minute there are 100. If the scientist represented these results with a graph, what would be the y–intercept?

A. 20

B. 40

C. 60

D. 100

2. What is the distance between point A with coordinates (−1,−2) and point B at coordinates (6, −2)?

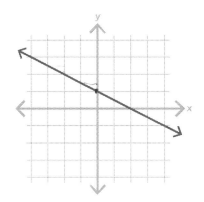

A. 5

B. 6

C. 7

D. 8

3. What is the equation of the line?

A. $y = -\frac{1}{2}x + 1$

B. $y = x - \frac{1}{2}$

C. $y = -2x + 1$

D. $y = \frac{1}{2}x + 1$

4. What is the slope of the line between the points (−6, 4) and (8, −12)?

A. 1/4

B. −8/7

C. 4

D. −7/8

5. If a rectangle has corners at the origin, (0,4), and (2,4), where is the fourth corner?

A. (0, 2)

B. (2, 0)

C. (4, 4)

D. (4, 0)

6. Which equations does the graph represent?

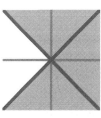

A. $y \le x$ or $y \ge -x$

B. $y \ge x$ or $y \le -x$

C. $y \le x$ and $y \ge -x$

D. $y \ge x$ and $y \le -x$

7. Which of the following best represents the data in the table?

x	f(x)
1	1
4	2
9	3
16	4

A.

B.

C.

D.

8. What is the slope of the line between the origin and (−3, 2)? (0, 0)

A. 2/3

B. −2/3

C. 3/2

D. −3/2

$$\frac{0-2}{0+3} = \frac{-2}{3}$$

9. If you have one point in Quadrant III and another point in Quadrant IV, and you found the product of their x−coordinates, what would you get?

A. Positive Number

B. Negative Number

C. Zero

D. Not enough information.

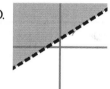 4x−3 = −12

III   IV

10. How would you graph: 80 − 20y > −15x + 40 ?

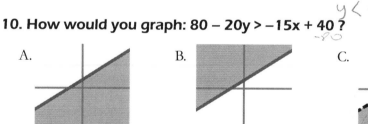

$$y < \frac{-15x - 40}{-20} \quad \frac{-80}{-20} \quad y < \frac{3}{4}x + 2$$

A.

B.

C.

D.

11. A line with a slope of −3 that passes through (−2, 4) has what y value when x is 3?

A. −11

B. −9

C. 6

D. 9

(3

y = −3x + b

4 = −3(−2) + b
     6

−2 = b

y = −3x − 2

y = −3(3) − 2

y = −9 + 0 = −11

12. Which of the following could be an explanation of why some lines have undefined slopes?

A. Horizontal lines have undefined slopes, since slope is change in y over change in x and the change in x can be any value depending on which two points you pick on the line.

B. Horizontal lines have undefined slopes, since slope is rise over run and there is no rise for horizontal lines.

C. Vertical lines have undefined slopes, since slope is rise over run and you can't determine the rise because you don't know which two points on the vertical line to test.

D. Vertical lines have undefined slopes. Slope is change in y divided by change in x, but any two points on a vertical line have a 0 change in x and dividing by 0 is undefined in math.

13. What is the midpoint of the line segment that connects point R at (−4, 6) and point S at (2, −1)?

   A. (−2, 3.5)

   B. (−2, 5)

   C. (−1, 2.5)

   D. (−1, 3)

14. What is the area of the square with the coordinates (2,2), (2, −1), (−1, 2), (−1, −1)?

   A. 2

   B. 4

   C. 8

   D. 9

15. Which of the following is the graph of the equation: −2x + y = −3 ?

A.    B.    C. 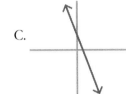   D.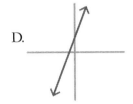

16. If a student wanted to find the equation of a line with a known y−intercept, which of the following could independently provide enough information?

   A. a coordinate pair on the line

   B. the slope

   C. the x−intercept

   D. all of the above

17. Sandra's Sunday afternoon consisted of walking for 15 minutes, running for 30 minutes, and then walking again for 15 minutes. Which graph best illustrates the distance she traveled over the course of her workout?

A. 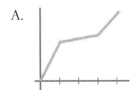   B. 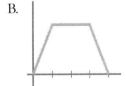   C. 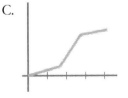   D.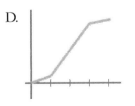

18. The graph to the right shows the distance that a car traveled over time. Which of the following graphs shows the same car's speed over time?

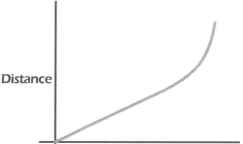

Distance

Time

A.

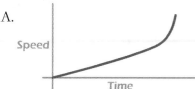

Speed

Time

B.

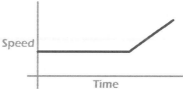

Speed

Time

C.

Speed

Time

D.

Speed

Time

19. A runner starts a race slowly and then picks up speed before sprinting to the finish line. Which graph could represent the position of the runner versus time?

A.

B.

C.

D. None of the above

20. This graph can be represented by the equation y = Zx−2. What is the value of Z?

A. –2

B. 2

C. 3 ½

D. 4 ½

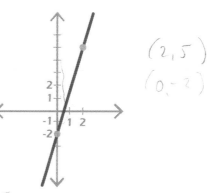

(2,5)

(0,-2)

$5 = 2(2) - 2$

$\dfrac{5}{2} = \dfrac{2x}{2}$ $x = 3.5$

Graphing: Chapter Review Answer Explanations

1. A   The scientist would graph the data with time on the x–axis and the number of bacteria on the y–axis because time is the independent variable, which is always graphed on the x–axis. The y–intercept on a graph is the point where the line crosses the y–axis. If a point is crossing the y–axis, that means that the x–value is zero.

If the x–value is zero, then we want the value when the scientist started his experiment. He starts with 20, and that is your y–intercept.

2. C Points A and B are graphed on the coordinate plane above. As you can see from the graph and their coordinates, points A and B have the same y coordinate. Therefore, we must find the difference in their x coordinates to figure out the distance between the points.

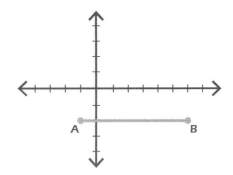

Point A's x–coordinate is at –1 and point B's x–coordinate is at 6. Subtract to find the difference or distance between them.

$6 - (-1) = 6 + 1 = 7$

3. A From the graph, you can see that the y–intercept (where the line crosses the y –axis) is at 1. b = 1

Now, to figure out the equation, pick any two points and determine the rise over the run or the slope. Let's use the points (0,1) and (2,0). From (0,1), the rise is –1 and the run is 2. Therefore, the slope is –1/2.

Using the slope and y–intercept you can determine the equation of the line.
y = mx + b, where m is slope and b is y–intercept.
$y = -\frac{1}{2} x + 1$

4. B The slope of a line is rise over run. You can also think of this as the change in y over the change in x.

(–6, 4) and (8, –12)
Slope = (change in y)/(change in x)
$= (4 - -12)/(-6 - 8)$
$= 16/-14$
$= -8/7$

5. B This problem gives you 3 of the coordinates of the rectangle and asks you to find the fourth. It is easy to see the solution to this problem when you graph the coordinates.

The last corner is at (2,0).

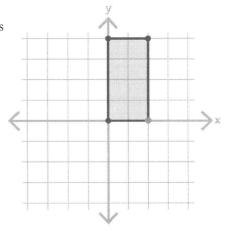

6. A First, you can tell that the graph represents an OR statement because all of the areas that satisfy either inequality have been shaded.

Let's look at the line y=x, which has the positive slope. All the points below that are shaded. Therefore, y ≤ x has been shaded.

Now, let's look at the line y=–x, which has the negative slope. All the points greater than that are shaded. Therefore, y ≥ –x has been shaded.

y ≤ x OR y ≥ –x

7. B In this table, you see as x increases, the y values also increase but at a slower rate.

A: In this graph, x and y increase at a steady rate. This is not represented in the table.

B: In this graph, x and y increase and x increases faster than y. This is represented in the table and is the answer.

C: y increases much faster than x in this graph.

D: this graph has negative values and rises too quickly.

8. B The slope between two points is the rise over the run, or the change in y over the change in x.
(0,0) and (–3,2)

From the first point to the second, y goes up by 2.
From the first point to the second, x goes down by 3.
Slope = $2/–3 = –2/3$

9. B If a point is in Quadrant III, then it's x–coordinate is negative. If a point is in Quadrant IV, it's x–coordinate is positive.

If you multiply a negative and a positive, you get a negative.
Therefore, the product of their x–coordinates will be negative.

10. C First, isolate y.
$80 – 20y > –15x + 40$

Subtract 80 from both sides.
$–20y > –15x – 40$

Divide everything by –20. When dividing by a negative, flip the sign.
$y < {}^{-15}\!/_{20}\, x – {}^{40}\!/_{20}$
$y < ¾\, x + 2$

Now graph the equation. The line should not be solid since the equation is $y <$ not $y ≤$. Finally, shade all the values less than the dashed line.

11. A First, find the equation of the line, then plug in x = 3 to solve for y.

The line has a slope of –3. Therefore, the basic form of an equation is y=mx+b. Plug in –3 for m.
$y = –3x + b$

Now, plug in the point (–2,4) to solve for b.
$4 = –3(–2) + b$
$4 = 6 + b$
$–2 = b$

Equation: $y = –3x – 2$
Plug in x = 3 to solve for y.
$y = –3(3) – 2$
$y = –9 – 2$
$y = –11$

12. D Horizontal lines have a slope of zero, and vertical lines have an undefined slope. Therefore, eliminate answer choices A and B.

Now, let's look at the explanations for answers C and D.

C: Vertical lines have undefined slopes, since slope is rise over run and you can't determine the rise because you don't know which two points on the vertical line to test.

The first part of the statement is true. Vertical lines do have undefined slopes, and slope is rise over run. However, when finding the slope of any straight line, you can pick any two points and you will always find the same slope. Eliminate answer C.

D: Vertical lines have undefined slopes. Slope is change in y divided by change in x, but any two points on a vertical line have a 0 change in x and dividing by 0 is undefined in math.

This is a valid explanation for the fact that vertical lines have undefined slopes. Slope is change in y divided by change in x, and, on a vertical line, the change will always be 0. Dividing by 0 is undefined.

13. C To find the midpoint of a line segment between (–4, 6) and (2, –1), find the average of the x–coordinates and the average of the y–coordinates.

The x coordinates are –4 and 2. The average can be found by adding and dividing by 2.

Average of x–coordinates = (–4 + 2)/2 = –1

The y coordinates are 6 and –1. The average can be found by adding and dividing by 2.

Average of y–coordinates = (6 + –1)/2 = 2.5

The midpoint's coordinates are (–1, 2.5)

14. D The easiest way to solve this problem is by first graphing the coordinate pairs and then finding the dimensions of the square. The coordinate pairs are graphed to the right.

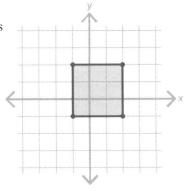

(2,2), (2, –1), (–1, 2), (–1, –1)

As can be seen in the graph, the square is 3 by 3. Therefore, the area is 9.

15. A Determine the intercept and slope of the equation. Put the equation in the form: y = mx + b.

–2x + y = –3
y = 2x – 3

From the equation, you can see the slope is positive 2 and intercept is –3.

Now, let's examine each answer choice.

Answer A has a positive slope and negative intercept.
Answer B has a negative slope and negative intercept.
Answer C has a negative slope and positive intercept.
Answer D has a positive slope and positive intercept.

Therefore, answer A is correct. It is the only graph with a positive slope and negative intercept.

16. D   There are various ways to find the equation of a line. The y–intercept is one point. Any other point on the line would provide enough information for the student to write the equation of the line. Therefore, answer A which says a coordinate pair would be enough. In addition, the x–intercept is just another point, so answer C would be enough.

Also, using the slope–intercept form of the equation, $y=mx+b$, the slope and y–intercept are the two pieces that are needed to find the equation. Answer B is enough.

Therefore, all would independently provide enough info.

17. D   Sandra walked for 15 minutes – this should be represented by a line with a positive slope.

Sandra ran for 30 minutes – this should be represented by a line with a positive slope greater than the slope of the walking line. In addition, this segment should be twice as long as the walking line since she ran for 30 mins.

Sandra again walked for 15 minutes – this should be represented by the same segment as the first walking segment in terms of slope and length.

The graph in answer D meets these requirements.

18. B   As can be seen in the graph, the distance that the car travels increasing steadily during the first part of the car's trip. If the distance increases at a steady rate that means the speed for that car is staying the same over that period of time.

During the second part of the trip, the car's distance increases exponentially. Therefore, the car is accelerating, and the speed is increasing.

The graph in answer choice B shows this pattern.

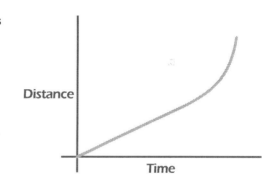

19. C   Since the graph is position versus time and the runner does not stop or turn around, then the graph will never have a negative slope. Eliminate answer B.

In addition, it says the runner picks up speed before sprinting to the finish line. Therefore, his graph will not be linear since the slope is not consistent. Eliminate answer A.

Graph C correctly shows a graph that could represent position over time. The runner starts slowly, therefore, his position does not change quickly. Towards the end of the race, the runner is sprinting and thus his position will be increasing quickly.

20. C   In the equation $y = Zx – 2$, Z is the slope of the line. You are given two points on the line: $(0, –2)$ and $(2,5)$. You can calculate the slope either by plugging in one of the points into the equation of the line and solving for Z or by using the formula for calculating slope.

Method 1: Plug into the equation. Use the point $(2,5)$ so Z does not get multiplied by 0.
$y = Zx – 2$
$5 = Z(2) – 2$
$2Z = 7$
$Z = \frac{7}{2} = 3\frac{1}{2}$

Method 2: Using both points in the slope formula. $(0, –2)$ & $(2, 5)$
Slope formula: $(y_2 – y_1)/(x_2 – x_1)$
$(5 – –2)/(2 – 0) = \frac{7}{2} = 3\frac{1}{2}$

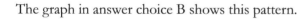

5. Geometry

Conversion Methods

To convert measurements from one type of unit into another type of unit, multiply the number by the appropriate conversion factor. You can determine which is the appropriate conversion factor when the units you want to change are cancelled and the units you want are the only ones left. For example, to convert 17 yards into feet, you know that you want to find a conversion factor where the units of yards cancel and you are left with only feet. We know that 1 yard equals 3 feet, and the conversion factor is a fraction with different units in the numerator and denominator. Since we want the yards to cancel and be left with feet, we put the yards in denominator and feet in numerator.

$$17 \text{ yards} \times \frac{3 \text{ feet}}{1 \text{ yard}} = 51 \text{ feet}$$

Try converting 64 ounces into pounds (1 pound = 16 ounces).

$$64 \text{ ounces} \times \frac{1 \text{ pound}}{16 \text{ ounces}} = 4 \text{ pounds}$$

There are some common unit conversions and conveniently they are provided on the ILTS TAP exam.

US Customary	Metric System
Length	**Length**
12 inches = 1 foot	10 millimeters = 1 centimeter
3 feet = 1 yard	100 centimeters = 1 meter
5280 feet = 1 mile	1000 meters = 1 kilometer
Volume (liquid)	**Volume**
8 ounces = 1 cup	1000 milliliters = 1 liter
2 cups = 1 pint	1000 liters = 1 kiloliter
2 pints = 1 quart	
4 quarts = 1 gallon	
Weight	**Weight**
16 ounces = 1 pound	1000 milligrams = 1 gram
2000 pounds = 1 ton	1000 grams = 1 kilogram

Metric System

Looking at the units above, a pattern is evident among the meters, grams, and liters. That is because they are the base units of the metric system. They all follow the following pattern of prefixes.

1000 = kilo–
.01 = centi–
.001 = milli–

Examples of metric system conversions.
Convert 1.2 kilometers to meters
$1.2 \text{ km} \times \frac{1000 \text{ m}}{1 \text{ km}} = 1200 \text{ m}$

Convert 340 meters to kilometers
$340 \text{ m} \times \frac{1 \text{ km}}{1000 \text{ m}} = 0.34 \text{ km}$

Multiple Unit Conversions

If required to perform multiple conversions in the same problem, you could either do one at a time or multiply all the conversion factors at once. For example, if you are required to convert from 3 gallons to cups, you could perform either steps to get the correct answer:

3 gallons = 3 gallons x (4 quarts/1 gallon) x (2 pints/1 quart) x (2 cups/1 pint) = 48 cups
3 gallons = 3 gallons x (4 quarts/1 gallon) = 12 quarts
12 quarts = 12 quarts x (2 pints/1 quart) = 24 pints
24 pints = 24 pints x (2 cups/1 pint) = 48 cups

Another instance when you may have to use multiple unit conversions is if you are dealing with square or cubic units. For instance, you may be asked to convert 27 square feet to square yards.

27 square feet = 27 feet x feet = 27 feet x feet x 1 yard/3 feet x 1 yard/3 feet = 3 yards x yards = 3 square yards

Unit Conversions: Practice

1. If you were on a trip when the exchange rate between Euros and dollars was 1 Euro = $1.54 and wanted to purchase a book that cost $10.78, approximately how many Euros would the book cost you?

   A. 7 Euros

   B. 9.24 Euros

   C. 12.32 Euros

   D. 16.60 Euros

2. If 1 kg is equal to approximately 2.2 lbs, how many ounces are there in 20 kgs?

   A. 44 ounces

   B. $1\frac{1}{4}$ ounces

   C. 96.8 ounces

   D. 704 ounces

3. Baking a chocolate cake requires 2 cups of flour. If you have 3 quarts of flour, how many cakes can you make?

   A. 3 cakes

   B. 6 cakes

   C. 12 cakes

   D. 24 cakes

4. If 1 inch = 2.54 centimeters, 200 inches is equal to how many meters?

   A. 0.508 m

   B. 5.08 m

   C. 50.8 m

   D. 50,800 m

5. If the volume of a box is 8 cubic meters, what is the volume in cubic centimeters?

A. 0.08 cubic cm

B. 800 cubic cm

C. 80,000 cubic cm

D. 8,000,000 cubic cm

6. Which of the following is the largest?

A. 1 sq yard

B. 9 sq feet

C. 1296 sq inches

D. All of the above are the same.

7. How many kilometers is 70 centimeters equal to?

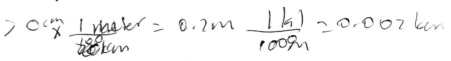

A. 0.0007 km

B. 0.7 km

C. 7000 km

D. 7,000,000 km

8. The formula for converting temperatures in degrees Celsius (°C) to degrees Fahrenheit (°F) is C = ⁵⁄₉(F – 32). If the temperature at the beginning of a day was 68°F and it increased by 50% on the Celsius scale, what was the temperature at the end of the day in degree Fahrenheit?

A. 30° F

B. 86° F

C. 98° F

D. 102° F

$$5/9 \left(68° - 32\right)$$

Unit Conversions: Answer Explanations

1. A   You are given a quantity in dollars and you want to convert it to Euros. Multiply by a unit conversion of Euros to dollars so that the dollars cancels and you are left with Euros.

$10.78 x ¹ ᴱᵘʳᵒ⁄$1.54 = 7 Euros

2. D   First, use the abbreviations provided on the ILTS mathematics definitions sheet to identify the units in the problem. Note that kg stands for kilograms and lbs is an abbreviation for pounds.

The question asks you to convert from kilograms to ounces. First, convert from kilograms to pounds and then convert that result to ounces.

20 kilograms x 2.2 pounds/1 kilogram
= 44 pounds
Note that the kilogram units canceled and you were left with pounds.

Now, convert from pounds to ounces. There are 16 ounces in 1 pound.
44 pounds x 16 ounces/1 pound
= 704 ounces

3. B   Convert 3 quarts to pints to cups and then figure out how many cakes can be made.

3 quarts x 2 pints/1 quart = 6 pints
6 pints x 2 cups/1 pint = 12 cups
12 cups x 1 cake/2 cups = 6 cakes

6 cakes
Note that the conversions are included on the formula sheet.

---

4. B   First, convert from inches to centimeters, then from centimeters to meters.

200 inches x 2.54 cm/1 in = 508 cm
508 cm x 1 m/100 cm = 5.08 m

5. D   Use three unit conversions to convert each dimension of meters to centimeters.

8 cubic meters x $^{100\ cm}/_{1\ m}$ x $^{100\ cm}/_{1\ m}$ x $^{100\ cm}/_{1\ m}$ = 8,000,000 cubic centimeters

6. D   Convert each answer choice to the same units and compare. Since the units are squared, use two unit conversions.

A: 1 square yard x $^{3\ feet}/_{1\ yard}$ x $^{3\ feet}/_{1\ yard}$ = 9 square feet
B: 9 square feet
C: 1296 square inches x $^{1\ ft}/_{12\ in}$ x $^{1\ ft}/_{12\ in}$ = 9 square feet

Answer D: All same

7. A   First convert centimeters to meters. Then from meters convert to kilometers.

70 centimeters x $^{1\ meter}/_{100\ cm}$ = 0.7 meters

0.7 meters x $^{1\ km}/_{1000\ m}$ = 0.0007 km

8. B   This problem involves many steps. First, convert the temperature from Fahrenheit to Celsius. Then, increase the temperature by 50% on the Celsius scale. Finally, convert the temperature back to Fahrenheit.

Convert from 68° Fahrenheit to Celsius
$C = \frac{5}{9}(F - 32)$
$= \frac{5}{9}(68 - 32)$
$= \frac{5}{9}(36)$
$= 20°\ C$

Increase by 50%
20 x 50% = 20 x 0.50 = 10
20 + 10 = 30
30° C

Convert from Celsius back to Fahrenheit.
$C = \frac{5}{9}(F - 32)$
$30 = \frac{5}{9}(F - 32)$
$30(\frac{9}{5}) = F - 32$
$54 = F - 32$
$F = 86$
86° F

Angles

An angle is formed by two rays that share the beginning point. The shared point is called the vertex, and the two rays are each the sides of the angles. An angle is referred to by its vertex, or by a series of three letters, where the first letter refers to a point on one ray, the middle letter is the vertex, and the third letter is a point on the 2nd ray.

A right angle is equal to 90 degrees. Right angles are formed by perpendicular lines. For example, a rectangle has four right angles as a rectangle has perpendicular sides. Angles that are less than 90 degrees are called acute and angles greater than 90 are obtuse.

Angles on a Line

Angles along a straight line will always add to 180 degrees.

For example, in the figure to the right, angles a, b, and c will sum to 180 degrees.

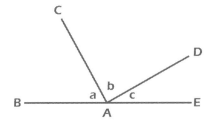

Angles in Shapes

The interior angles in a triangle will always sum to 180 degrees. The angles in a circle will always sum to 360 degrees. To determine the number of degrees in any other polygon, divide the polygon into triangles and multiply the number of triangles by 180°. The chart below shows a few common polygons and the sum of the degree measure of their angles.

Triangle = 180°

Rectangle = 2 Triangles
= 2 x 180°
= 360°

Pentagon = 3 Triangles
= 3 x 180°
= 540°

Hexagon = 4 Triangles
= 4 x 180°
= 720°

Supplementary Angles

Angles adding to 180 degrees are called supplementary angles.

The picture to the right contains three supplementary angles: a, b, and c. Each of those angles can also be named by referencing the three points that form the angle, for example, Angle c could also be called Angle DAE or EAD. When angles are referenced in this way, the point that forms the vertex of the angle, in this case A, will always be in the middle.

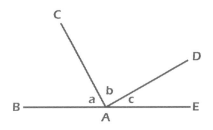

Complementary Angles

Two angles adding to 90 degrees are known as complementary angles.

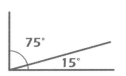

75°

15°

Bisectors

A line that cuts an angle in half is a bisector. Since the bisected angle is cut into halves, each angle created by the line is equal to one–half the measure of the whole angle. In the figure to the right, line LN is bisecting angle MNO.

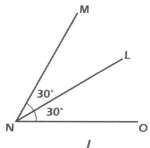

Opposite Angles

Angles adding to 180 degrees are supplementary, so any two intersecting lines create two sets of supplementary angles. In addition, angles on opposite sides of the intersecting lines are equal.

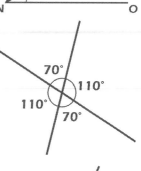

Parallel Lines

Lines are considered parallel if they have the same slope.

Any line intersecting two parallel lines will create identical sets of angles with each line. The lines LM and NP in the diagram are parallel, and the intersecting line has created equal sets of angles a and b.

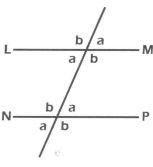

Perpendicular Lines

Perpendicular lines intersect to form four 90 degree angles. Lines C and D in the figure are perpendicular.

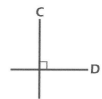

Angles: Practice

1. Angle b is how many degrees in the following triangle?

A. 242

B. 180

C. 142

D. 62

2. In the picture below, y is how many degrees?

A. 53

B. 127

C. 153

D. 180

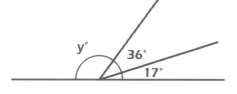

3. If triangle ABC is isosceles, with two angles equal, and angle CBA is a right angle, what is the measure of angle BAC?

A. 45°

B. 60°

C. 90°

D. 180°

4. In the diagram below, lines L and M are parallel. Choose the best answer to replace the question mark: a ? b .

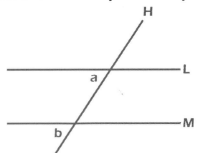

   A. >

   B. <

   C. =

   D. Not enough information.

5. In the figure, angle DCB = 50° and angle BDC = 60°. If angle DAB = angle BDA, find the measure of angle DAB.

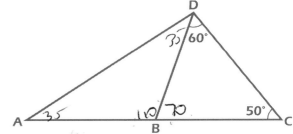

   A. 35°

   B. 50°

   C. 55°

   D. 70°

6. If angle CAB = 65°, what is the measure of angle ACD?

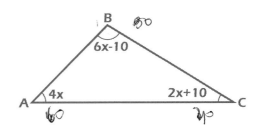

   A. 25°

   B. 65°

   C. 115°

   D. 155°

7. In the diagram, find the measure of angle x.

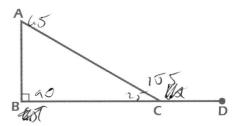

   A. 128°

   B. 54°

   C. 52°

   D. 26°

8. In triangle ABC, angle A = 4x, angle B = 6x − 10, and angle C = 2x + 10. What does x equal?

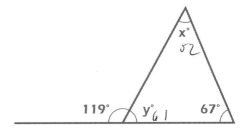

   A. 10

   B. 15

   C. 20

   D. 30

Angles: Answer Explanations

1. D   The angles of a triangle must add up to 180 degrees. Add the other two angles, and subtract their sum from 180 to find the measure of angle b.

180 − (75 + 43) = 180 − 118 = 62

62 degrees

2. B   There are 180 degrees on each side of a straight line. To find y, add the measures of the two angles and subtract their sum from 180.

180 – (36 + 17) = 127 degrees

3. A   We are told that one angle in the triangle is a right triangle and therefore equals 90°. We know that the sum of all the angles in a triangle are 180°. Subtract to find out the sum of the remaining two angles. The sum of the remaining two angles is 180 – 90 = 90°

An isosceles triangle has two sides that are equal and two angles that are equal. Therefore, the two remaining angles must be equal. If the two angles are equal and sum to 90°, then each angle must be 45°.
Angle BAC = 45°

4. C   Any line that passes through two parallel lines will create equal sets of angles with each line. Therefore, angle a = angle b.

5. A   First, let's find the measure of angle CBD. In a triangle, the measures of the angles must sum to 180°. In triangle CBD, you know the measure of two of the angles, so add them up and subtract the sum from 180 to determine the measure of the third angle. 180° – (50° + 60°) = 180° – 110° = 70°. angle CBD=70°

Now, let's find the measure of angle ABD. You know that angle ABD and angle CBD form a straight angle, which totals 180°. Therefore, angle ABD = 180° – angle CBD = 180° – 70° = 110°. angle ABD = 110°.

The problem stated that AB = BD. That makes triangle ABD an isosceles triangle. The angles opposite equal sides are equal, so angle ADB and angle DAB are equal. We know the third angle in triangle ABD is 110°, so we know the other two angles must sum to 70° so that the total of all three angles is 180°.

Therefore, we know that angle ADB + angle DAB = 70°. We also know that angle ADB = angle DAB, so each of the angles must equal 35°.

6. D   First, calculate angle BCA, the third angle in the triangle. We know two of the angles in the triangle are 65° (given in problem) and 90° (right angle) and we know that all the angles in a triangle add to 180°.

90° + 65° + angle BCA = 180°
155° + angle BCA = 180°
angle BCA = 25°

Now, find the measure of angle ACD. We know that angle BCA and angle ACD form a straight line, and the sum of the measures of angles that form a straight line is 180°.

angle BCA + angle ACD = 180°
25° + angle ACD = 180°
angle ACD = 155°

7. C   Solve for y, which is on a straight line and thus has a supplementary angle of 119 degrees.
180 – 119 = 61 degrees
Since y equals 61 degrees, you can use the fact that a triangle has 180 degrees to solve for x.
180 – (67 + 61) = 52 degrees

8. B   In a triangle, all 3 angles add up to 180°. Set up an equation and solve for x.
angle A + angle B + angle C = 180
4x + 6x – 10 + 2x + 10 = 180
12x = 180
x = 15

Perimeter

The perimeter of an object is the distance around its edge. Calculating the perimeter of any polygon simply requires finding the length of each side and then adding the lengths of all sides together.

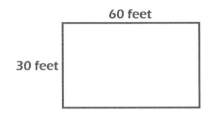

For example, the perimeter of the rectangle to the left is:

30 + 30 + 60 + 60 = 180 feet.

Since all sides of a square are of equal length, the perimeter of a square is the length of 1 side times 4. The perimeter of the square shown here is 20 yards x 4, or 80 yards.

20 yards

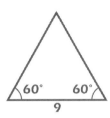

Finding the perimeter of a triangle sometimes requires you to use what you know about the properties of triangles, which you will learn more about in the "Triangles" lesson for this chapter. For example, if you were told that the triangle is equilateral, you would know the length of all sides of the triangle are equal. The perimeter is therefore 9 + 9 + 9, or 27 units.

Perimeter: Practice

1. If x = 3 inches, what is the perimeter of the following rectangle?

A. 6 inches

B. 1 foot

C. 18 inches

D. 2 feet

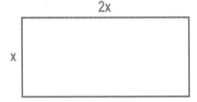

2. Find the perimeter of triangle ABC.

A. 12

B. 16

C. 20

D. 24

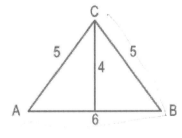

3. If the perimeter of the rectangle is 78, what is the value of x?

A. 14.5

B. 17

C. 24.5

D. 34

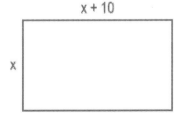

4. If the length of all the sides of a triangle are tripled, what would happen to its perimeter?

A. Increase by 3

B. Triple

C. Multiply by 6

D. Multiply by 9

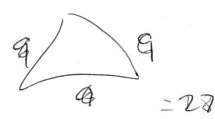

5. A gym teacher is painting a line around the outside of the rectangular basketball court. If he uses 2 gallons of paint for every 50 feet he paints, and the court is 50 feet wide and 100 feet long, how many gallons of paint will he need?

A. 10

B. 12

C. 14

D. 16

6. If the width of a rectangle is w and the length is 4 less than 3 times the width, what is the perimeter of the rectangle in terms of w?

A. $8 - 4w$

B. $3w^2 - 4w$

C. $4w - 4$

D. $8w - 8$

7. If the perimeter of a regular octagon is equal to the perimeter of an equilateral triangle, and each side of the octagon is 6, what is the length of each side of the triangle?

A. 4

B. 12

C. 16

D. 48

8. If the perimeter of the shape is 92, what is the length of a?

A. 17

B. 22

C. 34

D. Not enough information.

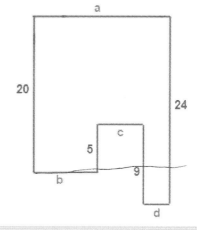

Perimeter: Answer Explanations

1. C   The width of the rectangle is x, which is 3 inches. The length of the rectangle is 2x, which is two times 3 inches or 6 inches.

To find the perimeter of the rectangle, add the lengths of all sides. There are two widths and two lengths.

Perimeter = (2 x width) + (2 x length)

= (2 x 3 in) + (2 x 6 in) = 6 in + 12 in = 18 in

2. B To find the perimeter, add the length of the three sides of the triangle. Be careful, the line with length 4 is not a side of the triangle.   Perimeter = 5 + 5 + 6 = 16

3. A Perimeter = width + width + length + length
= 2(width) + 2(length) = 2x + 2(x + 10) = 2x + 2x + 20 = 4x + 20

The perimeter equals 78, so set the equation equal to 78 and solve for x.
4x + 20 = 78
4x = 58
x = 14.5

4. B Let the sides of the original triangle be X, Y, and Z. Then the sides of the new triangle are 3X, 3Y, and 3Z.
Original perimeter = X + Y + Z
New perimeter = 3X + 3Y + 3Z = 3(X + Y + Z) = 3(Original perimeter)
The perimeter triples.

5. B Since the teacher is painting a line around the outside, you need to find the perimeter of the court.
Perimeter = 50 ft + 50 ft + 100 ft + 100 ft = 300 ft

Now, we can multiply it by the ratio of gallons of paint to feet, to find the amount of paint needed.
300 ft. x 2 gal./50ft. = 12 gal.

6. D First find the length in terms of w. The length is 4 less than 3 times the width and the width is w.
Length = 4 less than 3 times width = 4 less than 3w = 3w − 4

There are four sides on a rectangle, two widths and two lengths.
perimeter = (2 x width) + (2 x length) = 2w + 2(3w − 4) = 2w + 6w − 8 = 8w − 8

7. C We know the perimeters of the octagon and triangle are equivalent. First determine the octagon's perimeter.

Each side of the octagon has a length of 6 and there are 8 sides to the octagon.
Perimeter = number of sides x length of each side = 8 x 6 = 48

So, the perimeter of the triangle is equal to 48. Since there are three sides, divide the perimeter by 3 to find the length of each side.
48 ÷ 3 = 16.
Length of each side of the triangle is 16.

8. A We are given the total perimeter of the shape, 92. In addition, we are told the length of all the vertical sides. Therefore, let's first find the sum of the vertical sides and then determine the sum of all the missing sides.

Sum of length of given sides = 20 + 5 + 9 + 24 = 58
Sum of length of missing sides = Perimeter − Sum of length of given sides
a + b + c + d = 92 − 58 = 34

Let's now look at the figure and more closely examine the horizontal sides. We can see that the length of a is equal to the length of b + c + d.
a = b + c + d

We know from above that: a + b + c + d = 34. Let's substitute a for b + c + d.
a + a = 34
a = 17

Area – Rectangles

Area is the two–dimensional space inside a figure. Its units are always a length measurement squared.

On the definitions and formula sheet, you will find the area of a rectangle.

$A = lw$

To find the area of a rectangle, multiply the length by the width. For example, if a rectangular yard is 30 feet wide and 60 feet long, the area is 30 ft x 60 ft = 1800 sq ft.

On the definitions and formula sheet, you will also find the area of a square.

$A = s^2$

20 yards

A square is a rectange with all sides of equal length. Let's call the length of the square s, and thus the width is also s. Therefore, the area of the square is equal to s x s or s^2, the length of one side squared. The area of the square shown here is 20 yards x 20 yards, or 400 square yards.

Area – Triangles

The formula for the area of a triangle is:

½ x base x height

The height of a triangle is the length of a line from the base, or bottom, of the triangle to the opposite angle.

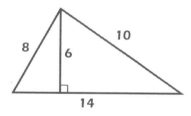

8 6 10

14

The line representing the height will always be perpendicular to the base. For example, in this triangle, the base length is 14, and the height is 6. Therefore, the area is ½ x 14 x 6 = 42 sq. units.

Area: Practice

1. You need to paint a huge outside wall that is 36 feet by 25 feet. If every 2 gallons of paint covers 50 square yards, how many gallons of paint do you need?

   A. 2

   B. 4

   C. 12

   D. 36

2. Daniel is painting a square wall with 9 foot sides. If he uses ⅓ gallon per square foot, how many gallons of paint will he need?

   A. 14 gal

   B. 27 gal

   C. 54 gal

   D. 81 gal

3. If you double all the sides of a rectangle, by how much does the area change?

A. doubles

B. increases by 2

C. quadruples

D. increases by 8

4. The outside edges of a picture frame are 8 inches by 12 inches. If the picture that is displayed is 54 sq. inches in area and the picture is 9 inches tall, what is the area of just the frame?

A. 6

B. 7

C. 24

D. 42

5. A 12 yard by 24 ft room will have a 30 ft by 18 ft dancing area in the middle. What percent of the room will not be used for dancing?

A. 12%

B. 37.5%

C. 46.7%

D. 62.5%

6. If a quilting club uses fabric to construct a quilt out of 4 inch squares, how many squares of fabric will it take to create a quilt measuring 3 yards by 3 yards?

A. 729

B. 162

C. 27

D. 11664

7. You have a picture that is 8 inches by 10 inches. You place it in a frame that is 2 inches wide all around. How much wall space will be covered up by the entire frame and picture?

A. 96 sq in

B. 100 sq in

C. 120 sq in

D. 168 sq in

8. If the area of the entire figure is 64 and the area of the triangle equals 14, what is the length of y?

A. 4

B. 5

C. 6

D. 7

Area: Answer Explanations

1. B   This problem involves many steps. First, find the area of the wall. Second, convert the units to square yards. Then, determine the gallons of paints needed.

Area of a rectangular wall is length x width = 36 ft x 25 ft = 900 sq. ft.

To convert from square feet to square yards, two unit conversions are necessary.
900 sq. ft x 1 yd/3 ft x 1 yd/3 ft = 100 square yards

You could also convert the dimensions from feet to yards first, and then find the area. Either way, you would end up with 100 square yards.

2 gallons/50 sq yds = x gallons/100 sq yds   –set up a ratio to find gallons
50x = 2 (100)   –cross multiply and set them equal
50x = 200   –multiply
x = 4   –divide both sides by 50
4 gallons

2. B   Calculate the area of the wall.
9 ft. x 9 ft. = 81 sq. ft.

Then multiply by the ratio of gallons to square feet.
81 sq. ft. x 1 gal/3 sq ft = 27 gal.

3. C   Let's say that the original rectangle has a width of w and a height of h. Therefore, the area of the original rectangle is wh.

If all the sides are doubled, the new rectangle has a width of 2w and a height of 2h. Therefore, the area of the new rectangle is (2w)(2h) = 4wh

Divide the new area by the original area to see how many times bigger the new area is:
4wh ÷ wh = 4
Area goes up 4 times, or quadruples

4. D   This is a relatively simple problem. The key here is to focus on relevant pieces of information. Find the area of the outside of the picture frame, and then subtract the area (54 sq. inches) of the picture inside.

Area of entire picture including frame:
8 inches * 12 inches = 96 sq. inches

Area of entire picture – Area of picture displayed:
96 sq. inches – 54 sq. inches = 42 sq. inches

5. B   The problem asks you to determine what percent of the room will not be used for dancing. First, you must determine the area of the room and the area that will be used for dancing.

Note that some of the units are in yards and some in feet. Always ensure that you have converted all quantities to the same units for accurate calculations. In this case, the units are: 12 yards by 24 feet for the entire room and 30 feet by 18 feet for the dance area. We could just convert the 12 yards to feet, however, that would make all of our numbers larger, so it may be easier to convert all the feet to yards.

To convert from feet to yards, you want the feet to cancel and be left with yards. Therefore, use the conversion factor: 1 yard/3 feet. The feet in the denominator will cancel leaving you with yards.

24 feet x 1 yard/3 feet = 8 yards
30 feet x 1 yard/3 feet = 10 yards
18 feet x 1 yard/3 feet = 6 yards

Therefore, the dimensions of room: 12 yards x 8 yards. Dimensions of dance area: 10 yards x 6 yards

Now, to find the areas:

Room = 12 yd x 8 yd = 96 sq yd

Dance = 10 yd x 6 yd = 60 sq yd

The area of the room that is not used for dancing is found by subtracting: 96 sq yd – 60 sq yd = 36 sq yd.

To calculate a percent, you can use the percent formula:

% = part/whole x 100

To find the percent of the room that won't be used for dancing, divide the area of the room not used for dancing by the total area of the room, then multiply by 100.

36 sq yd/96 sq yd x 100 = 3/8 x 100 = 37.5%

6. A   To calculate the number of squares needed to create the quilt, find the length of one side of the quilt, which is 3 yards, in inches.

3 yards x 3 feet/yard = 9 feet

9 feet x 12 inches/ foot = 108 inches

Now, let us convert the number of inches to quilt squares.

108 inches x 1 square/4 inches = 27 squares long

Since the quilt is 3 yards by 3 yards, it is 27 squares by 27 squares. Therefore, to find the number of squares needed, find the area by multiplying the length of the two sides.

27 x 27 = 729

7. D   Let's figure out the dimensions of the frame and picture.

Width of picture was 8 inches and the frame is 2 inches wide. That adds 2 inches to the left side of the picture and 2 inches to the right side. The total width is now 8 + 2 + 2 = 12 inches

Length of picture is 10 in. and frame adds 2 in. to top and bottom. Total length = 10 + 2 + 2 = 14 in

Area = 12 inches x 14 inches = 168 sq in.

8. C   If we know that the area of the entire figure is 64 and the area of the triangle is 14, then we know that the area of the remaining part of the figure is the difference. 64 – 14 = 50.

The remaining figure can be divided into two rectangles, as can be seen to the right.

The top rectangle has dimensions of 8 by 4. Thus, the area of that rectangle is equal to:

8 x 4 = 32.

So, the area of the remaining rectangle, at the bottom, is:

50 – 32 = 18

If the area of the rectangle is 18 and one side is 3, we can calculate the missing side, y.

3y = 18

y = 6

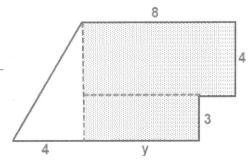

Geometry: Triangles & Circles

Triangles

A triangle is a closed polygon with three sides. In a triangle, all angles must add up to 180 degrees. The angles of a triangle are always proportionate to the sides opposite them, meaning that the longest side of a triangle will be opposite the largest angle, and the shortest side will be opposite the smallest angle. The relationship between sides and angles is shown by using a letter for an angle and the same letter for the corresponding side, with either all the angles with lower–case letters and sides with upper–case letters, or vice versa.

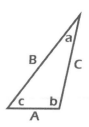

Types of Triangles

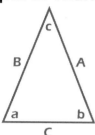

A triangle with two equal sides is called an isosceles triangle. Because angles are proportionate to the sides opposite them, the two angles opposite the two equal sides are also equal. In the isosceles triangle shown here, A = B and a = b.

An equilateral triangle has three equal sides and three equal angles. Because 180/3 = 60, the angles of an equilateral triangle will always equal 60 degrees. In the equilateral triangle to the right, A = B = C and a = b = c.

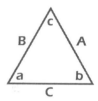

A right triangle is any triangle with a 90–degree angle, which is usually represented by a small square. In a right triangle, the side opposite the 90–degree angle, which will always be the longest side, is called the hypotenuse (C). The other two sides are labeled A and B, interchangeably.

Pythagorean Theorem

Right triangles are the only triangles for which The Pythagorean Theorem can be used to calculate missing side lengths. The Pythagorean Theorem states that the square of the hypotenuse is equal to the sum of the square of the other two sides. As a formula, this is written:

$$A^2 + B^2 = C^2$$

Note: The Pythagorean Theorem is provided on the Definitions & Formula Sheet.

Circles

A circle is a set of points equidistant (the same distance) from a center point. Imagine picking a point as the center and marking every possible point 4 units away from that point, you would create a continuous line around that point called a circle.

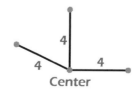

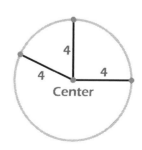

Circle Measurements

An important measurement for a circle is its radius (r). The radius is the distance between the center of a circle and any point on the circle itself. In the previous example, each point was 4 units from the center. Therefore, the circle's radius is 4.

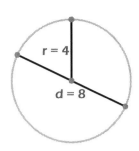

The diameter of a circle is any line beginning at one point on a circle, passing through the center, and ending at another point on the circle. The diameter of a circle is always twice as long as its radius. When working with circles, you will often need to use the diameter to find the radius so that you can calculate perimeter, arc length, or area.

In the diagram to the right, the radius is 4, and the diameter is 8.

Note that the following formula is provided on the exam. Diameter = 2r

Circumference and Area

The number pi, also represented by the Greek letter π, equals approximately 3.14. Pi is an irrational number (an unending decimal), but 3.14 is accurate enough for most purposes. Pi gives the ratio of a circle's perimeter – the distance around the outside of the circle – to its diameter (d). The perimeter of a circle is also called its circumference.

The equation can be expressed as: **Circumference = 2πr**

The area of a circle is also calculated using pi. The formula is: **Area = π x r x r = πr^2**

So, for a circle of radius 7 yards, the circumference is 14π yards and the area is 49π square yards.

Note that the formulas for the area and circumference of a circle are provided on your formula sheet.

Triangles & Circles: Practice

1. A student looks at a circle with a circumference of 24 and estimates that the radius is 8. Which of the following most accurately describes the estimate?

    A. The estimate is too low by a factor of 2.

    B. The estimate is too low by a factor of 3.

    C. The estimate is too high by a factor of 2.

    D. The estimate is correct.

2. A backdrop for a play is a triangle 9 meters tall. If the total area of the backdrop is 45 square meters, then how wide is the base?

    A. 4.5 m

    B. 5 m

    C. 9 m

    D. 10 m

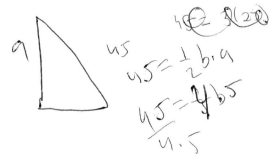

3. The area of Triangle T is how many times larger than the area of Triangle S?

A. 2

B. 4

C. 6

D. 8

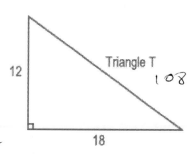

Triangle S

Triangle T

Handwritten: $A = \frac{1}{2} a \cdot b$ 27

Handwritten: 108

Handwritten: $a^2 + b^2 = c^2$ $36 + 81 = c^2$

4. Ken takes a 13-foot ladder to lean up against the side of a building. If the base of the ladder is 5 feet from the building, how high up the building does the ladder reach?

A. 9 feet

B. 10 feet

C. 11 feet

D. 12 feet

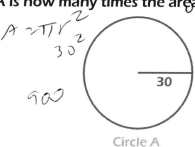

Handwritten: $5^2 + b^2 = 13^2$ $25 + b^2 = 13^2$ 144

5. The area of Circle A is how many times the area of Circle B?

A. 2

B. 4

C. 8

D. 15

Handwritten: $A = \pi r^2$ 30^2 900

Handwritten: 225

30

15

Circle A   Circle B

6. What is the perimeter of the figure below, which shows a quarter of a circle, if the entire circle had a diameter of 10m?

A. 2.5π meters

B. 10π meters

C. 10 + 6.25π meters

D. 10 + 2.5π meters

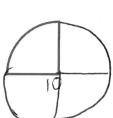

10

Handwritten: $\frac{2\pi r}{2 \cdot 5}$ 5π $2.5 = 10$ $\frac{2\pi 5}{4}$ 10π

7. Todd and Anne were standing together and talking after school. Todd walked 2 miles due north to get home. Anne walked 1.5 miles due east to get home. How far apart are their houses?

A. 1 mile

B. 2.5 miles

C. 3.5 miles

D. 5 miles

2   1.5

2m   1.5

Handwritten: $\frac{1.5}{+1.5}$ 3.0

Handwritten: $2^2 + 4.5$ $4 + 2.25 = c^2$ $\sqrt{6.25}$ 3.5

8. What is the distance between (−3,4) and (3,−4)? (hint: draw a right triangle on the coordinate plane)

A. 7

B. 8

C. 10

D. 14

Triangles & Circles: Answer Explanations

1. C   Estimate the radius, and then compare your estimate to the student's.

Note that the formula for finding the circumference of a circle is on the formula sheet of the ILTS TAP.

Circumference = 2π x radius = 24

π is approximately 3

Substitute that in to the formula

2π x radius = 24

$2(3)$ x radius $\approx$ 24

6 x radius $\approx$ 24

radius $\approx$ 4

The radius is approximately 4, and the student said the radius was approximately 8. The estimate is too high by a factor of 2.

2. D   Use the area of a triangle formula to calculate the length of the base.

Area = ½ x base x height

$45 = ½$ x b x 9

$45 = 4.5$ x b

b = 10 m

3. B   Let's calculate the area of each triangle using the formula = ½ x base x height

Triangle T's Area = ½ x 12 x 18 = 108

Triangle S's Area = ½ x 6 x 9 = 27

Divide to find how many times larger is Triangle T.

$108 \div 27 = 4$

4. D   The easiest way to solve this problem is to first draw a picture. The building, the ground, and the ladder create a right triangle as in the diagram.

To find how high up the building the ladder goes, use the Pythagorean Theorem.

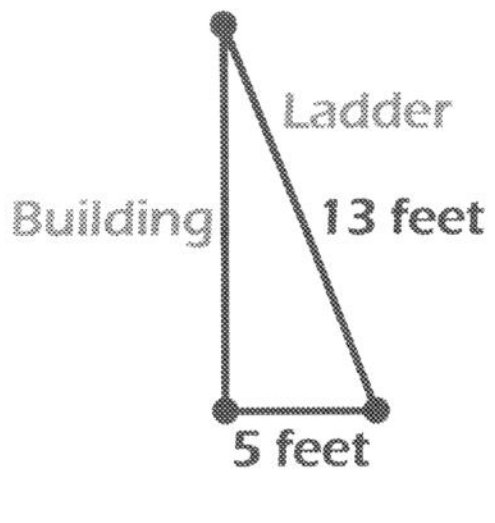

$5^2 + x^2 = 13^2$

$25 + x^2 = 169$

$x^2 = 144$

$x = 12$

12 feet

5. B   The radius of Circle A is 30 and the radius of Circle B is 15. Let's find the area of each and then create a ratio.

Area of Circle A = π x r^2 = π x 30^2 = 900π

Area of Circle B = π x r^2 = π x 15^2 = 225π

Now divide to find out how many times larger is the area of Circle A than the area of Circle B.

$900\pi \div 225\pi = 4$

6. D   If the circle had a diameter of 10m, then its radius must be 5m. Therefore, fill in the lengths of two of the sides of the figure.

To figure out the length around the curve, realize it is 1/4 the circumference of the entire circle. The circumference of a circle is found by multiplying π by the diameter.

Length of the Curve = 1/4 x π x 10 = $^{10}/_4\ \pi$ = 2.5π

The total perimeter is found by adding the lengths of all the sides: 5m + 5m + 2.5πm = 10 + 2.5π meters

7. B   Draw a picture to help solve the problem. If Todd and Anne both began walking at school, and Todd went north while Anne went east, their trips would look like the right triangle below.

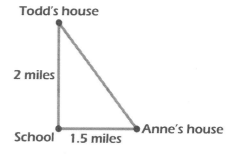

Use the Pythagorean Theorem to find the distance between their houses, which will be the hypotenuse of the right triangle.

$(1.5)^2 + 2^2 = c^2$

$2.25 + 4 = c^2$

$6.25 = c^2$

$c = 2.5$ miles

8. C   In the image below, you can see the two points have been graphed on the coordinate plane. Then, a right triangle was drawn with the hypotenuse representing the distance between the points.

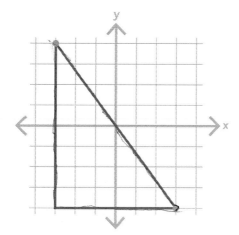

The vertical side of the right triangle has a length of 8. The horizontal side of the right triangle has a length of 6. Use the Pythagorean theorem to find the length of the hypotenuse.

$6^2 + 8^2 = \text{hypotenuse}^2$

$36 + 64 = \text{hypotenuse}^2$

$100 = \text{hypotenuse}^2$

$\text{hypotenuse} = 10$

Distance between the points is 10.

Volume

Volume is the three dimensional space filled by a figure. Its units are equal to a cubed length measurement.

Note that the formulas for volume are provided on the ILTS sheet of Mathematics Definitions and Formulas.

Rectangular Solid

These figures are also known as rectangular prisms or boxes. To find the volume, multiply length x width x height.

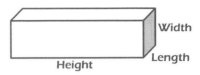

Volume = lwh

Cube

A cube is a type of rectangular solid where all dimensions are the same length. Thus, volume = lwh = s x s x s = s^3.

Volume = s^3

Cylinder

To find the volume, multiply the area of the base by the height. In this case, the area of the base is a circle with area of π x radius². Therefore, the volume = π x r^2 x height.

Volume = $\pi r^2 h$

Sphere

The volume of a sphere can be calculated by multiplying (⁴⁄₃) x π x r^3.

Volume = ⁴⁄₃ πr^3

Volume: Practice

1. Calculate the volume of a 9 foot tall cylinder with a base with a radius of 3 feet.

A. 81π ft. cubed

B. 270 ft cubed

C. 40.5 ft. cubed

D. 54 ft. cubed

$v = \pi(2)h$

$v = \pi \, 3^2 \, 9$

$v = 8\pi$

2. How many times bigger is the volume of a cube with sides of length 8m than the volume of a cube with sides of length 2m?

A. 4

B. 8

C. 16

D. 64

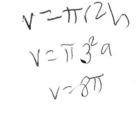

3. Calculate the volume of a sphere with a 12 yard diameter in cubic yards.

A. 144 π

B. 288 π

C. 566 π

D. 2304 π

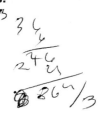

4. Which can hold more water, a plastic cube with 2 inch sides or a plastic box that is 4 inches long, 3 inches wide, and ¾ inch tall?

A. Cube

B. Box

C. Same

D. Not enough information.

5. If the width of a rectangular prism is w, and the length is twice the width, and the height is 4 more than the length, what is the volume of the prism in terms of w?

A. $5w + 4$

B. w^3

C. $2w^3 + 8w^2$

D. $4w^3 + 8w^2$

6. If the length of each side of a cube is doubled, what happens to the volume of the cube?

A. Doubles

B. Quadruples

C. Multiplies by 6

D. Multiplies by 8

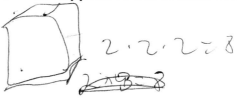

7. If the volume of a sphere is 288π, what is the diameter?

A. 6

B. 12

C. 24

D. 144

$288 \pi = \frac{4}{3}\pi r^3$

8. Which has the largest volume?

A. Cube with sides length 6m

B. Sphere with diameter 6m

C. Cylinder with height 6m and diameter 6m

D. Rectangular prism with sides length 5m, 6m, 7m

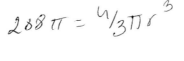

Volume: Answer Explanations

1. A First, find the area of the circle on the base of the cylinder. Area of circle = π x radius^2

Area of Base = π x 3^2 = 9π ft. sq.

Then multiply that area by the height of the cylinder.

9π ft. sq x 9 ft. = 81π ft. cubed.

Note: The formula is included on the ILTS sheet provided during the exam. Volume of Cylinder = $\pi r^2 h$.

2. D   The volume of a cube is side^3.

Volume of cube with sides of length 8m = 8^3 = 512

Volume of cube with sides of length 2m = 2^3 = 8

512 ÷ 8 = 64

3. B   Volume of Sphere = 4/3 x π x radius^3

In this case, the radius is 6 yards (half of the diameter).

Volume = 4/3 x π x 6^3 = 288π

Note: The formula for the volume of a sphere is included on the ILTS TAP sheet provided to you.

4. B   Find the volume of each to see how much water they can hold.

Plastic Cube: 2 in x 2 in x 2 in = 8 cubic inches

Plastic Box: 4 in x 3 in x 3/4 in = 9 cubic inches

Plastic Box can hold more.

5. D   The volume of a rectangular prism is the width x length x height. Let's put each dimension in terms of w.

Width = w

Length = twice the width = 2w

Height = four more than length = 2w + 4

Volume = Width x Length x Height = w x (2w) x (2w + 4) = $2w^2$(2w + 4) = $4w^3 + 8w^2$

6. D   Let each side of the original cube = S. Then, the volume of the original cube = S x S x S = S^3

Each side of the new cube = 2S. Then, the volume of the new cube = 2S x 2S x 2S = $8S^3$

= 8(volume of original cube)

Volume multiplies by 8.

7. B   The formula for the volume of a sphere is ⅓ π x radius^3.

288π = ⅓ π x radius^3	Divide both sides by π
288 = ⅓ x radius^3	Multiply both sides by 3/4
216 = radius^3	Take the cube root of both sides.
6 = radius	

If 6 is the radius, then double that will be the diameter. Diameter = 12.

8. A   Find the volume of each:

A: Cube with sides length 6m

Volume = side x side x side = 6 x 6 x 6 = 216m^3

B: Sphere with diameter 6m

Volume = 4/3 π radius^3 = 4/3 π 3^3 = 36π = approximately 110m^3

C: Cylinder with height 6m and diameter 6m

Volume = π radius^2 x height = π3^2 x 6 = 54π = approximately 170m^3

D: Rectangular prism with sides length 5m, 6m, 7m

Volume = length x width x height = 5m x 6m x 7m = 210m^3

The cube has the largest volume.

Surface Area

Surface area is the sum of the areas of all of the faces of an object. Its units are the same as those for area, a length measurement squared. *Note that the formulas for surface area are provided on the ILTS TAP.*

Rectangular Solid

This figure is also known as a rectangular prism or box. The surface area of a box is calculated by finding the area of each rectangle on the face of the box. There are 6 different faces, two with an area of length x width, two with an area of length x height, and two with an area of width x height. This can be written using the formula:(2 x length x width) + (2 x length x height) + (2 x width x height).

Surface Area = 2lw + 2lh + 2wh

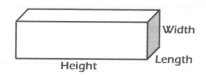

Cube

Since a cube has 6 sides, all with the same area of side^2, the surface area of a cube = 6 x side^2.

Surface area = 6s^2

Cylinder

To find the surface area of a cylinder, add the areas of three different faces, the top, the bottom, and the side. The top and bottom of the cylinder are circles, each with an area of π x r^2. If you think about unrolling a cylinder, the side makes a rectangle with a width equal to the circumference of the base and a length equal to the height of the cylinder. Therefore, the area of the side = π x diameter x height. The total surface area of a cylinder is = 2πrh + 2πr^2.

Surface Area = 2πrh + 2πr^2.

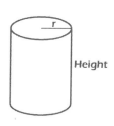

Sphere

The formula for the surface area of a sphere is: 4 x π x r^2.

Surface area = 4πr^2

Surface Area: Practice

1. A box is 9 m tall, 7 m long, and 3 m wide. What is its surface area?

A. 189 square meters

B. 189 cubed meters

C. 222 square meters

D. 222 cubed meters

2. What is the surface area of the cylinder in the diagram?

A. 10π

B. 50π

C. 70π

D. 100π

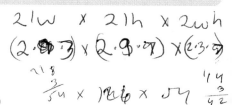

r = 5 yards

2 yards

3. Choose the best answer to replace the question mark.
The surface area of a sphere of radius y **?** the surface area of a cylinder of radius y and height y.

    A. >

    B. <

    C. =

    D. Not enough information.

4. A family is wallpapering their living room. If the room is 26 ft. by 19 ft. with 10 foot ceilings and they are only covering the walls, how much wallpaper will they need in square feet?

    A. 700

    B. 800

    C. 900

    D. 1000

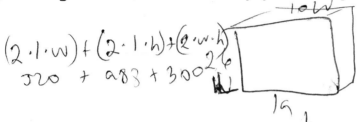

5. If the surface area of a cube is 150 square meters, what is the length of one side of the cube?

    A. 5m

    B. 10m

    C. 25m

    D. 50m

6. If a rectangular prism has a width of y, length of 2y, and height of 3y, what is its surface area?

    A. $6y^3$

    B. $12y^2$

    C. $22y^2$

    D. $36y^2$

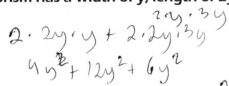

7. If the surface area of a cylinder is 320π and the radius is 10, what is the height of the cylinder?

    A. 6

    B. 12

    C. 16

    D. 32

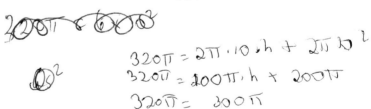

8. Which has a greater surface area: a cube with sides of length 8m or a rectangular prism which is 7m x 8m x 9m?

    A. Cube

    B. Rectangular Prism

    C. Equal

    D. Not enough information.

Surface Area: Answer Explanations

1. C   To find the surface area of a box, add the areas of each of the 6 faces. Plug the height, length, and width into the formula.

Surface Area of Box = Sum of Area of 6 faces =
(2 x length x width) + (2 x length x height) + (2 x width x height) =
(2 x 9 x 7) + (2 x 9 x 3) + (2 x 3 x 7)
= 126 + 54+ 42
= 222 sq meters

Note: The formula for the surface area of a rectangular solid is included on the ILTS TAP sheet provided during the exam. It states: Surface Area of Rectangular Solid = 2lw + 2lh + 2wh

2. C   To find the surface area of the cylinder, you must calculate the area of each of the faces.

Face 1: Top – The top of the cylinder is a circle with an area of πr^2.
$\pi r^2 = \pi 5^2 = 25\pi$

Face 2: Bottom – The top and the bottom have the same area.
$= 25\pi$

Face 3: Side – The side of the cylinder can be thought of as a rolled up rectangle with one side equal to the cylinder height and the other side equal to the circumference of the base, which is found by multiplying $2\pi r$.
height x $2\pi r$ = 2 x 2π x 5 = 20π

Total Surface Area = $25\pi + 25\pi + 20\pi = 70\pi$

Note: The formula for the surface area of a cylinder is included on the ILTS TAP sheet provided during the exam. It states: Surface Area of Cylinder = 2\pi rh + 2\pi r^2

3. C   Solve algebraically by plugging in y for the radius and the height of each of the formulas. Note that the formulas are provided on the ILTS TAP.

Surface area of a sphere:
$= 4\pi \times radius^2 = 4\pi y^2$

Surface area of a cylinder:
$= 2\pi \times radius^2 + 2\pi \times radius \times height$
$= 2\pi \times y^2 + 2\pi \ y \times y$
$= 2\pi y^2 + 2\pi y^2$
$= 4\pi y^2$

The surface areas are equivalent for all values of y.

4. C   The two shortest walls will be 19 feet long and 10 feet tall, find the area by multiplying and then multiply by 2 since there are 2 walls.
19 x 10 x 2 = 380 ft. sq.

The two longest walls will be 26 feet long and 10 feet tall, find the area by multiplying.
26 x 10 x 2 = 520 ft. sq.

Find the sum.
520 + 380 = 900 ft. sq.

5. A   A cube has 6 faces, all with the same area. The area of each face is side x side or side^2.

So, surface area of a cube = 6 x side^2

$150 = 6 \times$ side^2

$25 =$ side^2

$5 =$ side

Length of one side = 5m

Note: The formula for the surface area of a cube is included on the ILTS sheet provided during the exam.

6. C   A rectangular prism has 6 faces.

Two faces with dimensions: width x length
2 x width x length = 2 x y x 2y = $4y^2$

Two faces with dimensions: width x height
2 x width x height = 2 x y x 3y = $6y^2$

Two faces with dimensions: length x height
2 x length x height = 2 x 2y x 3y = $12y^2$

Total surface area = $4y^2 + 6y^2 + 12y^2 = 22y^2$

7. A   A cylinder has 3 faces.

Top Circular Base: Area = πradius^2 = $\pi10^2$ = 100π

Bottom Circular Base: Same Area as top base = 100π

Around side of Cylinder: can be thought of as a rolled up rectangle
Area of the rectangle = Circumference of base x height
= 2πradius x height
= 2π10 x height
= 20πheight

Total surface Area = Area of top base + Area of bottom base + Area of side
$320\pi = 100\pi + 100\pi + 20\pi$height
$320\pi = 200\pi + 20\pi$height
$120\pi = 20\pi$height
$120 = 20$ x height
$6 =$ height

8. A   Cube: A cube has 6 equal faces, therefore the surface area is found by multiplying 6 by the area of one face.
Surface Area = 6 x side^2
= 6 x 8^2 = 6 x 64 = 384

Rectangular Prism: There are 6 faces. Two with area of length x width; two with area of width x height; two with area of length x height.

Surface Area = 2(length x width) + 2(width x height) + 2(length x height)
= 2(7 x 8) + 2(8 x 9) + 2(7 x 9)
= 2(56) + 2(72) + 2(63)
= 112 + 144 + 126
= 382

The cube's surface area is larger.

1. A man is painting one of the walls in his dining room. He uses 1 gallon of paint to cover 14 square yards of wall space. If the wall is 12 feet high and 21 feet long, how many gallons of paint will he need?

    A. 1 gallons

    B. 2 gallons

    C. 6 gallons

    D. 18 gallons

2. You have a right triangle and you double the length of all the sides. How does the area change?

    A. Increases by 2

    B. Doubles

    C. Triples

    D. Quadruples

3. Choose the best answer to replace the question mark:
Perimeter of Circle A **Perimeter of Square B**

    A. >

    B. <

    C. =

    D. Not enough information.

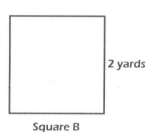

Circle A   Square B

4. Julian is 6 feet 3 inches tall. Barbara is $^{14}/_8$ yards tall, and Sandra is 70 inches tall. Order them from shortest to tallest.

    A. Julian, Sandra, Barbara

    B. Julian, Barbara, Sandra

    C. Barbara, Julian, Sandra

    D. Barbara, Sandra, Julian

5. What is the area of the circle shown here?

    A. 13π

    B. 144π

    C. 169π

    D. 225π

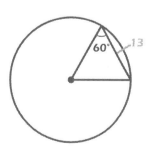

6. What is the area of the figure?

    A. 34

    B. 74

    C. 90

    D. 98

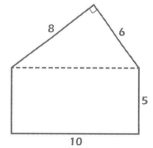

7. Find the perimeter of the following triangle.

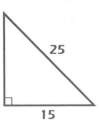

A. 20

B. 40

C. 55

D. 60

8. A dart board has a red bull's eye that is 6 inches in diameter. No other part of the dartboard is red. If the dart board is 30 inches in diameter, what area of the dartboard is not red?

A. 576π sq. in.

B. 396π sq. in.

C. 216π sq. in.

D. 144π sq. in.

9. What is the perimeter of the shape?

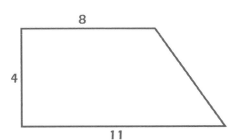

A. 23

B. 26

C. 28

D. 32

10. The field below is made up of two half circles on either end with a straight line of 50m connecting them. If the height of the field is 20m, what is the perimeter of the entire field?

A. 120m

B. 140m

C. 162.8m

D. 414m

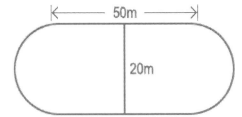

11. The field above is made up of two half circles on either end with a straight line of 50m connecting them. If the height of the field is 20m, what is the area of the entire field?

A. 3140 sq. m.

B. 1000 sq. m.

C. 1062.8 sq. m.

D. 1314 sq. m.

12. If the width of a box is w, the length is ½ the width, and the height is 6 more than the length, what is the volume of the box in terms of w?

A. $2w + 12$

B. $w^3 + 3w^2$

C. $2w^3 + 12w^2$

D. $\frac{1}{4}w^3 + 3w^2$

13. A circular track is 63 meters long. Approximately how long is the diameter of the circle formed by the track?

    A. 8m

    B. 15m

    C. 20m

    D. 30m

14. Choose the best answer to replace the question mark.

surface area of sphere with radius 9m **?** surface area of cylinder with radius 9m and height of 9m

    A. $<$

    B. $>$

    C. $=$

    D. Not Enough Information

15. Which of the following is the largest?

    A. 8 square yards

    B. 70 square feet

    C. 10,000 square inches

    D. 5 square yards, 20 square feet, and 500 square inches

16. George is a kindergartener coloring in wedges of circles for a project on fractions. If the diameter of a circle is 6 inches, and the circle is divided evenly into 6 wedges, what is the area that George colored if he carefully colors in 1 wedge?

    A. π

    B. 1.5π

    C. 2π

    D. 3π

17. If the volume of a cube is 216 m³, what is its surface area?

    A. 108 m^2

    B. 144 m^2

    C. 216 m^2

    D. 432 m^2

18. The trailer of a truck measures 10 feet by 15 feet by 30 feet. The trailer is to be filled with identical cube–shaped cartons, each having sides measuring a whole number of feet. What number of identical cartons with the largest possible side length could be packed into the trailer with no empty space remaining?

    A. 11

    B. 36

    C. 55

    D. 4500

19. In the figure below, if line L is parallel to line M, what is the measure of angle c in degrees?

A. 38

B. 52

C. 128

D. 180

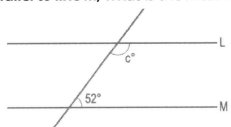

20. If AB = AC and angle BAC = 80°. What is the measure of angle ACD?

A. 50°

B. 100°

C. 130°

D. 180°

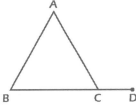

Geometry: Chapter Review Answer Explanations

1. B   This problem has many steps:

Convert wall dimensions from feet to yards.

12 feet x 1 yard/3 feet = 4 yards

21 feet x 1 yard/3 feet = 7 yards

Find area of the wall. 4 yards x 7 yards = 28 square yards

Find number of gallons of paint needed.

28 sq yds x 1 gallon/14 sq. yds = 2 gallons

2 gallons of paint

2. D   The area of a triangle = ½ x base x height = ½ bh

If you double the length of all sides, the length of the base and height will each double. The new area can then be found: New Area = ½(2b)(2h) = 4(½ bh) = 4(original area)

The area quadruples.

3. B   Don't forget to first convert the units so that they are the same.

Square B: First, convert the units from yards to feet. There are 3 feet in each yard, therefore the length of the side is 6 feet. To find the perimeter of the square, multiply the length of the side times 4. Therefore, the perimeter is 4 x 6 feet = 24 feet.

Circle A: The formula for calculating the perimeter or circumference of a circle is π x diameter. The diameter is 4.5 feet and pi is a little more than 3. A quick estimate will show that this is definitely less than the perimeter of the square.

Perimeter of Circle A < Perimeter of Square B

4. D   *Note that the unit conversions are provided on the ILTS TAP.* Convert all of the heights to mixed numbers with a common denominator. Remember that 1 foot equals 12 inches and 1 yard equals 3 feet.

Julian: 6 feet 3 inches = 6 $\frac{3}{12}$ feet

Barbara: $1\frac{4}{8}$ yards x 3 feet/1 yard = $\frac{42}{8}$ feet = $2\frac{1}{4}$ feet = 5 ¼ feet

Sandra: 70 inches x 1 foot/12 inches= $\frac{70}{12}$ feet = 5 $\frac{10}{12}$ feet

From shortest to tallest: Barbara, Sandra, Julian

5. C   Two sides of the triangle are radii of the circle. Thus, they are equal. One of those sides is opposite a 60 degree angle, so the other side must also be opposite a 60 degree angle. Since the angles of a triangle add up to 180 degrees and two of the angles add up to 120, the third angle must also be 60 degrees, making this an equilateral triangle. Equilateral triangles have three equal sides, so each side of the triangle is 13 units long.

Now that we know the sides of the triangle, we must determine the area of the circle. We know that the radius is 13, so we can calculate the area by squaring radius and multiplying by pi.

Area of circle = $\pi r^2 = \pi \times 13^2 = 169\pi$

6. B   To find the area of the entire shape, find the area of the triangle and add that to the area of the rectangle.

Area of triangle = ½ x base x height = ½ x 6 x 8 = 24
Area of rectangle = length x width = 5 x 10 = 50

Area of shape = 50 + 24 = 74

7. D   To find the perimeter, you need to add the length of all the sides. Unfortunately, only two sides of the triangle were given. But, since the triangle is a right triangle, you can use the Pythagorean Theorem to find the length of the other side.

$15^2 + B^2 = 25^2$
$225 + B^2 = 625$
$B^2 = 400$
$B = 20$

Now, add up all the sides. 15 + 20 + 25 = 60

8. C   Find the area of the dartboard and subtract the area of the bullseye to find the area that is not red.
Area of dartboard = $\pi 15^2 = 225\pi$
Area of bullseye = $\pi 3^2 = 9\pi$
Area of dartboard – area of bullseye = $(225 - 9)\pi = 216\pi$

9. C   The perimeter of a shape is the distance around its edges. The last side must be found.
Draw a vertical line through the middle of the shape to create a rectangle and a right triangle. The rectangle has dimensions of 4 by 8. The right triangle's sides are 4 and 3.

To find the missing side, use the Pythagorean Theorem.
$3^2 + 4^2 = \text{hypotenuse}^2$
$9 + 16 = \text{hypotenuse}^2$
$25 = \text{hypotenuse}^2$
$5 = \text{hypotenuse}$

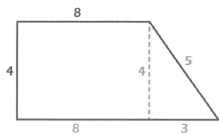

To find perimeter, sum the length of all the sides.
Perimeter = 8 + 5 + 11 + 4 = 28

10. C   The perimeter of the field is the total distance around the outside. First, let's find the perimeter around the two half–circles and then we can add in the two straight lines.

Since the two half–circles will equal one total circle, we need to find the perimeter, or circumference, of one circle, which equals π times diameter. In this case, the height of the field, 20m, is equal to the diameter.
Circumference of Circle = π x 20m ≈ 62.8m

Now, there are two straight edges, the top and bottom, each 50m.
Total Perimeter = 62.8m + 50m + 50m = 162.8m

11. D To find area of the entire field, first find area of the two half–circles and add in the area of the rectangular middle of the field.

The two half–circles will add up to one whole circle. The area of a circle = π x radius². The diameter of the circle is the same as the height of the field, 20m. Therefore, the radius = 10m.
Area of Circle = π x 10^2 ≈ 314 sq. m.

The area of the middle rectangular portion can be found by multiplying the base by the height. The base is 50m and height is 20m.
Area of Rectangle = 50m x 20m = 1000 sq. m.

Total Area = 1000 + 314 = 1314 sq. m.

12. D Volume of a box is found by multiplying length, width, and height. First put the dimensions in terms of w.
Width = w
Length = ½ w
Height = ½ w + 6
Volume = w (½ w) (½ w + 6) = (½ w^2) (½ w + 6) = ¼ w^3 + $3w^2$

13. C If the distance around the track is 63m, that means the circumference or perimeter of the circle is 63m.
The circumference is equal to 2 x π x radius = π x diameter
63 = π x diameter
63 = 3.14 x diameter
diameter = 63 ÷ 3.14

The diameter is approximately 20 meters.

14. C Let's calculate the surface area of each shape. *Note the formulas for surface area are provided on the ILTS TAP.*

Sphere: To calculate the surface area of a sphere, you can use the following formula: 4 x π x r^2.
In this case, sphere's surface area = 4 x π x 9^2 = 324π

Cylinder: To calculate the surface area of a cylinder, you must find the area of all the surfaces. The top and bottom are circles with an area of $πr^2$. The side of a cylinder can be found by taking the circumference of the base and multiplying by the height = 2πrh
2 x area of base + area of side =
$2πr^2$ + 2πrh =
$2π9^2$ + 2π x 9 x 9 =
162π + 162π = 324π

The surface areas are equal.

15. A Let's convert each answer to square inches, so that you can easily compare the quantities.

A: 8 square yards: 8 sq yards x 36 in/1 yard x 36 in/1 yard = 10368 sq. inches
B: 70 square feet: 70 sq feet x 12 in/1 foot x 12 in/1 foot = 10080 sq. inches
C: 10,000 square inches
D: 5 square yards, 20 square feet, and 500 square inches
5 sq yards x 36 in/1 yard x 36 in/1 yard = 6480 sq. inches
20 sq feet x 12 in/1 foot x 12 in/1 foot = 2880 sq inches
6480 + 2880 + 500 = 9860 sq inches

Answer A is the largest.

16. B   Find the area of the entire circle. Then, find 1/6 of the area since he colored 1 of the 6 evenly sized wedges. Since the diameter is 6 inches, the radius is 3 inches.

Area of the circle = $\pi \text{ radius}^2 = \pi 3^2 = 9\pi$

Now, find 1/6 of the area of the circle. $\frac{1}{6} \times 9\pi = 1.5\pi$

17. C   The volume of a cube is found by cubing the length of the side. Volume = side^3
$216 = \text{side}^3$
$6 = \text{side}$

The surface area of a cube is found by multiplying the area of each face by the 6 faces.
Surface Area = 6 x Area of each face = $6 \times \text{side}^2 = 6 \times 6^2 = 216$
Surface Area = 216 m^2

18. B   The problem deals with filling the container, so we know it relates to volume. However, we must figure out the size of the containers to determine the minimum number to be used. If you are confused on how to start the problem, first find one possible answer so you can understand how to approach the problem.

The easiest container size to start with that involves a whole number of feet for each side, is a container whose dimensions are 1 ft for each side of the cube. If so, the number that would fit in the trailer would be 10 x 15 x 30 = 4500.

Now, we at least know the maximum number of containers and hopefully it is now clear that you want to find the GCF of 10, 15, and 30 to determine the side length of the cube that each side can be divided into. The GCF of 10, 15, and 30 is 5. Therefore, if there was a cube with sides of length 5 ft, we know that the cubes would fit into the trailer with no empty space.

Ok, if the cubes are 5 feet on each side, to find the number that would fit into each side of the box, you must divide. Therefore, you can fit: 10ft ÷ 5ft = 2   by   15ft ÷ 5ft = 3   by   30ft ÷ 5ft = 6
Now, find the number of cartons that can fit: 2 x 3 x 6 = 36.

Another way to think about this problem is that if we know the cubes are 5 ft on each side, the volume of each cube is $(5 \text{ feet})^3$ or 125 cubic feet. We have previously determined that the volume of the trailer is 4500 cubic feet, so the number of cubes that would fit into the truck is:
4500 cubic feet x 1 cube / 125 cubic feet = 36 cubes

19. C   Using what you know about parallel lines and angles, fill in the angles you know. Remember that vertical angles and alternate interior angles are equal.

You can see that angle c and 52 degrees make a straight line.
Therefore, c and 52 must equal 180 degrees.
c + 52 = 180
c = 128

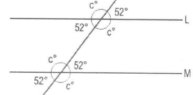

20. C   Since AB = AC, you know the triangle is isosceles, and therefore angle ABC = angle ACB.

Let angle ACB = y. Also, note agnles in a triangle add to 180 and angles along straight line add to 180.

angle ABC + angle ACB + angle BAC = 180
y + y + 80 = 180
2y = 100
y = 50

Angle ACB + angle ACD = 50 + angle ACD = 180
Angle ACD = 130 degrees

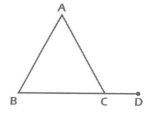

6. Data Analysis & Statistics

Graphs & Charts

Graphs, charts, and tables are useful tools for organizing information and making it easier to interpret. When presented with any form of visual display, start by looking at the titles, headings, labels, legends, units, and sources of data, which will help you to figure out how to interpret the data.

Line Graphs

A line graph displays information by showing a line that connects a series of data points over time. Line graphs compare two types of information on an x–y (horizontal–vertical) axis. Typically, the horizontal axis represents time, and the vertical axis represents the amount or quantity. Line graphs are suitable for showing how measured data increases, decreases, or fluctuates over time.

An important thing to note is that line graphs can only be used when the data between the measured data points has a meaningful value. For instance, suppose you want to record a group of children's favorite ice cream flavors, showing the flavors on the horizontal axis and the number of students on the vertical axis. A line graph could not be used as there is no value to the points in between flavors.

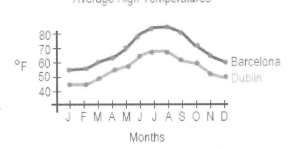

The line graph to the right shows the average high temperatures for two cities: Barcelona and Dublin. The horizontal axis shows the time in months. The vertical axis shows the temperature. You can quickly see that Barcelona's average high temperature is always about 10 degrees warmer than Dublin's. A line graph is very suitable for comparing measured values over time.

To interpret a specific data point on a line graph, trace the point with a straight line to each axis to determine its value. For instance, if you want to analyze the first dot on the lower line, you should start by noting that this line shows the temperatures for Dublin. Next, using a vertical line from this point, you see that it is above "J," representing January. Tracing a horizontal line from the point tells you that the temperature is approximately 45°F. Therefore, the average high temperature for Dublin in January is about 45°F.

Bar Graphs

Like line graphs, bar graphs involve plotting two pieces of information against each other; however, bar graphs differ in that they deal with discrete pieces of data. For example, the simple bar graphs below show the favorite foods of students in a certain classroom. It is obvious that there is no meaning for the values in between pizza and chicken nuggets.

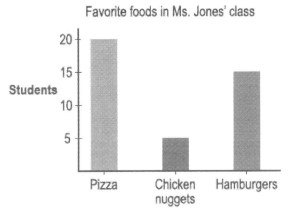

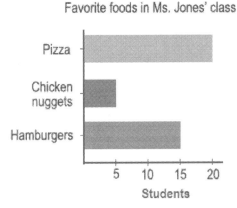

Bar graphs are typically used to compare values. Rectangular bars are used to proportionately represent the data. The graphs above show that 20 students in Ms. Jones' class chose pizza as their favorite food; 15 chose hamburgers; and 5 chose chicken nuggets. Note that the information contained in each bar graph is identical and can be analyzed in the same way. There is no difference in interpreting horizontal and vertical bar graphs.

Pie Charts

Pie charts, also called pie graphs, are fairly easy to interpret. Pie charts are always used to show one data series that adds to 100%. The circle is divided into slices to proportionally represent each set of values from that data series. You can quickly analyze and compare information in pie graphs by looking at the size of each slice.

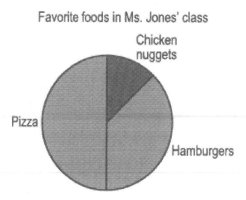

Favorite foods in Ms. Jones' class

The data for Ms. Jones' class can easily be represented in pie chart form. Since there are 40 students in the class and 20 of them chose pizza, pizza takes ½ or 50% of the chart. The 5 chicken nugget responses are ⅛ of the whole, and the 15 hamburger responses are ⅜.

Line of Best Fit & Independent/Dependent Variables

For data that is best represented by graphing, which is often the case for a large sample, a line of best fit can be use to examine the relationship between the independent and dependent variables. A line of best fit shows the data as a straight line that is drawn to minimize the distances of all the points from that line. In the graph to the right, the month is the independent variable, which is always graphed on the x–axis, and the rainfall in inches is the dependent variable. The data points are represented by dots. The line of best fit on the graph is represented by the line.

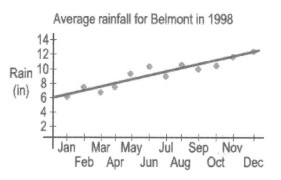

Average rainfall for Belmont in 1998

Discrete vs Continuous Data

The choice of which graph is appropriate to use depends on whether your data is discrete or continuous.

Discrete data has only a finite number of possible values. For example, the number of students that like a certain food has only a finite number of possible values as you can not have a fraction of a child. Bar graphs and pie charts are used to graph discrete data.

Continuous data represents all data that is not discrete. Continuous data has values in between data points. For instance, if you were measuring the temperature, you could have temperatures of 70, 71, and 70.523 degrees. Line graphs are used to represent continuous data.

Graphs & Charts: Practice

1. Which is the independent variable in the graph below?

A. time

B. weight

C. neither

D. both

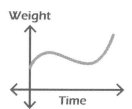

2. The graph represents that growth of a student's plant over the course of his 7 day science experiment. Which of the following equations best models the relationship between days, d, and plant height in centimeters, h, as shown in the graph?

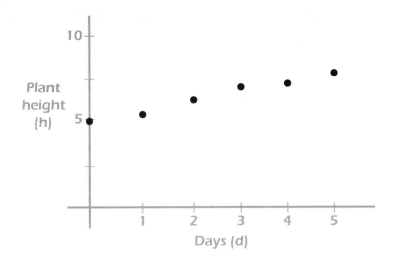

A. d = ½ h + 5

B. d = 5 h + ½

C. h = ½ d + 5

D. h = 5 d + ½

3. Which set of data can be best represented by a straight line of best fit?

A. 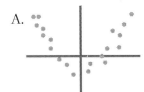   B.    C. 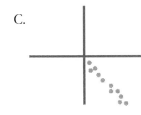   D.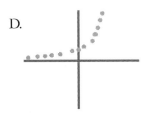

4. What percentage of the annual budget is for Other?

A. 18%

B. 24%

C. 30%

D. 34%

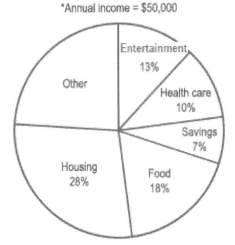

5. What can be determined about the value of the total budget for Other and Housing?

A. It is more than $25,000.

B. It is less than $25,000.

C. It is equal to $25,000.

D. Not enough information.

6. Which of the following graphs could be used for discrete data?
   I. Pie Chart
   II. Bar Graph
   III. Line Graph

A. I only

B. I and II

C. II and III

D. I, II, and III

7. Which would be the best way to represent data from a survey of languages spoken by college students if the goal is to illustrate the proportion of students who speak each language?

    A. line graph

    B. table

    C. pie chart

    D. bar graph

8. A teacher measured the heights of students in a certain class and then generated two graphs. The first graph was used to compare the heights of the students on that day. The second illustrated the rank of each student from tallest to shortest. What type of data is the teacher graphing?

    A. 1st: discrete, 2nd: discrete

    B. 1st: continuous, 2nd: discrete

    C. 1st: continuous, 2nd: continuous

    D. 1st: discrete, 2nd: continuous

Graphs & Charts: Answer Explanations

1. A   Time is graphed on the x–axis which is where the independent variable will be, while the dependent variable will be on the y–axis. Also, common sense tells us that time is not dependent on anything, it will keep going regardless. However, weight is being influenced by or is dependent on the amount of time that has passed.

        Independent variable = time

2. C   The data on the graph is close to a straight line, so it can best be represented by an equation of the form $h = md + b$, where h is the dependent variable and d is the independent. The y–intercept is 5, so substitute 5 for b.

        None of the points are obvious outliers, so you can use any of them to calculate an approximate slope. The final point appears to be at approximately $(5, 7.5)$. Plugging that point into the equation gives a slope of $\frac{1}{2}$.

        $7.5 = m(5) + 5$

        $2.5 = 5m$

        $m = 0.5$

        $h = \frac{1}{2}d + 5$

3. C   The data in answer choice C roughly conforms to a straight line. The data in A is most closely parabolic in shape, and the data in D best matches an exponential function. The data in B does not have a pattern.

4. B   In a pie graph, the percentages will always add to 100%. Therefore, you can solve this question by summing the percentages given to you and then subtracting from 100%.

        Other + Entertainment + Health Care + Savings + Food + Housing = 100%

        Other + 13% + 10% + 7% + 18% + 28% = 100%

        Other + 76% = 100%

        Other = 24%

        Another way to solve this problem is by visually comparing the Other category to the categories which list the percentages. For instance, it can be seen that Other is smaller than Housing and Housing is equal to 28%, so we can eliminate any answer larger than 28%. It can also be seen that Other is larger than Food, which is 18%, eliminating answer A. This leaves only answer B.

5. A   From the pie chart, we can quickly see that Other and Housing are more than half, or 50%, of the total budget. The title tells us that the annual income is $50,000. Therefore, we know that those two categories will be more than half of $50,000, or more than $25,000.

6. B   Discrete data has a finite number of possible values.

A pie chart is a graphical representation which divides a circle into a number of slices, each of those slices represents a proportion of the whole and is equivalent to a certain value. As the pie chart is divided into a finite number of slices, it is used for discrete data.

A bar graph has bars of certain heights for each data point. A bar graph is used to represent a finite set of values and not all the data points in between. Therefore, a bar graph is used for discrete data.

A line graph plots data points and then connects the dots with a line. All the interim data can be inferred by the line. Therefore, a line graph is used for continuous data not discrete.

I and II are used for discrete data.

7. C   To show proportionality, the best method to choose would be the pie chart.

A line graph is only appropriate for continuous data and the number of students who speak each language is discrete. It is hard to quickly glance at a table to see the proportion of students. A bar graph would be one appropriate way to illustrate this data, however it is better for comparing quantities as opposed to proportions.

8. A   Let's examine each graph to understand what data is being graphed.

1st: The first graph was used to compare the heights of the students on that day.

This is a tricky question as often graphs of height measurements show continuous data. However, those graphs are heights over time which can have in between values. In this case, the graph is showing the height of each student on a certain day. In other words, we may be graphing that Susie is 5'2" and Michael is 5'4" and there are no data points in between those data points. Therefore, the data for this graph is discrete.

2nd: The second graph illustrated the rank of each student from tallest to shortest.

Each student is being assigned a rank based on their height in comparison to the other students. Therefore, the data will be values such as 1st, 2nd, 3rd, 4th, and so on. There are no values in between each of those rankings. The possible values are finite and therefore the data is discrete.

Logic

Logic is a method of reasoning. For any problem you solve, you are using some form of logic. There are some rules and definitions which will help you with logic statements.

There are declarative statements, which can be either true or false. For example, "Patrick is 14 years old," is a declarative statement. This is either true or false depending on Patrick's age. If it is used as part of a problem statement, then assume it is true.

Some statements will use the words, "at most" or "at least".
There are at most 30 monkeys at the zoo. This statement means the number of monkeys is less than or equal to 30.
There are at least 30 monkeys at the zoo. This statement means the number of monkeys is greater than or equal to 30.

You can also use logic to combine statements. For instance, if you know that Mike is taller than Luke and Luke is taller than Andy, then you can combine the first two statements and can determine that Mike is taller than Andy. Be careful though that you are combining in the correct sequence. For instance, if you know that Melissa is taller than Lucy and Melissa is taller than Carrie, you can not make any determinations about how the heights of Lucy and Carrie compare.

Conditional Statements

Conditional statements have two parts, if and then. For example, "If you study, then you will pass," is a conditional statement. Now, let's analyze how this statement can be used.

If you study, you will pass. Now, let's see possible scenarios to see what this means.

    You study. — Then you definitely will pass.
    You do not study. — We do not know if you will pass.
    You pass. — We do not know if you studied or not.
    You do not pass. — Then you definitely did not study.

The above statement is in the form, "If A, then B". The same analysis can be applied to the statement, if A then B.

    A true. — B true.
    A false. — We can not make any statements about B.
    B true. — We can not make any statements about A.
    B false. — A false.

Deductive Reasoning

Deductive reasoning is a valid method of proof in mathematics. This type of reasoning follows a step–by–step process of making conclusions based on facts.

Here is an example of deductive reasoning:

    All rectangles have 90 degree angles.
    A square is a type of rectangle.
    Therefore, a square has 90 degree angles.

The first two statements were facts and a conclusion was drawn based on those facts.

As long as the premises are true, then all the facts or conclusions drawn from them are true. A common problem for deductive reasoning involves starting with an incorrect premise.

One common method of deductive reasoning follows this form:

    If A, then B.

    A.

    Then B.

Here is an example that follows the above form:

    If someone is taller than 5'6", then they can reach the top shelf.

    Sandra is 5'8".

    Then, Sandra can reach the top shelf.

Inductive Reasoning

Unlike deductive reasoning, inductive reasoning is not a valid form of proof. In inductive reasoning, a conclusion is reached based on identifying a trend or pattern in a series of observations. As inductive reasoning involves making generalizations or predictions, it is not always valid.

Here is an example of inductive reasoning:

    Every ant that has ever been seen is less than 2 inches long.

    Therefore, every ant is less than 2 inches.

Note that just because every observed instance of an ant was shorter than 2 inches it is not necessarily true, though it is likely. Inductive reasoning is most often used to construct hypotheses which are then tested or confirmed with other methods of reasoning.

While deductive reasoning can be thought of as going from general to a specific instance, inductive reasoning is going from specific observations to a general conclusion.

Math Reasoning & Logic: Practice

1. Maggie chose three toppings for her pizza from the list below.
    Standard: Onions, Mushrooms, Ham, Pepperoni, Pineapple
    Premium: Chicken, Goat Cheese, Roasted Peppers

Based on the following information, which topping did Maggie definitely choose for her pizza?
Maggie is a vegetarian.
Maggie chose only one premium topping.
Maggie loves pineapple, but not on pizza.

    A. Goat Cheese

    B. Roasted Peppers

    C. Ham

    D. Onions

2. The length of a rectangle is 5 feet less than 3 times the width. If the perimeter must be less than 86 feet, and the dimensions of the rectangle are all whole numbers of feet, what is the largest possible width for the rectangle?

    A. 10 ft

    B. 11 ft

    C. 12 ft

    D. 13 ft

3. In the Bronx Zoo, there are at least as many monkeys as reptiles and as least as many reptiles as cats. Which of the following statements are true?

A. There are at least as many cats as monkeys.

B. There are just as many cats as monkeys.

C. There are at least as many monkeys as cats.

D. There are more reptiles than cats.

4. Line AB is parallel to line CD. Another line EF is perpendicular to line AB. What can be said about the relationship between CD and EF?

A. CD and EF are parallel lines

B. CD and EF are perpendicular lines

C. CD and EF are axiomatic lines

D. CD and EF are tangent lines

5. Patricia needs at least a 75 on her final test and at least a C on her final report to pass her class. She is also told that if she completes the extra credit assignment, her final report score will be raised by a letter grade. In which scenario will Patricia pass her class? Note the scenarios presented below include the original scores on the final reports before extra credit is taken into account.

A. 74 on final test, B+ on final report, extra credit complete

B. 75 on final test, D on final report, extra credit complete

C. 95 on final test, D on final report, no extra credit

D. 72 on final test, A on final report, no extra credit

6. Which of the following arguments would best lead to a deductive conclusion as opposed to an inductive conclusion?

A. My plant seeds generally grow better when they are planted a few inches below the surface.

B. Currently, my outdoor plants are growing better than my indoor plants as my house does not get much light.

C. This indoor plant needs to be watered weekly, yet it has been neglected for one month.

D. The outdoor plants from Home Depot seem to yield better results than those from the local florist.

7. Which of the following statements are true about the quantities in the columns, if x is a positive number?

A	B
x^2	x^3

A. The quantity in column A will always be bigger.

B. The quantity in column B will always be bigger.

C. The quantities in A and B are always equal.

D. Not enough information to determine relationship.

8. A particular function is defined as follows: Take any negative integer and multiply it by −2. What is the range, or all the possible outputs, of the function?

A. Negative integers

B. Positive integers

C. All real numbers.

D. Positive even integers

Math Reasoning & Logic: Answer Explanations

1. D Let's analyze each statement to determine what information we know about Maggie's choice of toppings. Below is the list of all possible toppings.
Standard: Onions, Mushrooms, Ham, Pepperoni, Pineapple
Premium: Chicken, Goat Cheese, Roasted Peppers

Maggie is a vegetarian.
Since we are told that Maggie is a vegetarian, we can assume she would not choose a meat topping. Therefore, eliminate Ham, Chicken, and Pepperoni. This leaves us with the following possible toppings:
Standard: Onions, Mushrooms, Pineapple
Premium: Goat Cheese, Roasted Peppers

Maggie chose only one premium topping.
There are still two possible premium toppings, so we can not eliminate any based on this information. However, we know that Maggie chose only three toppings total and if only one was a premium topping, we know that she chose two standard toppings.

Maggie loves pineapple, but not on pizza.
We can therefore eliminate pineapple as a possible topping for her pizza. This leaves only two standard toppings, Onions and Mushrooms. We know that she chose two standard toppings and therefore both of those toppings must be chosen.

The toppings that Maggie definitely chose are onions and mushrooms. We are not sure whether she chose goat cheese or roasted peppers.

2. B Let the width of the rectangle be w. Then, set up an equation for the length.
"The length of a rectangle is 5 feet less than 3 times the width"
length = 3w – 5

The perimeter is the length + length + width + width
Perimeter = 3w – 5 + 3w – 5 + w + w = 8w – 10

The perimeter must be less than 86 feet
8w – 10 < 86
8w < 96
w < 12

If the width must be a whole number and is less than 12 ft, then the largest possible width is 11 ft.

3. C Let's examine the statements in the problem stem and then review each answer.

There are at least as many monkeys as reptiles. — This means that the number of monkeys is greater than or equal to the number of reptiles. If you want to think of it as a mathematical statement, it can be written: monkeys ≥ reptiles

There are at least as many reptiles as cats. — This means that the number of reptiles is greater than or equal to the number of cats. Written as a mathematical statement: reptiles ≥ cats

A. There are at least as many cats as monkeys. Let's combine the two mathematical statements above.
monkeys ≥ reptiles ≥ cats

Now, we can quickly see that the number of monkeys is greater than or equal to the number of cats. However, this does not mean that there are at least as many cats as monkeys as that would mean the number of cats is greater than or equal to the number of monkeys. For instance, here is a counterexample, that holds true for original statements but not answer choice A: Monkeys: 10, Reptiles: 9, Cats: 8

B. There are just as many cats as monkeys.

This statement implies that the number of cats is greater than or equal to the number of monkeys. Again, using the combined mathematical statement, we can see that this statement is not always true.

monkeys $\geq$ reptiles $\geq$ cats

We know that the number of monkeys is greater than or equal to the number of cats and not the other way around. A counterexample: Monkeys: 10, Reptiles: 9, Cats: 8

C. There are at least as many monkeys as cats.

If we translate this statement into a mathematical expression, it would be the following:

monkeys $\geq$ cats

This is true. We know that the number of monkeys is greater than or equal to the number of reptiles which is greater than or equal to the number of cats. Therefore, we can see that the number of monkeys is greater than or equal to the number of cats.

D. There are more reptiles than cats.

We know that the number of reptiles is greater than or equal to the number of cats. Therefore, the number of reptiles could be equal to the number of cats. For instance, there could be 12 Reptiles and 12 Cats and that would still meant that the number of reptiles is at least as many as the number of cats, but it makes answer D wrong.

4. B   If two lines are parallel, then lines perpendicular to one line are also perpendicular to the other.

Since EF is perpendicular to AB, it will cross AB at a 90 degree angle. As AB and CD are parallel, then any line crossing AB will cross CD at the same angle. Therefore, EF will cross CD at a 90 degree angle. Therefore, EF and CD are perpendicular.

The above is a form of deductive reasoning and it was a step by step proof of true statements to reach a conclusion.

5. B   These are simple scenarios which we probably all calculate as it gets close to the end of a semester. Let's examine the criteria that Patricia needs to pass the class.

There are two conditions which must be met for her to pass:
1.   At least a 75 on final test
2.   At least a C on final report

The last statement provides information on the grading of the final report. Patricia is told that if she completes an extra credit assignment her final report score wil be raised by a letter grade.

Let's now go through each answer choice to see if Patricia meets the two conditions to pass.

A. 74 on final test, B+ on final report, extra credit complete

She does not meet the first condition and therefore she can not pass the class.

B. 75 on final test, D on final report, extra credit complete

The 75 on the final test meets the first condition. Since she completed the extra credit assignment, her final report score is increased by a letter grade to C. Therefore, she meets the conditions and passes the class.

C. 95 on final test, D on final report, no extra credit

Patricia definitely met the condition of receiving a high enough grade on her final test. However, since she did not complete any extra credit she did not pass the second condition and therefore does not pass the class.

D. 72 on final test, A on final report, no extra credit

Patricia's score on her final test is not high enough for her to pass the class.

6. C   Inductive reasoning is based on a series of observations. Deductive reasoning is a valid form of proof based on series a facts. This problem wants to know which of the following arguments would lead to a deductive conclusion. Therefore, we want to find the answer choice that includes a fact as opposed to an observation.

A. My plant seeds generally grow better when they are planted a few inches below the surface.
This statement is a general observation based on an individual noticing what happens with their plants. It is unlikely that a deductive argument will be able to use this statement as a fact.

B. Currently, my outdoor plants are growing better than my indoor plants as my house does not get much light.
Again, this statement is an observation about a person's outdoor plants versus their indoor plants. It would not lead to a valid proof about whether indoor plants or outdoor plants would always grow better at this individual's home.

C. This indoor plant needs to be watered weekly, yet it has been neglected for a month.
This statement does sound like a fact that could be used to prove why this particular indoor plant is not growing well. It states that this plant "needs to be watered weekly". The statement sounds like it has been tested and proven. Furthermore, the statement does not say anything about "it seems" this plant needs to be watered weekly, or an individual has "noticed that" this plant likes to be watered weekly, etc. This statement could lead to a deductive conclusion.

D. The outdoor plants from Home Depot seem to yield better results than those from the local florist.
The words "seem to" help to demonstrate this statement is based on observations not facts. There is nothing concrete in this statement that could be used to definitely prove anything about plants from Home Depot versus the local florist. This could only lead to an inductive conclusion.

7. D   This question is asking us to compare two quantities, x^2 and x^3. Let's try a few values for x and see what happens.

If $x = 2$, $x^2 = 4$ and $x^3 = 8$. In this case, column B is larger.
If $x = 1$, $x^2 = 1$ and $x^3 = 1$. In this case, column A is equal to column B.

Therefore, sometimes column B is larger, sometimes they are equal. Thus, there is not enough information to determine what the relationship will be.

8. D   The range of a function is the output, or all possible y values. Let's try a few inputs to see the outputs.

Function: Take any negative integer and multiply it by –2.
$x = -1$, $y = -1(-2) = 2$
$x = -2$, $y = -2(-2) = 4$
$x = -3$, $y = -3(-2) = 6$

Multiplying a negative integer by a negative will always result in a positive.
Multiplying any number by an even will always result in an even number.
Therefore, multiplying a negative integer by –2 will result in a positive even integer.

Range = Positive Even Integers

Sample Space

A random experiment is one for which the outcome is unknown before the experiment is performed. An example of a random experiment is flipping a fair coin with one side heads and the other tails.

A simple event is one that relies on one independent outcome. For the example of flipping a coin, a simple event would be flipping the coin once. The outcome of that experiment would be whichever side lands face–up: heads or tails.

To calculate the probability (or likelihood of occurrence) for an event, you must first determine the sample space or total number of possible outcomes for that event.

For the simple case of flipping a coin once, the sample space includes heads and tails, the only two possible outcomes. For rolling a dice, the sample space includes 1, 2, 3, 4, 5, and 6, the six possible outcomes for the dice.

Counting Principle

Determining sample space by writing out all possible outcomes works for very simple experiments but it can be quite cumbersome for even slightly complex situations.

For example, if a woman is making a sandwich with three types of bread: white, wheat, and rye and four kinds of meat:turkey, ham, roast beef, and pastrami. Listing possibilities will take quite a bit of time:

> White–Turkey, White–Ham, White–Roast Beef, White–Pastrami, Wheat–Turkey, Wheat–Ham, Wheat–Roast Beef, Wheat–Pastrami, Rye–Turkey, Rye–Ham, Rye–Roast Beef, Rye–Pastrami

Notice the number of possibilities is 12, which is equal to 3 x 4, the number of outcomes for event A (the type of bread) multiplied by the number of outcomes for event B (the type of meat). This is called the counting principle or multiplication rule. The counting principle works for any number of events.

possible outcomes for n events = possible outcomes for 1st event x possible outcomes for 2nd event x possible outcomes for 3rd event x ...

Probability

The probability that an event will occur is the number of favorable outcomes divided by the total number of outcomes.

Finding the probability of rolling a dice and getting an even number, would involve first finding the favorable outcomes: 2, 4, and 6 then finding the total number of outcomes: 1, 2, 3, 4, 5, and 6. There are 3 favorable outcomes and 6 total outcomes, therefore the probability of getting an even number is $3/6 = 1/2 = 0.5$

Finding the probability of picking a card and getting an Ace, would involve first finding the favorable outcomes: 4 aces, and then finding the total number of outcomes: 52 cards. There are 4 favorable outcomes and 52 total outcomes. Therefore, the probability of picking a card and getting an Ace is $4/52 = 1/13$

Compound Events

In statistics, the probability that 2 or more events will occur sequentially is referred to as the probability of a compound event. For example, the probability of flipping a fair coin and having it land heads up is 1/2. How do you calculate the probability of getting heads twice in a row?

One way, which you have already learned, is to list out all of the possible outcomes for flipping two coins.

> Heads – Heads, Heads – Tails, Tails – Heads, Tails – Tails

There are 4 possible outcomes, and one is favorable with heads–heads, therefore, the probability is 1/4.

This method will not work if there are a large number of outcomes and events. For example, finding the probability of getting heads 20 times in a row by this method would be quite tedious.

Determining Probability of Compound Events

To find the probability of independent compound events, multiply the probability of each of the individual events. Independent events are events that do not affect the outcome of each other. For example, flipping a coin that lands heads up does not affect the probability of a heads–up result for the next coin flip. To answer a question that asks for the probability of rolling a die and getting a 3 and flipping a coin that lands heads–up, you should find the product of the probabilities of each event.

Prob of getting a 3 on die x Prob of getting heads = 1/6 x 1/2 = 1/12
To find the probability of getting 3 heads in a row, multiply the probability of each head = 1/2 x 1/2 x 1/2 = 1/8

Dependent Events

Dependent events are those with outcomes that affect the probability of another. When calculating the probability of a combination of dependent events, you must consider how the sample space of the second is affected by the first event, and so on.

Example: A bag contains 8 marbles, 3 red and 5 blue. What is the probability of pulling a red marble and then a blue marble from the bag if you do not replace the marbles as you take them?

This example has two dependent events. The first event is pulling the first marble and it being red, and the second event is pulling a blue marble next. Therefore, to find the probability of these dependent events, we must find the probability of each event and then multiply.

The probability of drawing a red marble from the bag is 3/8, since there are 3 red marbles and 8 marbles total.

After that marble has been removed, there are 2 red marbles and 5 blue marbles remaining for a total of 7 remaining marbles. Therefore, the probability of pulling out a blue marble on the second draw is 5/7.

To find the probability of drawing a red and then drawing a blue, multiply the two probabilities.
3/8 x 5/7 = 15/56

If the marbles were replaced on each round, then these events would be independent and not dependent.

Trees

Trees can be useful diagrams for illustrating and visualizing a set of decision–making rules.

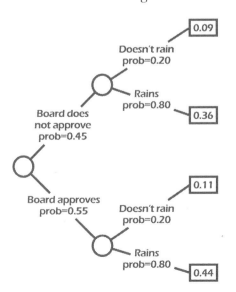

The graph to the left shows a tree diagram.

For this tree, you can see the probabilities of various decisions and combinations of decisions. For instance, the probability it rains is 80% or 0.80. If you wanted to find out the probability that the board approves and it rains, you would multiply the two probabilities together = 0.55 x 0.80 = 0.44. All the calculated probabilities are displayed in this tree, but common problems will have missing information somewhere along the decision paths.

Probability: Practice

1. A student rolls two dice. One die has six faces that are marked with 1, 2, 3, 4, 5, or 6 spots. The other is a special die with eight faces that are marked with A, B, C, D, E, F, G, or H. How many outcomes are in the sample space for this experiment?

    A. 14

    B. 28

    C. 48

    D. 64

2. If there are 120 red marbles and 5 green marbles in a bag of 1200 marbles, what is the probability that a marble drawn from the bag will be red or green?

    A. 5/1200

    B. 120/1200

    C. 125/1200

    D. 600/1200

3. What is the probability of drawing a red skittle out of a bag of 100 skittles that are 20% red and then rolling a 2 on a fair die?

    A. 1/120

    B. 11/30

    C. 1/11

    D. 1/30

$$20/100$$

$$\frac{20}{100} \times \frac{1}{6} = \frac{20}{400} = \frac{1}{30}$$

4. What is the probability of spinning purple 300 times in a row on the spinner below?

    A. $\frac{1}{1200}$

    B. $\frac{300}{4}$

    C. ¼

    D. $(¼)^{300}$

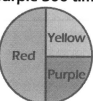

5. Francisco is trying to guess a letter of the alphabet that has been randomly selected. What is the probability that Francisco will guess the letter correctly on the 2nd try?

    A. 1/26

    B. 1/25

    C. 1/13

    D. 25/26

6. If a card is drawn at random from a standard 52 card deck, what is the probability that it will be a 10 or a spade?

    A. 17/52

    B. 4/13

    C. 1/13

    D. 1/4

$$1/52 \quad ^{10} \; spade$$

$$\frac{2}{104}$$

7. There is a circular dart board with a bulls–eye in the middle. The radius of the board is ten inches, and the radius of the bulls–eye is 2 inches. If a dart thrown randomly hits the board, what is the probability that it hits the bulls–eye?

A. 1/25

B. 1/5

C. 1/8

D. 1/96

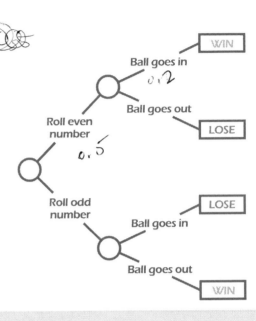

8. If the probability of getting the ball in is 0.2 and if the probability of rolling an even number is 0.5 as it is a standard die, what is the probability of winning this game?

A. 0.1

B. 0.2

C. 0.5

D. 0.7

Probability: Answer Explanations

1. C   To find the number of possible outcomes in a sample space, multiply the number of outcomes for each part of the experiment.

There are 6 outcomes for the first die.

There are 8 outcomes for the second die.

Therefore, the total number of outcomes = 6 x 8 = 48

2. C   To calculate the probability of an event occurring you need to find the the number of favorable outcomes and divide by the total number of outcomes.

In this case, the favorable outcomes are the number of red and green marbles. There are 125 marbles that are red or green.

The number of total outcomes is 1200 as that is the total number of marbles.

The probability is the favorable outcomes divided by the total outcomes = 125/1200.

Note that you do not want to multiply the probability of getting a red with the probability of getting a green marble as there are not two separate independent events. In this problem, you are only getting one marble which is one event and you want to determine whether it is red or green.

3. D   For independent compound events, multiply the probability of each of the events.

Probability of drawing a red skittle out of 100 skittles that are 20% red = 20% = 1/5

Probability of rolling a 2 on a fair die = Favorable outcomes/total outcomes = 1/6

Probability of both events happening = Probability of drawing a red x Probability of rolling a 2
= 1/5 x 1/6 = 1/30

4. D   The probability of multiple independent events occurring is the product of the probabilities of the individual events. The probability of spinning purple once is ¼ since that is the fraction of the circle that is purple.

This question asks for the probability of spinning a purple 300 times. Therefore, you need to multiply ¼ times itself 300 times. You can use exponents to represent this. $(¼)^{300}$

5. A   For Francisco to guess it correctly on his 2nd try it means that Francisco did not guess it correctly on his first try. Therefore, we need to find the probability of these two events which can be found by multiplying the probability of each individual event.

Probability of Francisco not guessing correctly on his first try.
= Number of letters he could have guessed divided by Total number of letters = 25/26

Probability of guessing correctly on 2nd try.
= Number of correct letters divided by Total number of letters left to guess = 1/25

Multiply the two probability to find the probability that Francisco guesses the letter on his 2nd try.
25/26 x 1/25 = 1/26

Another way to think about this problem is that Francisco will have an equal likelihood of guessing correctly on any of his first 26 guesses. Therefore, the probability of guessing correctly on any of his guesses is 1/26

6. B   We need to figure out the number of favorable outcomes. We want a 10 or a spade.
The number of 10s in a deck is 4.
The number of spades in a deck is 13.

However, note that the 10 of spades is counted in both of the above totals. Therefore, we must subtract out 1 from total to account for overlap.

Therefore, the number of cards in a deck that are 10s or spades is 4 + 13 − 1 = 16
Also, remember that the total number of outcomes is the total number of cards in a deck which is 52.

Probability of 10 or spade = 16/52 = 4/13

7. A   To find the probability that the dart hits the bulls–eye, find the area of the bulls–eye, and divide that by the area of the dart board. Remember, the area of a circle is πr^2.

The bulls eye has a radius of 2 inches, the area is $\pi 2^2 = 4\pi$.
The dartboard has a radius of 10 inches, the area is $\pi 10^2 = 100\pi$.

The probability is 4π divided by $100\pi = 4/100 = 1/25$.

8. C   There are two ways to win this game: the first is rolling an even number and ball goes in, and the second is rolling an odd number and ball goes out. To calculate the total probability of winning the game, add the probabilities of each individual option.

Rolling even number and ball goes in:
To find this probability, multiply the probabilities of each event since you need both to occur to win. Probability of rolling an even number is 0.5 and the probability of ball going in is 0.2.
0.5 x 0.2 = 0.1

Rolling odd number and ball goes out:
Multiply the probabilities of each event. The probability of rolling an odd number on a die is 0.5. Probability of the ball going out is 1 − the probability of ball going in. Prob of ball going out = 1 − 0.2 = 0.8.
0.5 x 0.8 = 0.4

Probability of winning: 0.1 + 0.4 = 0.5

Measures of Central Tendency

There are several ways to describe a set of data. One of the most important is to find the "average" or middle value. Generally, when people discuss averages, they are referring to the mean of one or more sets of data. Mathematicians also use other methods of finding the center or describing a set of data: median, mode, and range. In this section, you will learn how to calculate each of these important aspects of data sets.

Mean

In words, the mean value of a set of numbers is equal to the sum of those numbers divided by the number of numbers. For example, to take the mean of 2, 3, 4, 5, and 6, you would add them and divide the sum by 5, because there are 5 numbers being averaged. Their sum is 20 and their mean is 4.

The formula for mean: (sum of numbers)/(# of numbers)

Median

Like the median on a road, the median number in a set is the one located in the middle. To find the median of 29, 113, 1, 4, and 76, order the numbers from least to greatest, and then locate the middle number: 1, 4, 29, 76, and 113. For this set, 29 is in the middle, so it is the median.

For a set containing an even number of numbers, take the average of the two middle numbers. Example: Find the median of 9, 17, 82, and 9. First, order the numbers: 9, 9, 17, and 82. There are two numbers in the middle 9 and 17. Take the average of those two numbers: $(9+17)/2 = 13$. The median = 13.

Note, the median of a set of numbers can be a number that is not in the original set of numbers.

Mode

The mode of a set of data is the most frequently occurring number or piece of data. If this was your set: 1, 1, 1, 7, 8, 9, 9, 10, 11, 12. Then the mode would be 1, since it occurs the most often. If two or more numbers occur the same number of times within a set, then that set can have multiple modes.

Example: Find the mode of: 62, 0.9, 0.5, 3.75, 0.5, 0.9, 27
First order the numbers: 0.5, 0.5, 0.9, 0.9, 3.75, 27, 62
Since 0.5 and 0.9 each occur twice, they are the two modes of the set.

Measures of Central Tendency: Practice

1. Which is greater, the median or mean of the following set?   23, 75, 16, 91, 100

    A. Median

    B. Mean

    C. They are equal.

    D. Not enough information.

2. If a scale is off by 5 lbs, what measure changes?
    I. mean
    II. median
    III. mode

    A. I and II

    B. I only

    C. II and III

    D. I, II, and III

3. For the data set: 16, 16, 24, 96, and 3, 16 is the:
   I. mean
   II. median
   III. mode

A. I and II

B. II and III

C. III only

D. I, II, and III

4. A researcher lost one piece of data from his set. He knows that the median is 83. Which of the following could be the missing element if the rest of the set is: 81, 92, 85, 76, 80?

A. 78

B. 82

C. 84

D. 90

5. If n is an odd, prime integer and 10 < n < 19, which is true about the mean of all possible values of n?

A. It is greater than the median and greater than the mode.

B. It is greater than the median.

C. It is equal to the median.

D. It is less than the median.

6. Of the following set, which statistical measure is the largest? 7, –3, 11, –4, 8, 2, 9, 2

A. Mean

B. Median

C. Mode

D. All of the above are equal.

7. Which of the following is/are true?
   I. The median and mean of a data set are always different.
   II. The median of a data set is always a member of the set.
   III. There can be more than one mode in a data set.

A. I and II

B. II and III

C. III only

D. None of the above.

8. If the median of the data set is 14, what could be the value of x?   Set: 13, 92, 0, 15, 6, x

A. –10

B. 14

C. 15

D. 13

1. A   To answer this question, you must calculate both the median and mean of the set: 23, 75, 16, 91, 100.

Median: First put the numbers in order and then find the middle number:
16, 23, 75, 91, 100. The middle number is 75, so that is the median.

Mean: Add the numbers and divide that sum by 5.
$23 + 75 + 16 + 91 + 100 = 305$
$305 \div 5 = 61$
Mean $= 61$

Median is greater than the mean for this data set.

2. D   Let's go through each measure and see what would happen.

I. mean: The mean is the average of the numbers. If each number changes by 5 lbs, the average will also change by 5 lbs.

II. median: The median is the middle value. If each value changes by 5, so does the middle value. Therefore, the median changes.

III. mode: The mode is the value that appears most often. If all values change by 5, so will that value. Therefore, the mode changes.

Mean, Median, and Mode change.

3. B   Let's calculate the mean, median, and mode for the data set: 16, 16, 24, 96, and 3

I. mean: To calculate the mean, add all the numbers and divide by 5 since there are 5 numbers in the set.
mean $= (16 + 16 + 24 + 96 + 3) \div 5 = 155 \div 5 = 31$
16 is not the mean.

II. median: To find the median, order the set and find the middle number.
3, 16, 16, 24, 96
The middle number in the set is 16. Therefore, 16 is the median.

III. mode: To determine the mode, find the number that appears most often in the set. 16 appears twice and is the only number that appears more than once. Therefore, 16 is the mode.

16 is the median and mode. II and III.

4. D   The data set is missing an element, let's call it n.

Place the rest of the elements in order: 76, 80, 81, 85, 92.

The median is the middle element in a list. If there are an even number of elements in your set, the median is the average of the two middle elements. In this case, when the missing element is included there will be 6 elements, and the median must be the average of the two middle terms.

The median is 83, which is the average of 81 and 85. Therefore, 81 and 85 must remain the middle elements. The only way this can happen is if the missing element is greater than or equal to 85.

90 is the only answer that fits this requirement.

5. B The possible values of n are 11, 13, and 17 (15 is not prime).

To find the median, put the numbers in order and take the middle number. 11, 13, 17. Median = 13.

Mean is found by adding the numbers and dividing by 3. $(11+13+17)/3 = {}^{41}\!/_3 = 13\,{}^2\!/_3$.

Mode is the number that appears the most frequently. However, each number is used exactly once.

Mean is greater than the median.

---

6. B Let's calculate each of the statistical measures of the following set: 7, –3, 11, –4, 8, 2, 9, 2

A: Mean: Mean is the average of the data. It is found by adding all the elements and dividing by the number of elements.
Mean = (7 + –3 + 11 + –4 + 8 + 2 + 9 + 2) ÷ 8 = 4

B: Median: The median is the middle value when the numbers are in order. First, order the numbers from smallest to largest.
–4, –3, 2, 2, 7, 8, 9, 11
Since this data set has an even number of elements, you must find the average of the two middle numbers, 2 and 7.
Median = (2 + 7) ÷ 2 = 4.5

C: Mode: The mode is the element that appears most often. In this case, 2 is the only number that appears more than once.
Mode = 2

Median is the largest.

---

7. C I. The median and mean of a data set are always different.
You could have a set where the mean and median are the same value. For example, the set: 2, 3, 4 has a mean of 3 and a median of 3. I – False.

II. The median of a data set is always a member of the set.
If there are an even number of elements in a set, the median may not be a member of the set. For example, the set: 2, 4, 6, 8, the median is the average of the two middle numbers 4 and 6. The median of that set is 5, but 5 is not a member of the set. II – False.

III. There can be more than one mode in a data set.
The mode of a set is the element that appears most often. You could have multiply elements that appear the same number of times, therefore having multiple modes. For example: the set: 1, 2, 2, 3, 4, 4, 5, 6 has two modes: 2 and 4 since they both appear twice. III is true.

III is the only one that is true.

---

8. C To find the median of a data set, order the elements, and then find the middle element. If there are an even number of elements in a set, then the median is the average of the two middle numbers. In this case, there are 6 elements, so the median must be the average of the two middle values.

First order the set with the values you know: 0, 6, 13, 15, 92

If 14 is the median, it must be the average of the two middle numbers. If 13 and 15 are the two middle numbers, then 14 would be the median. X must be greater than or equal to 15, so that the middle numbers are 13 and 15.

The only answer choice that would make the median equal to 14 is 15.

Measures of Dispersion

Several statistical measures describe how data is dispersed within a series. Range, variance, and standard deviation are commonly used measures of dispersion.

Range

The range of a set of numbers is their spread. This is the easiest measure of dispersion to calculate. To find the range, subtract the smallest number from the largest number.

Example 1: Find the range of 1, 45, 5, 9, 73.   Range = 73 – 1 = 72.

Example 2: Find the range of –27, 32, 58, 96.   Range = 96 – (–27) = 123

Standard Deviation & Variance

Standard deviation is a measure of the dispersion of a set of data from its mean, or how spread out the data is. For example, if every student on an exam scored between 80 and 85, the standard deviation would be smaller than if some students got below 20, and others got perfect 100s. The better the data matches the mean, the smaller the standard deviation. If data has a standard deviation of 0, that means you can easily predict all the data points as they do not vary from the mean. Data with high standard deviations means there is a lot of variation in the data.

On a graph, standard deviation can be thought of as the distances of all the data points from the line of best fit. The better the line fits the data, the smaller the standard deviation. If all the data is directly on the line of best fit (in other words, equal to the mean), the standard deviation is 0.

Variance is another measure for finding the amount of variation among the data points. In fact, if you were performing calculations to solve for the standard deviation, it would be equal to the square root of the variance.

Correlation

Correlation is a statistic that measures how closely one variable tracks with another. The range of the correlation statistic is –1 to 1.

Correlations close to +1 indicate that variables track very closely with one another. For example, the amount of time studied and test scores are likely to be positively correlated. A correlation of 1 is a perfect correlation. For example, the length of a side of a square and the perimeter of the square are perfectly correlated. If length goes up, the perimeter goes up.

Correlations close to –1 indicate that variables track inversely. For example, grades and time watching television might be negatively correlated.

A correlation close to 0 means that there is no apparent relationship between the variables.

Note that correlation does not necessarily imply causation. For example, a child's grades in school might be correlated to the number of books in her house, which does not mean that buying more books will directly affect a child's grades.

Measures of Dispersion: Practice

1. If you have the highest score on a math test, which measure would you need to determine the lowest score on the test?

    A. Mean

    B. Median

    C. Mode

    D. Range

2. Find x if the range of the data set is 16.   Set: x, 2.3, 9.8, 12.9

   A. –16

   B. 16

   C. –3.1

   D. 3.1

3. You obtained the salaries of ten of your friends who graduated college with you. Nine had salaries in between $50,000 to $70,000 per year. One very successful friend was making over $250,000 per year. Which of the following statistical measures is least affected by the outlier?

   A. Range

   B. Median

   C. Mean

   D. Standard Deviation

4. Which of the following sets of numbers has a higher standard deviation?
Set A = 5, 5, 5, 5, 6, 16
Set B = 8, 9, 10, 10, 11, 12

   A. Set A

   B. Set B

   C. Equal

   D. Not enough information

5. If the range of a set of test scores is 85 and median 75, which of the following could be the set of all test scores?

   A. 50, 85, 75, 80, 55

   B. 75, 10, 95, 55

   C. 75, 15, 85, 90, 75

   D. 85, 70, 20, 80, 5, 90

6. If you own a mutual fund, and the standard deviation of the return increases while the mean stays the same, what happens to the fund's risk? (A return is a measure of how much the mutual fund has increased or decreased in value over any given time period.)

   A. increases

   B. decreases

   C. stays the same

   D. don't know

7. Adding a zero to a set may change which of the following:
I. median
II. mean
III. range

   A. I only

   B. I and III

   C. II and III

   D. I, II, and III

8. At the end of a growing season, a farmer measures the amount of a certain crop produced. He then compares that amount with amounts he has produced in past years. Then, he finds some historical information about average temperatures for each of the past growing season. Finally, the farmer calculates the correlation between temperature and the amount of crops produced. He calculates a correlation of –93%.

What can be said about the relationship between crop production and temperature?

A. As the temperature increases, the crop production tends to increase.

B. As the temperature decreases, the crop production tends to decrease.

C. As the temperature decreases, the crop production tends to increase.

D. The temperature has no relationship to crop production.

Measures of Dispersion: Answer Explanations

1. D   A: Mean. The mean is the average of all the numbers. Only knowing the highest score and the mean would not help you find the lowest score. Eliminate A.

B: Median. This is the middle number if you order the numbers. Therefore, knowing the median would only help you find the middle score not the lowest score. Elimiante B.

C: Mode. This is the score that appears most often. This can be any score from the highest, to the lowest, to any score in between. This would not help. Eliminate C.

D: Range. This is the highest score minus the lowest score. Therefore, if you knew the range and the highest score, you could easily find the lowest score. This is the answer.

2. C   To find the range, subtract the largest number from the smallest number.
Range = 12.9 – smallest = 16.
The smallest number that is given in the set, 2.3, is too large to give a range of 16, therefore x must be the smallest number.
12.9 – x = 16
x = –3.1

3. B   As you are dealing with a rather small data set of just 10 data points, an outlier can drastically affect the statistical measures. Let's analyze each answer and use the following sample data to help with the analysis.
Sample: 55,000; 55,000; 55,000; 60,000; 60,000; 60,000; 65,000; 65,000; 65,000; 260,000

A. Range: If the outlier was not part of the data set, then the range would be at a maximum of $20,000 as the remaining friends' salaries were between $50,000 to $70,000. In this case, the range is going to be much higher. For instance, in the above sample data the range is 260,000 – 55,000 = 205,000. The range is greatly affected by the outlier.

B. Median: The median is found by ordering the data points and finding the middle value. Regardless of the outlier, the median will be between $50,000 to $70,000. For instance, in the sample data above, the median is $60,000. This statistical measure is not greatly affected by a single outlier.

C. Mean: The mean is calculated by adding all the data points and dividing by the number of data points. Without the outlier, the mean would be between $50,000 to $70,000. However, with the outlier and the small data set, as in the sample data above, the mean will be much higher. For instance, the mean of the sample data is $80,000.

D. Standard Deviation: The standard deviation is measuring the spread of the data from the mean. As you have a data point that is extremely far from the mean, this would greatly increase the standard deviation.

4. A   The standard deviation measures how spread out the data is, or how far the data points lie from the mean.

In set A = 5 ,5, 5, 5, 6, 16, you can see that many of the terms are the same and therefore would not have a large variance. However, the data point 19 has a value far from the others and thus would increase the standard deviation drastically. If you calculated the mean of this data, it would be

Mean = (5 + 5 + 5 + 5 + 6 + 16)/6 = 42/6 = 7

You can see that each data point is different from the mean and that the 16 is quite far away.

In set B = 8, 9, 10, 10, 11, 12, you can see that all the terms are close together and there are no outliers. Let's calculate the mean of this data set.

Mean = (8 + 9 + 10 + 10 + 11 + 12) / 6 = 60 / 6 = 10

Now if you compare each data point to the mean, you see that the greatest spread is only 2 units away. Therefore, there is very little variance in the data and the standard deviation would be relatively low.

5. D   The range of a set is calculated by subtracting the lowest score from the highest score. The median is the middle number when the scores are put in order from lowest to highest. Below, the set of numbers for each answer choice is ordered from least to greatest and the range and median are given for each.

A. 50, 55, 75, 80, 85. Range = 85 − 50 = 35. The median is 75.

B. 10, 55, 75, 95. Range = 95 − 10 = 85. Since there are an even number of numbers, you take the average of the middle numbers. Median = (55+75)/2 = 65

C. 15, 75, 75, 85, 90. Range = 90 − 15 = 75. Median = 75.

D. 5, 20, 70, 80, 95, 90. Range = 90 − 5 = 85. Median = (70+80)/2 = 75.

6. A   If the mean of the return remains the same, that means the average doesn't change. If the standard deviation increases, that means that the variability in the return increases. Therefore, the risk increases.

7. D   Let's go through each measure to see how adding a zero could affect the value.

I. median: Adding a zero could change the median since there are now more numbers in the set and the number that used to be in the middle will no longer be there.
Example: The set 2, 4, 6 has a median of 4.
Add a zero to the set: 0, 2, 4, 6, now the median is 3 (average of the 2 middle numbers). Median changes

II. mean: Adding a zero to a set could change the mean since the number of elements in the set is changed.
Example: the set: 3, 4, 5 has a mean = (3 + 4 + 5) ÷ 3 = 4
Add a zero to the set: 0, 3, 4, 5, mean = (0 + 3 + 4 + 5) ÷ 4 = 3. Mean changes

III. range: Adding a zero to the set could change the range since the smallest or largest number may change.
Example: the set 3, 4 , 5 has a range = 5 − 3 = 2
Add a zero to the set: 0, 3, 4, 5 and the range = 5 − 0 = 5. Range changes.

8. C   The correlation is strongly negative at −93%, since the limits of the correlation are −100% to 100%. Sometimes it is easier to convert the percents to decimals. If so, the correlations are always between −1 and 1 and in this case the correlation is −0.93. A negative correlation means that when one variable goes up, the other variable tends to go down (and vice versa).

Therefore, as the temperature decreases, the crop production tends to increase.

You already reviewed graphs and charts in the first section of this chapter. This section will cover a few additional graphical representations of statistical concepts.

Frequency & Cumulative Distributions

A frequency distribution is an organization of raw data. Often, data is grouped into bins, and the frequency of occurrence is counted for each bin. The first two columns in the table below show an example of a frequency distribution. It shows the number of houses sold per day, where each day is a bin. The third column shows the cumulative distribution, which indicates the total number of houses sold up to that day of the week.

Day of the Week	Number of Houses Sold	Cumulative Number of Houses Sold
Monday	2	2
Tuesday	1	3
Wednesday	2	5
Thursday	1	6
Friday	4	10

Histograms are used to show the distribution of a data. They are created like bar graphs, where the x–axis contains the bins from a frequency distribution and the y–axis represents the number of items in each bin. To the right is an example of a histogram which shows the data from the table above.

Percentile Ranks

A percentile rank is the proportion of scores in a frequency distribution that a score is less than or equal to. You calculate the percentile rank by counting the number of occurrences less than or equal to a given score. Then, divide that result by the total number of occurrences in the sample.

Day of the Week	Number of Houses Sold	Percentile Rank
Monday	2	2/10 = 20%
Tuesday	1	3/10 = 30%
Wednesday	2	5/10 = 50%
Thursday	1	6/10 = 60%
Friday	4	10/10 = 100%

The median statistic is the 50th percentile value.

Another way to approach calculating percentiles is to first order all your data points. Then, multiply the percentage by the number of data points, to find which data point would be equal to that percentile. For instance, use the following data points: the heights of students are 61 in, 64 in, 65 in, 65.5 in, 66 in, 66.5 in, 68 in, 68 in, 69 in, 70 in.. Note, the data points are already in order and there are 10 data points. Therefore, to find the height in the 50th percentile, multiply 10 by 50% = 5. So, the 5th data point, or 66 in, would be equal to the 50th percentile.

Probability Distributions

There are many probability distributions. Two of the most common are uniform and normal distributions.

A uniform distribution means that each value in the distribution has an equal opportunity of being selected. For example, the distribution of one six–sided die would be considered uniform, since each number has an equal likelihood of occurring.

A normal distribution has a familiar bell–shape curve. In a normal distribution, the numbers in the center have a higher likelihood of occurring than those at the tails (i.e. the right or left side).

Classifying probability distributions helps to get an idea quickly of what a distribution will be like. For instance, if you were told that choosing a lottery number in a game has a uniform distribution, you would instantly know that every value has the same likelihood of occurring, and there is no reason to choose one number over another. If you were told that test scores followed a normal distribution, you would know that the students received scores around the average and a few students received high scores and some low scores.

Regression Models and Curve Fitting

Regression attempts to model the relationship between one variable (i.e. the dependent variable) and one or more other variables (i.e. the independent variables). Regression is often used to attempt to predict future events based on history or an experiment.

A simple linear regression is often written in slope–intercept form, $y = mx + b$. Here, y is the dependent variable and x is the independent variable; b is the y–intercept.

Other types of regression can be used to fit data that has a curved relationship. For this type of data, a quadratic equation can be used instead of a linear equation.

One measure of the predictive capability of a regression is the r–squared. The r–squared statistic is a measure of how well a regression line approximates real data points. Simply square the statistic r, which is the correlation coefficient, to get r–squared.

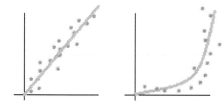

To the left, you can see two examples of regression lines. In the first graph, the data points are represented by the dots, and you can see that the data matches a linear regression model. Using this regression line, you can then predict future data points. The r–squared statistic and correlation would describe how well the data matches the line.

The second graph shows that the data points are more closely modeled with a quadratic equation. If a straight line were drawn through the data points, the correlation and r–squared statistics would be low, indicating that the model doesn't fit as well.

Graphical Representations of Statistical Concepts: Practice

1. What is the cumulative frequency on Wednesday?

Day of the Week	Number of Cars Sold
Monday	4
Tuesday	2
Wednesday	1
Thursday	3
Friday	5

A. 1

B. 4

C. 6

D. 7

2. A histogram of the age of cars is shown to the right. The mean age of cars is 7 years and the standard deviation is 2 years.

How many cars are within one standard deviation of the mean?

    A. 90

    B. 110

    C. 260

    D. 350

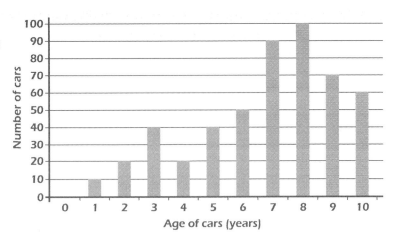

3. What type of visual representation would be most suitable for the following information? A student's science project data, recorded daily over 3 weeks, on the height of two plants that have been given different amounts of water.

    A. Pie Chart

    B. Bar Graph

    C. Line Graph

    D. Histogram

4. The graphs below show the distribution of test scores on the x-axis with the same scale for each graph. Which of the following sets of data has the greatest mean?

A.    B.    C. ⊢—————————   D.

5. The following are scores that were received on a Social Studies test: 82, 75, 62, 80, 91, 86, 71, 54, 61, 92, 78, 68, 89, 85, 88, 100, 94, 76, 72, 76. The scores are also represented using the score intervals 50–54, 55–59, ..., 95–100 in the histogram:

What score is at the 85th percentile?

    A. 85

    B. 88

    C. 89

    D. 91

6. The entire student population in the high school senior class of 400 took a math test. Marissa was ranked 40th out of the senior class while Isabella scored at the 92nd percentile. How much higher is Isabella's rank?

    A. 52

    B. 32

    C. 16

    D. 8

7. A local organization is trying to determine whether to run its annual festival outdoors or indoors. Based on data from similar regions, a simulation was run on how many days of the week it might rain in the particular month.

What is the likelihood that it will rain 3 or more days in the month?

A. 0.6%

B. 4%

C. 6%

D. 25%

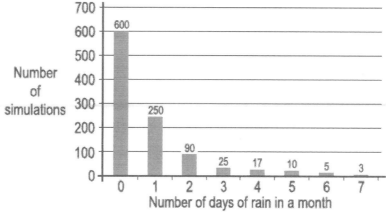

Number of simulations

Number of days of rain in a month

8. If the likelihood of a sale is the same for any day of the week, what is the expected number of sales on a day?

Day of the Week	Number of Houses Sold
Monday	6
Tuesday	5
Wednesday	1
Thursday	3
Friday	5

A. 3

B. 4

C. 5

D. 12

Graphical Representations of Statistical Concepts: Answer Explanations

1. D The cumulative frequency is the frequency up to and including that bin for the frequency distribution. Therefore, the cumulative frequency on Wednesday is the total number of cars sold up to that day of the week. $4 + 2 + 1 = 7$

2. D With a mean of 7 and a standard deviation of 2 years, the range of plus or minus one standard deviation is [5, 9]. We want to total the number of cars between 5 to 9 years inclusive.

The total number of cars is $40 + 50 + 90 + 100 + 70 = 350$

3. C The data from this project is continuous. In other words, if the first plant was measured at 8 inches on day 3 and 10 inches on day 4, we can assume that it grew from 8 to 10 inches between those times. This type of continuous data, which is measured over time, is best represented with a line graph. In this case, the x–axis would be time, the y–axis would be the height of the plant, and two lines would be used to represent the two plants. As the plant growth continues between the data points, a line graph is better than a bar graph (choice B). The information presented does not add to 100%, so a pie graph would not make sense (choice A). This data does not fall into ranges, so a histogram would not work (choice D).

4. B The problem notes that the distribution graphs all have the same scale. Therefore, the graph that shows data with the greatest mean will be the graph that has the mean farthest to the right. The mean is the average of all the data points, so the greater the data points, the greater the mean.

A. The mean of this data set will be less than the half way point on the graph. There are more data points less than half.

B. The mean of this data set will be greater than the half way point on the graph. There are more data points greater than half. This has the greatest mean.

C. The mean of this data set will be equal to the half way point as all the data is evenly distributed.

D. The mean of this data set will be less than the half way point on the graph.

5. D   When solving a question involving finding the percentiles, you must first order your data points.

54, 61, 62, 68, 71, 72, 75, 76, 76, 78, 80, 82, 85, 86, 88, 89, 91, 92, 94, 100

Next, figure out how many data points you are dealing with. In this case, we have 20 scores.

Finally, simply multiply the percentile as a percent by the number of data points. This will give you the data point that is at that percentile.

85% x 20 = 0.85 x 20 = 17

Thus, the 17th data point will be at the 85th percentile. Count out 17 data points from the start. The score of 91 is the 85th percentile.

In addition, using the histogram, you can count out 17 data points on the histogram from lowest to highest noting the number of scores in each interval. The interval 50–54 has 1 score, the interval 55–59 has no scores, the interval 60–64 has 2 points, the interval 65–69 has 1 score, the interval 70–74 has 3 scores, the interval 75–79 has 4 scores, the interval 80–84 has 2 scores, and the interval 85–89 has 3 scores. At this point there are 16 scores recorded in the score intervals and the next score, the 17th score, which is the 85th percentile, would be recorded in the interval 90–94. This 17th score is a 91.

6. D   Isabella scored in the 92nd percentile. This means that 92% of the class is less than or equal to her score. Therefore, if you take 92% of 400, you will calculate where Isabella falls in her class.

92% x 400 = 0.92 x 400 = 368

Therefore, Isabella is better than 368 students. Subtract that from 400.   400 – 368 = 32.

So, Isabella is ranked 32nd out of the entire group of 400 students.
Since Marissa ranked 40th, Isabella is 8 rankings ahead of her.

7. C   First, we need to determine the total number of simulations run by adding the numbers from each bar:

600 + 250 + 90 + 25 + 17 + 10 + 5 + 3 = 1000 total simulations

Since we need the probability of 3 or more days of rain, add the numbers from bins 3 and above, then divide by 1000: (25 + 17 + 10 + 5 + 3)/1000 = 0.06 or 6%

Or, add the numbers for 0, 1, and 2 days, and divide by 1000. Then, subtract the number from 100%.
(600 + 250 + 90)/1000 = 0.94 or 94%
100% – 94% = 6%

8. B   Since the likelihood is the same on each day, you can find the expected value by averaging the number of houses sold on each day.

(6 + 5 + 1 + 3 + 5)/5 = 20/5 = 4

The expected number of houses sold on a day is 4.

A more involved way to think about the expected value, is that the expected value is the sum of each occurrence multiplied by its probability. Since the likelihood is the same in each, the probability is always 1/5. The expected value is

6(1/5) + 5(1/5) + 1(1/5) + 3(1/5) + 5(1/5) = (6 + 5 + 1 + 3 + 5)/5 = 20/5 = 4

1. Which pie chart best reflects the data?

Monthly Finances
Rent $1500
Food $500
Entertainment $1000
Car $500

A.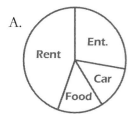

B.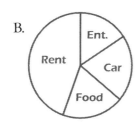

C.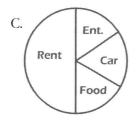

D.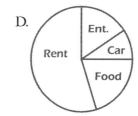

2. The following is a list of house prices for a given area. What is the best way to describe the average house price to a family interested in purchasing there?

$750,000	$595,000
$10,000,000	$800,000
$830,000	$840,000

A. Range

B. Median

C. Mean

D. Mode

3. On Sophie's report card, there are at least as many A's as B's, and at least as many A's as C's. She has no D's or F's and she hopes these grades make her family proud. Which of the following statements is true about the grades on Sophie's report card?

A. She has at least as many B's as C's.

B. She has the same number of B's and C's.

C. She has at least as many A's as B's and C's combined.

D. At least one third of the grades on her report card are A's.

4. A young child picks a number of balls out of a large bin. The chosen balls are then put back in the bin after selection. The colors of the chosen balls are, in order, Blue, Green, Red, Red, Green, Red, Green, Blue, Red, Green.

If the child picks 60 additional balls, how many Red balls would be expected to be chosen out of the 60 additional balls?

A. 4

B. 20

C. 24

D. 28

5. The following are student's test scores. Which student is at the 60th percentile?

George = 73	Brad = 59	Michael = 63	Steve = 71
Sandra = 52	William = 86	Patricia = 89	Sophie = 90
Marissa = 78	Joseph = 62	Chris = 69	Cyndi = 51
Richard = 91	Terry = 94	Kate = 82	

A. Chris

B. Marissa

C. George

D. Kate

6. What can be said about the following statement?
The area of a square is greater than the perimeter of the square if the length of the sides are whole numbers.

A. Always true.

B. Sometimes true.

C. Never true.

D. Not enough information.

7. If an even number is multiplied by an odd number and then added to an odd number, the result will be:

A. Even

B. Odd

C. Zero

D. Not enough information.

8. Find a counterexample to the following scenario.
n is a prime number. The square of (n + 1) is always even.

A. n = 4

B. n = 7

C. n = 1

D. n = 2

9. Given are two non-parallel lines, both intersected by a third line as shown in the diagram below.

Proof: $\angle$ b $\ne$ $\angle$ c

1. $\angle$ b = $\angle$ a
2.   The two lines are not parallel.
3.   Therefore, $\angle$ a $\ne$ $\angle$ c
4.   If $\angle$ a $\ne$ $\angle$ c and $\angle$ b = $\angle$ a, then $\angle$ b $\ne$ $\angle$ c

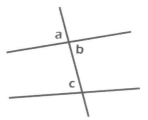

What is this proof an example of?

A. Inductive reasoning

B. Deductive reasoning

C. Hypothesizing

D. Generalizing

10. Assuming that every order includes one sandwich, one bag of chips, and one drink, how many different combinations of lunch orders are possible for 5 types of sandwiches, 4 types of chips, and 6 different drinks?

    A. 15

    B. 26

    C. 60

    D. 120

11. A flight will only takeoff if there are enough customers and if the weather is good. Based on the tree diagram below, calculate the probability that the flight will take off.

    A. 45%

    B. 56%

    C. 70%

    D. 80%

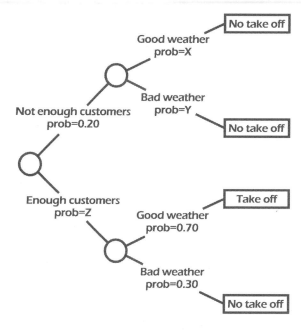

12. Of City High's varsity athletes, there are 30 that play football and there are three sports which City High is offering this season: football, soccer, and baseball. You know that 6 play only football and soccer, 5 play only baseball and soccer, 3 play only football and baseball, and 3 play all three sports. How many athletes play only football?

    A. 13

    B. 16

    C. 18

    D. 24

13. Which of the following is likely to be the correlation between the heights and weights of students at a school?

    A. –0.5

    B. 0.9

    C. 1

    D. 2.5

14. Which of the following distribution graphs shows data with the smallest standard deviation?

A.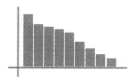

B.

C.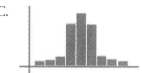

D.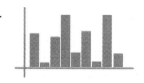

15. If you roll 2 dice, what is the probability that the numbers rolled will have a sum of 10?

    A. 5/18

    B. 1/36

    C. 1/18

    D. 1/12

16. The statement "If Sandra finishes her report, she will get extra credit" is true, which other statement must be true?

    A. If Sandra receives extra credit, she finished her report.

    B. If Sandra does not finish her report, she will not receive extra credit.

    C. If Sandra does not receive extra credit, she did not finish her report.

    D. Sandra received extra credit because she finished her report.

17. The mean of your 5 test scores for the semester is 82, and you know that your scores for the first four tests were 84, 72, 98, and 86. What did you score on that last test?

    A. 68

    B. 70

    C. 82

    D. 85

18. There is a bag with 5 green marbles, 2 red marbles, and 6 yellow marbles. If you reach into the bag and take out two marbles without replacing, what is the probability that both are green?

    A. 25/169

    B. 5/26

    C. 5/39

    D. 9/25

19. The graph below shows the stock value of a company for the past 9 years. During which years did the company have the greatest increase in value?

    A. Between years 1 and 2.

    B. Between years 3 and 4.

    C. Between years 7 and 8.

    D. Between years 8 and 9.

20. Each of the numbers in a normally distributed data set is added to the number 10. How does this transformation affect the mean, median, and the standard deviation of the frequency distribution curve?

    A. The mean stays the same, but the median and standard deviation increase by 10.

    B. The median stays the same, but the mean and standard deviation increase by 10.

    C. The standard deviation stays the same, but the mean and median increase by 10.

    D. The mean, median, and standard deviation all increase by 10.

1. A   Pie charts should represent the data proportionately. The total amount spent per month is $3500. Rent is slightly less than half of the month spending, therefore, rent should take up slightly less than half the pie. This is only true in answers A and B, therefore eliminate C and D.

Next, we see that entertainment should have twice as large a slice of the pie as both food and car. In answer choice A this is true.

2. B   Notice that the data set has an outlier, or a data point whose value is very different than the rest of the sample. The outlier is the $10,000,000 home. Let's see how this affects each of the measures.
Range: The range does not describe the average of a set, only its spread. Therefore, this would not be useful.
Median: The median of this set is $815,000. This would give the family a good indication of the average house price.
Mean: The mean house price is $2,302,500. This is not a good description of the average house price since it was obviously affected greatly by the outlier.
Mode: There is no data point that occurs more than once, eliminating the usefulness of the mode as a descriptor.

3. D   Let's examine the question stem before reviewing each answer choice.
There are 5 possible grades: A, B, C, D, or F.
We are told that she has no D's or F's.
She has at least as many A's as B's. Thus, the number of A's is greater than or equal to the number of B's.
She has at least as many A's as C's. Thus, the number of A's is greater than or equal to the number of C's.

A. She has at least as many B's as C's: We know how the number of A's compares to B's and C's. However, we do not know how B's and C's compare. For instance, you could have the following scenarios: 5 A's, 4 B's, and 3 C's or 5 A's, 1 B's, and 3 C's. Both of those scenarios are valid for the problem statement but show that you can not make any conclusions about how the number of B's and C's compare.

B. She has the same number of B's as C's: For the same reasons stated above in the explanation for answer choice A, we can not say that this statement is true.

C. She has at least as many A's as B's and C's combined: Again, see explanation above. There are possible scenarios that make the original statements true where there are at least as many A's as B's and C's combined and there are possible scenarios that the make the original statements true where there are not at least as many A's as B's and C's.

D. At least one third of the grades on her report card are A's: We know that Sophie received only A's, B's, and C's. We also know that the number of A's is greater than or equal to the number of B's and that the number of A's is greater than or equal to the number of C's. If they were all equal, than the number of A's would be exactly one third of the grades of the report card. Therefore, we know that the number of A's is equal to or greater than one third of the grades. Another way to say this is that at least one third of the grades are A's. This is correct.

4. C   We are not told how many of each color balls there are in the bag. However, we can find the experimental probability of choosing a Red ball from the small sample that was given. The child picked 10 balls and 4 of them were red. Therefore, the experimental probability of choosing a Red ball is 4/10.
Now, the question asks the expected number of Red balls to be chosen out of the additional 60 balls that will be picked from the bag. We multiply the probability of choosing a Red ball by the total number of balls to be chosen to get the expected value.
4/10 x 60 = 24.   24 Red balls

5. B   First, put the scores in order:

Cyndi = 51, Sandra = 52, Brad = 59, Joseph = 62, Michael = 63, Chris = 69, Steve = 71, George = 73, Marissa = 78, Kate = 82, William = 86, Patricia = 89, Sophie = 90, Richard = 91, Terry = 94

To find the 60th percentile, multiply the number of scores by 60%.

$15 \times 60\% = 15 \times 0.60 = 9$

Thus, the student at the 60th percentile is the student with the 9th highest score, which is Marissa.

6. B   When presented with a problem like this where the answer is not obvious, try a few numbers to understand how the area and perimeter compare with different side lengths.

You should always try the end values to see if they are exceptions to the pattern. In this case, try the smallest possible value. We are told that the lengths of the sides are whole numbers, and the smallest possible whole number that is a possible side length is 1.

Side: 1, Area: 1, Perimeter: 4
Side: 2, Area: 4, Perimeter: 8
Side: 3, Area: 9, Perimeter: 12

From the first few values tested, the perimeter is greater than the area and the statement is false. Now, try a number that is completely different to the ones tested. For instance, try a rather large number.
Side: 100, Area: 10000, Perimeter: 400
As you can see, in this case the area is much larger than perimeter.

Therefore, the statement is sometimes true.

7. B   An even number multiplied by an odd number will always be even. The reason is that an even number has 2 as a factor, and if you multiply a number with 2 as a factor, the product will also have 2 as a factor. Therefore, the product will be even.

Now, we will take the even number and add it to an odd number. An odd number is just one more than any even number. Therefore, even + odd = even + even + 1.

Two even numbers added will always give you an even number since both numbers have 2 as a factor, their sum will also have 2 as a factor. So, even + even = even.

even + odd = even + even + 1 = even + 1 = odd
Result will always be odd.

8. D   Let's first remember the definition of a prime number. It is a number whose only factors are itself and 1. Now, let's examine each answer choice.

A. n = 4: This breaks the first statement that n is a prime number. Therefore, eliminate answer A.

B. n = 7: n, which equals 7 in this case, is a prime number. n + 1 = 8. The square of 8 is 64. 64 is even. This is an example, not a counterexample.

C. n = 1: n, which equals 1 in this case, is not a prime number. n + 1 = 2. The square of 2 is 4. 4 is even. This is not a counterexample.

D. n = 2: n, which equals 2 in this case, is a prime number. n + 1 = 3. The square of 3 is 9. 9 is odd. This is a counterexample and proves that the statement is false.

9. B   This is a proof that uses deductive reasoning by building step by step until a conclusion is reached. It is a valid proof showing that the two angles are not equal based on information stated in the problem. It uses a series of facts to draw a conclusion. This is deductive reasoning.

10. D   The counting principle states that to determine the total number of possible outcomes, multiply the number of ways each event can occur.

In this problem, there are 5 types of sandwiches, 4 types of chips, and 6 different drinks.
To find the number of possible outcomes, multiply 5 x 4 x 6 = 120
There are 120 different lunch combinations.

11. B   Based on the tree, the flight will take off only if there are enough customers and the weather is good.

The probability of enough customers is 1 – prob(not enough) = 1 – 0.20 = 0.80. This is prob = Z on the diagram.

To find the probability of having enough customers and good weather, multiply the individual probabilities.
0.80 x 0.70 = 0.56.
Multiply 0.56 times 100 to get a percentage of 56%.

12. C   The easiest approach to solving this problem is with the use of a Venn Diagram.
Start with the innermost combination – those who play all three sports. Put a 3 in the area that all three circles overlap.

Then, move on to the combinations of two sports each.

6 play only football and soccer. Put a 6 in the area of those students who play football and soccer only.
5 play only baseball and soccer. Put a 5 in the area of baseball and soccer overlapping.
3 play only football and baseball. Put a 3 in the area with football and baseball overlapping.

Now that we have filled out the Venn Diagram with information from the problem, we have to solve for the missing piece of information.

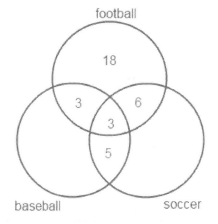

The question is asking for those students who only play football. We know that 30 students total play football. In the football circle now, we have 3, 3, and 6 for a total of 12 students. These 12 students play football and at least one other sport. To reach 30 students total, we must subtract the 12 students that play football and another sport and that leaves 18 students who play only football.

13. B   Correlations are only calculated on a range of –1 to 1. Therefore, you can quickly eliminate answer D as that is not a possible correlation.

If we think about the heights and weights of student, we would note that as height goes up it is likely that weight goes up also. In other words, taller students are likely to be heavier than shorter students. However, we also know that this is not a perfect correlation, as there may be tall, thin students who are not very heavy. Therefore, heights and weights are likely to be positively correlated, but not equal to 1.

A negative correlation would mean that as one variable goes up the other goes down. This is not the case with height and weight. Eliminate A.

A correlation of 1 would mean that height and weight are perfectly correlated and as one goes up the other also goes up. This is not always the case. Eliminate C.

A correlation of 0.9 shows a positive correlation and fits our assumptions about the data. This makes sense as the correlation between the heights and weights of students. Answer B is correct.

14. C   The standard deviation is a measure of how disperse a data is from its mean. Therefore, a data set with a small standard deviation would have data points very close to the mean. Let's examine each answer choice.

A. This data does seem to follow a pattern, but the data is not centered around a mean. This data set would have a rather large standard deviation.

B. Again, this data follows a pattern, but the data is not centered around the mean. In fact, the data is evenly spread out among all possible values. As the data is spread out, this set has a large standard deviation.

C. This graph shows a data set that is centered around the mean. The majority of the data points are at a certain value and as you get further away from the mean, there are fewer and fewer data points. Therefore, the standard deviation of this data would be small.

D. This data is spread out all over the place with no consistency and pattern, thereby resulting in a high standard deviation.

15. D   Probability is the number of favorable outcomes divided by the total number of outcomes. We must calculate how many favorable outcomes and how many total outcomes.

The number of favorable outcomes is how many ways you can get a sum of 10 if you roll 2 dice. Let's list out the possible ways: 4 and 6, 5 and 5, 6 and 4
3 possible ways

The number of total outcomes can be found by multiplying how many possible outcomes on the first die multiplied by how many outcomes for the 2nd die.
$6 \times 6 = 36$

Probability $= 3/36 = 1/12$

16. C   This type of question poses a common structure for logic statements.   If A, then B.
In this case, we are told if Sandra finishes her report, then she will receive extra credit.
Let's go through each answer choice to see which must also be true based on that statement being true.

A. If Sandra received extra credit, she finished her report.
This statement is not true. In logic, you can not take a statement, "If A, then B" and turn it into "If B, then A" as it would not necessarily hold true. For instance, in this case, Sandra could have received extra credit in another way. We have no knowledge from the original statement that the only way to obtain extra credit was by completing the report. Therefore, we can not say that this statement must be true.

B. If Sandra does not finish her report, she will not receive extra credit.
This statement is also not necessarily true for the same reasons as the explanation for answer choice A. You can not turn the statement, "If A, then B" into "If not A, then not B". As noted above, there may be other ways to obtain extra credit.

C. If Sandra does not receive extra credit, she did not finish her report.
This statement is true. The fancy name for this statement is the contrapositive, which is always true. If we know that "If A, then B" then we know "If not B, then not A". We know that if Sandra finishes her report, she will definitely receive extra credit. This was clearly stated in the original statement. If she does not receive extra credit, there is no way she could have finished her report, otherwise there would be a contradiction. This statement is true.

D. Sandra received extra credit because she finished her report.
This statement may be true, but not necessarily. We do now know whether or not Sandra received extra credit or finished her report. We just know what would happen if she does finish her report. We can not make a definitive statement about Sandra's actions without further information.

17. B   If the mean or average of the 5 tests is 82, then you can calculate the total number of points that you got on all 5 tests by multiplying.

Total number of points on 5 tests = 5 x 82 = 410

You remember the scores on 4 of your tests, so find the total of those 4 tests.

Total number of points on 4 tests = 84 + 72 + 98 + 86 = 340

Find the score on the last test by subtracting your total points on 4 tests from your total points on all the tests.

Last test = 410 − 340 = 70.

18. C   Probability is the number of favorable outcomes over the total number of outcomes. To find the probability of multiple independent events, you multiply the probabilities of each of the individual events.

First, find the probability that the first marble drawn will be green, and then multiply that by the probability that the second marble drawn will be green.

For the first draw, there are 5 green marbles and a total of 13 marbles. The probability of drawing a green marble is 5/13.

For the second marble, there are only 12 marbles left, 4 of which are green. The probability of drawing a second green marble is 4/12, which reduces to 1/3.

The product of the two probabilities is the probability of drawing two green marbles in a row. 5/13 x 1/3 = 5/39

19. C   This question asks you to interpret a bar graph to determine during what years the company experienced growth. Even though there are no specific values listed on the y–axis, each unit on the y–axis is consistent. Therefore, you can determine the greatest increase.

Let's examine each answer choice.

A. Between years 1 and 2.
The stock went from 1 unit to 5 units. Therefore, an increase of 4 units during those years.

B. Between years 3 and 4.
The stock had a value of 0 in year 3 and a value of 4 units in year 4. Therefore, also an increase of 4 units during those years.

C. Between years 7 and 8.
The stock had a negative value in year 7 of −2 units and then increased to 3 units in year 8. The difference was 3 − (−2) = 5. An increase of 5 units.

D. Between years 8 and 9.
The stock increased just 2 units in those years.

20. C   In a normal distribution, adding a number simply shifts the mean. As the same number is added to every value, the mean will just increase by that amount.

In a normal distribution, the mean and median are identical. Therefore, if the same number is added to each data point, it will increase the median by that number.

You can think of the standard deviation as an indicator of the spread of the data – shifting every data point by the same amount will not change how much the data is spread.

7. Diagnostic Exam

1. Which scenario can be solved with the following expression? 2(7.5 ÷ 0.75)

A. You want to find the diagonal of a rectangle with width of 7.5 inches and height of 0.75 inches.

B. You want to find the total amount of time worked over two days, each 7.5 hours long, if you know that out of every hour, you had to work for 45 minutes and then take a 15 minute break.

C. You want to find the area of two triangles, each has a base of 7.5 and height of 0.75.

D. You want to know how many ¾ foot long pieces can be made from 2 long strings that are each 7 ½ feet long.

2. What is the distance between A and B on the number line?

A. 0.14

B. 0.15

C. 1.2

D. 7

3. Which of the following is true?
I. There are no even prime numbers.
II. The greatest common factor of 2 numbers will always be smaller than both numbers.
III. The least common multiple of 2 numbers will always be greater than both numbers.

A. I only

B. II and III

C. I, II, and III

D. None of the above.

4. If P^3 is an odd negative number, which of the following is an even positive number?

A. 2P

B. P^2

C. $4P^4$

D. Not enough information.

5. Order the following from least to greatest:
I. 3 ÷ ½
II. 3 x ½
III. ½ ÷ 3

A. I, II, III

B. III, II, I

C. III, I, II

D. II, III, I

6. The ratio of fiction to nonfiction books in a store is 4 to 5. If the store contains 810 books, how many are fiction?

    A. 360

    B. 450

    C. 648

    D. 720

7. You have a string of beads that starts with the following beads: Red, Yellow, Blue, and Green. This sequence continues throughout the entire string. What color is the 49th bead?

    A. Red

    B. Yellow

    C. Blue

    D. Green

8. Choose the best answer to replace the question mark.
The area of the circle is **?** times that of the triangle inscribed in it.

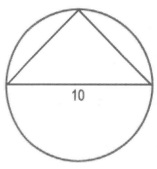

    A. π

    B. 2π

    C. 5π

    D. 10π

9. A line with a slope of 7 that passes through (12,44) has what x–value when y=100?

    A. –20

    B. –10

    C. 10

    D. 20

10. Patricia drove the first 120 miles of her trip at 40mph and the remaining 120 miles at 60mph, what was her average speed for the entire trip?

    A. 45 mph

    B. 48 mph

    C. 50 mph

    D. 52 mph

11. If 3y – 2 = 7, what does ($\frac{2}{3}$) y + 5 equal?

    A. $11\frac{1}{3}$

    B. 11

    C. 7

    D. 8 $\frac{2}{3}$

12. If the number 720 is written as a product of its prime factors in the form: ab^2c^4. Then what is the sum of a, b, and c?

    A. 10

    B. 19

    C. 25

    D. 27

13. In the figure below, AB = AC and angle ABC = 55°. What is the measure of angle ACD?

    A. 70°

    B. 110°

    C. 125°

    D. 155°

14. An electronics store owner buys products from the manufacturer and then marks them up 20%. For the Labor Day weekend, the store owner has a 10% off sale. What is the percent change from the manufacturer's price to the sales price?

    A. 8% increase

    B. 10% increase

    C. 12% increase

    D. 18% increase

15. At the same moment, two trains leave Chicago and New York. They move towards each other with constant speeds. The train from Chicago is moving at speed of 40 miles per hour, and the train from New York is moving at speed of 60 miles per hour. The distance between Chicago and New York is 1000 miles. How long after their departure will they meet? (hint: distance = rate x time)

    A. 10

    B. 15

    C. 17

    D. 20

16. Bob is buying supplies for his office. He has $60 to spend on pens and pencils. Each pen costs $3 and each pencil costs $1. Which graph represents his buying options?

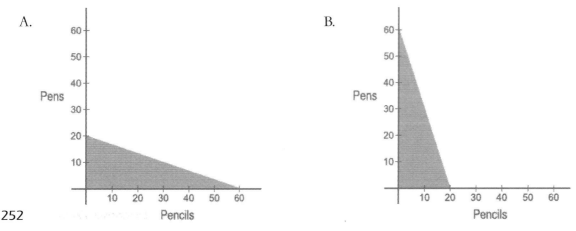

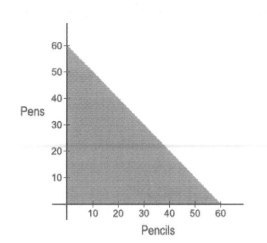

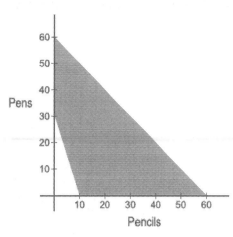

17. What does one circle equal?

A. –3

B. –1

C. 4

D. 7

$$\square + \square + \bigcirc + \bigcirc + \bigcirc + \bigcirc = 0$$

$$\square + \square + \square - \bigcirc = 7$$

18. Everyone in a group is being assigned a secret code of 3 characters. The first character must be a letter and the second and third are numbers which can not be the same. How many possible codes can be made?

A. 46

B. 126

C. 2340

D. 2600

19. There are 60 marbles in a bag. The probability of a marble being green or red is ⁵⁄₁₂, and there are 5 green marbles. How many red marbles are in the bag?

A. 5

B. 12

C. 20

D. 25

20. Phone plan T costs $25/month plus $0.10/minute and plan R is $10/month plus $0.25/minute. How many minutes of talking in one month would cost the same on either plan?

A. 10 minutes

B. 25 minutes

C. 100 minutes

D. 250 minutes

21. Steve reads 80 pages in 2 hours and 40 minutes. If Cassandra reads twice as fast as Steve, how long will it take her to read a 300 page book?

    A. 4 hours 40 minutes

    B. 5 hours

    C. 5 hours 20 minutes

    D. 5 hours 40 minutes

22. Which of the following CANNOT be true of the triangle?

    A. The hypotenuse equals 1000

    B. The side lengths add up to 20.

    C. Two of the angles are equal.

    D. One of the angles measures 60 degrees.

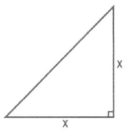

23. A rather clumsy researcher spilled coffee on one of the pages of his notebook and couldn't read one of his data points. He had already performed some statistical calculations. If the median of his data is 19 and the mean is greater than the median, what could be the missing element from the data points below?

18, 18, 19, 19, 21, ?

    A. 17

    B. 18

    C. 19

    D. 20

24. If you have a circle with radius r, then the area of the circle is equal to how many times the circle's circumference?

    A. 2r

    B. 4r

    C. r/2

    D. r/4

25. Which of the following best represents the area of an isosceles right triangle as a function of the length of the sides?

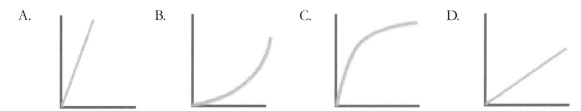

1. D To solve this problem, you must analyze and set up each answer choice to see which matches the expression. Also, it is generally nice to quickly solve the expression so that if you estimate or solve one of the answer choices you can see whether the answers align and the approach was different.

$2(7.5 \div 0.75) = 2(750 \div 75) = 2(10) = 20$

A. You want to find the diagonal of a rectangle with width of 7.5 inches and height of 0.75 inches.

If you use two adjacent sides of the rectangles and the diagonal of a rectangle, you will form a right triangle with the diagonal as the hypotenuse. Now, we are told the lengths of the sides of the rectangle, therefore we have the lengths of both sides of the right triangle and want to find its hypotenuse. We do this using the Pythagorean Theorem. $7.5^2 + 0.75^2 = c^2$. This equation is nothing like the one in the problem.

B. You want to find the total amount of time worked over two days, each 7.5 hours long, if you know that out of every hour, you had to work for 45 minutes and then take a 15 minute break.

In this scenario you want to find the total time worked. Therefore, you will multiply. First, multiply the number of days by the number of hours in each.

2 x 7.5. Next, you are told that you only work 45 minutes out of every hour, or $3/4 = 0.75$ of an hour. Thus, you want to multiply the total number of hours by the fraction of each that you worked. 2 x 7.5 x 0.75. Not the correct equation.

C. You want to find the area of two triangles, each has a base of 7.5 and height of 0.75.
The area of a triangle is found by multiplying 1/2 x base x height. In this case you have two triangles, so you would multiply:

2 x ½ x base x height = 1 x 7.5 x 0.75. Not the correct equation.

D. You want to know how many 3/4 foot long pieces can be made from 2 long strings that are each 7 ½ feet long.

You want to divide up long strings into $3/4 = 0.75$ foot long pieces. Therefore, to figure out how many pieces can be made from one string, divide the total length of the string by the length of each piece you want. $7.5 \div 0.75$. Next, you know that you have two strings, so multiply the number from each string by 2.

2 x (7.5 ÷ 0.75). This is our answer.

2. A First, determine the value of each space. Between 3.4 and 3.5, there are 5 spaces.

$3.5 - 3.4 = 0.1$
$0.1/5 = 0.02$

Each space is worth 0.02.

Now, let's determine the values of A and B.

A is one space, or 0.02, below 3.4.
$A = 3.4 - 0.02 = 3.38$.

B is one space above 3.5
$B = 3.5 + 0.02 = 3.52$.

The distance between A and B.
$B - A = 3.52 - 3.38 = 0.14$

3. D   Let's examine each option.

I. There are no even prime numbers.

This is not true. There is one even prime number, 2. The only factors of 2 are 2 and 1, and a prime number is a number whose only factors are itself and 1. I is false.

II. The greatest common factor of 2 numbers will always be smaller than both numbers.

The greatest common factor can equal one of the numbers. For instance, the GCF of 6 and 12 is 6, since 6 is a factor of both 12 and 6. Therefore, GCF is not always smaller since it can be equal. II is false.

III. The least common multiple of 2 numbers will always be greater than both numbers.

The least common multiple can equal one of the numbers. For instance, the LCM of 6 and 12 is 12, since 12 is a multiple of both 12 and 6. Therefore, LCM is not always bigger since it can be equal. III is false.

None of the above are true.

4. C   When there are variables in the question prompt and the answer choices, you could plug in a value for the variable and then try the same value in each answer choice to see which makes the statement true. Or, you could analyze the problem using the properties of the variable P in the problem.

Method 1: Plugging in a value for the variable

You have to choose a value that makes the original statement true and makes your calculations easy. So, the problem states P^3 is an odd negative number. Let's think of a value for P such that P^3 is odd and negative. Well, for P^3 to be negative, we know that P must be negative. Also, if P^3 is odd, then P must be odd. Let's try P as -3. If P is -3 then P^3 is $-3 \times -3 \times -3 = -27$. This works, therefore, lets keep P as -3.

Now, let's go through each answer choice to see which yields an even positive number.

A. $2P = 2(-3) = -6$. Not positive.

B. $P^2 = -3 \times -3 = 9$. Not even.

C. $4P^4 = 4 \times -3 \times -3 \times -3 \times -3 = 324$. Positive, even. Correct Answer.

Method 2: Analyze variables.

Let's reason about the problem while keeping the terms as variables.

The problem states that P^3 is odd and negative.

For P^3 to be negative, this means that P x P x P is negative. Well, the only way that the same number multiplied by itself 3 times will be negative is if the original number is negative. A positive times a positive times a positive will yield a positive, while a negative times a negative times a negative will be negative. Ok, we know that P must be negative.

For P^3 to be odd, this means that P x P x P is odd. The only way for the same number multiplied by itself 3 times will be odd is if the original number is odd. An even number times any other number will always be even as an even number has 2 as a factor and therefore the resulting product will also have 2 as a factor making it even. Therefore, we know that P must be odd, because if P was even then P^3 would be even. Ok, we know that P must be odd.

Now, let's examine each answer choice knowing that P is odd and negative and we want the answer to be even and positive.

A. 2P. A positive times a negative is negative. 2 x P will be negative. Not the answer.

B. P^2. An odd number multiplied by an odd number will be odd. Not the answer.

C. $4P^4$. Multiplying an even number, in this case 4, by any number will always yield an even number since 2 is a factor of 4 and thus will be a factor of the product. A negative times a negative times a negative times a negative will yield a positive number since we are multiplying an even number of negative numbers. So, this answer will give an even positive number. This is the answer.

D. We have enough information to reason the answer.

5. B   Let's solve each equation and then determine the order.

I. $3 \div \frac{1}{2} = 3 \times \frac{2}{1} = 6$

II. $3 \times \frac{1}{2} = \frac{3}{2} = 1\frac{1}{2}$

III. $\frac{1}{2} \div 3 = \frac{1}{2} \times \frac{1}{3} = \frac{1}{6}$

Order from least to greatest: $\frac{1}{6}$, $1\frac{1}{2}$, 6

III, II, I

6. A   If the ratio of fiction to nonfiction books is 4 to 5, then the fraction of fiction books in the store is $\frac{4}{9}$.

To determine the number of fiction books, multiply the fraction of fiction books in the store by the total number of books in the store.

$\frac{4}{9} \times 810 = 360$

360 Fiction books.

7. A   Every four beads, the pattern "Red, Yellow, Blue, Green" repeats. Therefore, the bead in any position that is divisible by 4 will be Green.

Since 48 is divisible by 4, the 48th bead will be green. The 49th bead must be red, since a red bead always comes after a green bead.

8. A   Calculate the area of the circle and the area of the triangle.

Circle: Area of a circle = $\pi \times r^2$. The radius of the circle is half the diameter, therefore the radius = 5.
Area of Circle = $\pi \times 5^2 = 25\pi$

Triangle: Area of a triangle = $\frac{1}{2} \times$ base $\times$ height. The base of the triangle is 10. The height of the triangle equals the radius of the circle = 5.
Area of Triangle = $\frac{1}{2} \times 10 \times 5 = 25$

To find how many times bigger the area of the circle is divide the areas.
Area of circle $\div$ Area of triangle = $25\pi \div 25 = \pi$

9. D   The slope of a line can be calculated by dividing the change in y by the change in x. The problem stated the slope = 7, one point is (12,44) and y=100. Therefore, use the slope equation to solve for x.

Slope = (Change in y)/(Change in x)
$7 = (100-44)/(x-12)$
$7 = 56/(x-12)$
$7(x-12) = 56$
$7x - 84 = 56$
$7x = 140,\ x = 20$

10. B   To find the average speed, divide the total number of miles by the total time.
Patricia drove the first 120 miles at 40 mph. Therefore, divide the distance by the speed to find the time it took. 120 miles $\div$ 40 mph = 3 hours

She drove the remaining 120 miles at 60 mph. Divide to find the time this part of the trip took.
120 miles $\div$ 60 mph = 2 hours

The total number of miles driven = 120 miles + 120 miles = 240 miles.

The total time for the trip = 3 hours + 2 hours = 5 hours.

Average speed = Total miles $\div$ Total time = 240 miles $\div$ 5 hours = 48 mph

11. C   This problem has multiple steps. First, solve the first equation for y.

$$3y - 2 = 7$$
$$3y - 2 + 2 = 7 + 2$$
$$3y = 9$$
$$3y \div 3 = 9 \div 3$$
$$y = 3$$

Plug into the second expression. $(\frac{2}{3}) y + 5 = (\frac{2}{3})(3) + 5 = 2 + 5 = 7$

12. A   If the number 720 is written as a product of its prime factors in the form: ab^2c^4. Then what is the sum of a, b, and c?

The easiest way to solve this problem is to first make a factor tree. Then, take the bottom "leaves" of this factor tree.

$720 = 3 \times 2 \times 3 \times 2 \times 5 \times 2 \times 2$

Then, write the product of any repeated factors, as the factor to a power.
$720 = 5 \times 3^2 \times 2^4$

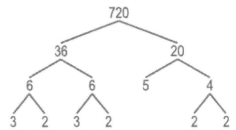

We can now see that a = 5, b = 3, and c = 2.
$a + b + c = 5 + 3 + 2 = 10$

13. C   If AB=AC, that means that the angles opposite the equal sides are equal. Therefore, if angle ABC=55°, then angle ACB=55°.

angle ACB and angle ACD form a straight line, and so their angles total 180°.
angle ACB + angle ACD = 180°
55° + angle ACD = 180°
angle ACD = 125°

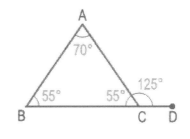

14. A   The easiest way to solve percent problems is to set the original price of the product to $100 and see how the price changes. The manufacturer sells the product for $100, and the store owner marks it up 20%.

$100 x 20% = $100 x 0.20 = $20
The store sells it for $100 + $20 = $120.
The store has a 10% off sale.
$120 x 10% = $120 x 0.10 = $12
The sale price is $120 – $12 = $108.
The sale price of $108 is an 8% increase from the manufacturer's price of $100.

15. A   The classic train problem. This is a travel word problem, where the important equation to remember is that distance = rate x time. First, let us assign a variable to the unknown. In this case, we want to find out how long after they departed that they meet. So let's assign the variable t to represent this time.

The distance the train that left Chicago travels, is the rate x time = 40(t)
The distance the train that left New York travels, is the rate x time = 60(t)

If the distance between the two cities is 1000 miles, then the total distance the trains travel is 1000. Thus, add the distances and set them equal to 1000.
40t + 60t = 1000
100t = 1000
t = 10, Time = 10 hours

16. A   First, use the variables x and y to represent the two unknown quantities.

Let x = number of pencils Bob purchases.

Let y = number of pens Bob purchases.

Set up an equation to represent the amount Bob can spend.

Each pen costs $3, so the total cost of pens = 3y.

Each pencil costs $1, so the total cost of pencils = 1x.

Bob has only $60 to spend.

$$3y + 1x \leq 60$$

Isolate y and then graph.

$$3y + x \leq 60$$
$$3y \leq -x + 60$$
$$y \leq -x/3 + 20$$

The graph of that inequality will have a y–intercept of 20 and a slope of $-\frac{1}{3}$. You want to shade below the line. Also, since x and y can not be negative, only shade in quadrant I.

17. B   The easiest way to deal with problems involving shapes is to substitute variables for each shape. Let each circle be represented by the letter c and each square by the letter s. Now, create equations with these variables.

$$s + s + c + c + c + c = 0$$
$$s + s + s - c = 7$$

Now, simplify each equation.

$$2s + 4c = 0$$
$$3s - c = 7$$

Rearrange the first equation.

$$2s + 4c = 0$$
$$2s = -4c$$
$$s = -2c$$

Now, substitute the value for s into the second equation.

$$3s - c = 7$$
$$3(-2c) - c = 7$$
$$-6c - c = 7$$
$$-7c = 7$$
$$c = -1$$

One circle equals –1.

18. C   To find the total number of possibilities, multiply the number of possible characters for each space in the code.

The first character must be a letter, therefore there are 26 possibilities.

The second character must be a number, therefore there are 10 possibilities.

The third character must be a distinct number, therefore there are 9 possibilities (since one number was already used).

Total possibilities = 26 x 10 x 9 = 2340.

19. C   If there are 60 marbles in a bag and the probability of being green or red is $\frac{5}{12}$, then you can multiply the probability by the total number to find the number of red or green marbles.

Red or Green marbles = 60 x $\frac{5}{12}$ = 25

The problem also states that there are 5 green marbles. Therefore, the number of red marbles is 25 − 5 = 20 marbles.

20. C   The unknown variable in this is case is the number of minutes of talking. Let's call that m.
Cost for Plan T: $25 + 0.10m
Cost for Plan R: $10 + 0.25m

Set the costs equal to solve for m, the number of minutes.
25 + 0.10m = 10 + 0.25m
15 + 0.10m = 0.25m
15 = 0.15m
100 = m
100 minutes

21. B   First, convert the 2 hours and 40 minutes to minutes.
2 hours and 40 minutes = 160 minutes.

Steve reads 80 pages in 160 minutes.
That's 1 page every 2 minutes.

If Cassandra reads twice as fast, then she reads 1 page per minute. It would take her 300 minutes, or 5 hours, to read a 300 page book.

22. D   Let's examine each answer choice to see which can be true.

Answer A: The hypotenuse equals 1000 — This can be true. We know nothing about the lengths of the sides.

Answer B: The side lengths add up to 20. — There is no reason why this could not be true.

Answer C: Two of the angles are equal. — This is definitely true. The triangle has two sides that are the same size; therefore the angles opposite those sides must also be equal.

Answer D: One of the angles measures 60 degrees. — This is false. Since there are two sides that each equal x and one right angle, the triangle is a 45–45–90, or right isosceles triangle. None of the angles can equal 60 degrees. This is the answer.

23. D   Let's start with examining the median and see if we can eliminate any of the answer choices.
The original data set: 18, 18, 19, 19, 21

We know that the median of the new data set is 19. With the new element, there will be 6 elements total in the data set and therefore the median will be the average of the two middle elements, one of which is the current middle element 19.

If the missing element was less than 19, then the two middle elements would be 19 and a number less than 19, which would not have an average of 19. Therefore, the missing element can not be less than 19.

If the missing element is greater than or equal to 19, then the two middle elements would both be 19, their average would also be 19, and this is the median that we are looking for. Therefore, the missing element is greater than or equal to 19.

We can eliminate answer choices A and B as they violate the requirement that the median is equal to 19.

Next, let's examine the mean. We are told that the mean is greater than the median. We can try the remaining answer choices to find the mean and see whether it is greater than the median.

Let's try answer C: 19. The mean is found by adding all the elements and dividing by the total number, which in this case would be 6 elements.

$(18+18+19+19+21+19)/6 = 19$

Here the median equals the mean and therefore can not be the answer.

24. C   Note that the formulas for area and circumference are provided on the ILTS.

The area of the circle $= \pi r^2$
The circumference of the circle $= 2\pi r$

Now you must use algebra to solve this question. Let y represent the answer to this question which states that the area is how many times the circumference. This can be set up as:

Area = y x Circumference
$\pi r^2 = y \times 2\pi r$

Divide both sides by π
$r^2 = y \times 2r$

Divide both sides by r
$r = y \times 2$

Divide both sides by 2
$r/2 = y$

25. B   The area of a triangle is found by multiplying ½ x base x height. For an isosceles triangle, the base and the height are equal.

Therefore, the area $= ½$ x side x side $= ½$ side^2.

Thus, as the length of the side increases, the area will go up as the length squared. For example, if the length triples, the area will increase by $3^2 = 9$.

The graph must show that the increase in the y direction is exponential.

8. Final Exam

1. A sweater is originally $80. It was marked down 10% and still didn't sell, so the store marked it down an additional 25%. What percentage of the original price does the sweater cost?

    A. 35%

    B. 45%

    C. 65%

    D. 67.5%

2. Which of the following is the farthest from 1?

    A. 7/8

    B. 1.12

    C. 0.9^2

    D. 7/6

3. If N is a positive number, which of the following products could be a negative number?

    A. (N+1)(N–1)

    B. (N+1)(N+2)

    C. N(N–2)

    D. N(N)

4. You are making oatmeal raisin cookies and a recipe calls for ¾ cups of raisins and ⅔ cups of brown sugar. You have 2 cups of brown sugar and decide to increase the recipe in order to use all of it. How many cups of raisins should you use to keep the ratio the same as the original recipe?

    A. 1 ⁷⁄₉

    B. 2 ¼

    C. 2 ⅚

    D. 3

5. There are four monkeys stealing bananas from the trees, monkeys A, B, C, and D. Monkey A steals 9 bananas. Monkey B steals 3 less than 4 times what A stole. C steals the difference of A and B. Monkey D steals 2 more than twice C. How many bananas total did the four monkeys steal?

    A. 80

    B. 82

    C. 116

    D. 118

6. Beth can type 40 words per minute, and Vanessa can type 3 words for every 2 that Beth types. If they both start typing at the same time, how many words has Beth typed when Vanessa has finished 4200 words?

    A. 157.5 words

    B. 2800 words

    C. 6300 words

    D. 7000 words

7. If the figure, the distance from B to C is twice the distance from A to B, and the distance from C to D is equal to half the distance from A to C. If the distance from B to C is x, what is the distance from A to D?

A. ½ x

B. ¾ x

C. 2 ¼ x

D. 2 ½ x

8. A manufacturing company produced 500 units in a single day. 40% of the units were type A. Unfortunately, 5% of the type A units were defective and could not be sold. How many type A units were <u>not</u> defective on that day?

A. 25

B. 190

C. 275

D. 475

9. Which of the following problems could be solved by using the following equation: 3.5 ÷ 0.5 ?

A. A concert lasts three and a half hours and you missed a half hour. How much of the concert did you see?

B. The base of a triangle is 0.5cm and the height is 3.5cm, what is the triangle's area?

C. The length of the wooden plank is three and a half feet and you need pieces that are half a foot long, how many pieces can you get from the plank?

D. Jimmy's house is 5 miles from Susie's. If Jimmy can run 3.5 miles per hour, how long will it take him to reach Susie's?

10. What is the sum of the following 2 numbers in proper expanded form?
First number: 200,000 + 30,000 + 8,000 + 70 + 6
Second number: 400,000 + 80,000 + 900 + 10

A. 700,000 + 10,000 + 8,000 + 900 + 80 + 6

B. 600,000 + 10,000 + 8000 + 900 + 80 + 6

C. 600,000 + 110,000 + 8000 + 900 + 80 + 6

D. 700,000 + 10,000 + 8,000 + 900 + 70 + 16

11. At the same moment, two trains leave a station on parallel tracks. Train A travels the 700 miles from Station 1 to Station 3 in the same amount of time that it takes Train B to travel the 500 miles to Station 2. If the total route is 1500 miles long and both trains travel to the very end before turning around and traveling back to Station 1, which of the following proportions shows the total distance Train A has traveled when Train B reaches the end of the route?

A. 500/700 = x/1000

B. 500/700 = 1000/x

C. 500/700 = x/1500

D. 700/500 = x/1500

12. Use the diagram below to determine what shape is the 61st element if the pattern continues.

A. Circle

B. Triangle

C. Square

D. Hexagon

13. If 20 red, 30 purple, and 40 yellow marbles are in a bag, and marbles are drawn from the bag without replacement, how would you find the probability that a red will be selected on the first random draw, a purple on the second, and a yellow on the third?

A. $\frac{2}{9} \times \frac{1}{3} \times \frac{4}{9}$

B. $\frac{2}{9} \times \frac{30}{89} \times \frac{5}{11}$

C. $\frac{2}{9} + \frac{1}{3} + \frac{4}{9}$

D. $\frac{2}{9} + \frac{30}{89} + \frac{5}{11}$

14. You take the square root of a number, multiply it by 3, add 4, and then divide by 2 to get 26. What was the original number?

A. 4

B. 32

C. 256

D. 2601

15. What is the difference between A and B?

A. $\frac{3}{4}$

B. $2\frac{1}{4}$

C. $2\frac{4}{7}$

D. 18

16. Which of the following is/are true?

I. The greatest common factor of two numbers can be equal to one of the numbers.
II. The least common multiple of two numbers can be equal to one of the numbers.
III. The product of the LCM and GCF of two numbers can equal the product of the two numbers.

A. I only

B. I and II

C. I, II, and III

D. None of the above.

17. Noah is papering one of the walls in his bedroom. He uses 3 rolls of paper to cover 20 square yards of wall space. If the wall is 15 feet high and 18 feet long, how many rolls of paper will he need to purchase?

A. 2

B. 3

C. 4

D. 5

18. If the midpoint of a line segment is (−3, 5) and one endpoint is (1, −2), what is the other endpoint?

    A. (−2, 3)

    B. (−3, −10)

    C. (−7, 12)

    D. (5, −9)

19. In the figure below, angle a is 30 degrees. What is the measure of angle d?

    A. 45 + c

    B. 90 − c

    C. 120 − c

    D. 180 − c

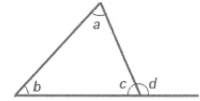

20. Louise's shoe is $^{17}/_{24}$ feet long, and Andrew's shoe is $^{55}/_{120}$ feet long. What is the average length of their shoes?

    A. 7 inches

    B. $^{7}/_{6}$ feet

    C. 1 foot

    D. 6 inches

21. The ratio of the number of marbles Mike has to the number David has is 5 to 8. If David has 12 more marbles than Mike, how many marbles does Mike have?

    A. 7 marbles

    B. 9 marbles

    C. 20 marbles

    D. 28 marbles

22. If the area of a circle is A and the circumference is C, what happens to the area and circumference in terms of A and C when you triple the diameter of the circle?

    A. 3A, 3C

    B. 9A, 3C

    C. 9A, 9C

    D. A + 3, C + 3

23. Triangle PQR is an isosceles triangle. If angle P = 70°, which of the following is not a possible measure for angle Q?

    A. 20°

    B. 40°

    C. 55°

    D. 70°

24. A door is 3 times as long as it is wide. If the area is 108 square feet when the length and width are each doubled, how wide was the door originally?

    A. 2

    B. 3

    C. 4

    D. 5

25. An airplane takes 6 hours to fly from San Francisco to Boston and only 5 hours to return. The wind velocity is 50 mph and increases the plane's speed from Boston to San Francisco, but decreases the plane's speed from San Francisco to Boston. What is the average speed of the airplane? (hint: rate x time = distance)

    A. 450 mph

    B. 500 mph

    C. 550 mph

    D. 600 mph

26. It takes a painter 2 hours to paint a wall that is 10m x 10m. How long would it take 2 painters working at the same rate to paint a wall that is 40m x 40m?

    A. 2 hours

    B. 4 hours

    C. 8 hours

    D. 16 hours

27. Students at Watertown high participate in three different types of extracurricular activities, music, sports, or yearbook. There are 50 students who participate in extracurriculars, 5 who participate in only yearbook, and 30 play sports. How many participate in only music?

    A. 3

    B. 8

    C. 10

    D. Not enough information.

28. If each triangle in the equations is equal to 2. What does one square plus one circle equal?

    A. –7

    B. 1

    C. 9

    D. 11

$$\square + \square + \square + \square + \triangle + \triangle = \bigcirc + \bigcirc$$
$$\square + \square - \bigcirc - \bigcirc - \bigcirc = \triangle + \triangle + \triangle$$

29. How many integers between 600 and 700, inclusive, are divisible by both 5 and 3?

    A. 7

    B. 15

    C. 33

    D. 53

30. You have a circle centered at (−2, −2) and with a diameter of 8. What are the coordinates of the point that is on the circle and has the largest x−coordinate?

    A. (2, −2)

    B. (6, −2)

    C. (8, −2)

    D. (2, 2)

31. The sum of 4 times a number y and 21 is greater than 45 and less than 73. What are all possible values for that number?

    A. $6 < y < 13$

    B. $y > 6$ or $y < 13$

    C. 8, 9, and 10

    D. $y > 6$

32. In Rebecca's coin jar, there are at least as many nickels as quarters and as least as many nickels as dimes. Which of the following statements must be true?

    A. There are an equal number of dimes and quarters.

    B. There are at least as many quarters as dimes.

    C. The number of nickels is at least as much as the sum of the number of dimes and quarters.

    D. None of the above.

33. If the dimensions of a rectangular prism (length = l, width = w, height = h) are all doubled, what happens to the surface area of the prism?

    A. Doubled.

    B. Quadrupled.

    C. Multiplied by 8.

    D. Not enough information.

34. What equations represent the graph?

    A. $y \leq x$ or $y \geq -x$

    B. $y \geq x$ or $y \leq -x$

    C. $y \leq x$ and $y \geq -x$

    D. $y \geq x$ and $y \leq -x$

35. You have two different types of bacteria in petri dishes. Dish A contains Bacteria A, and Dish B contains Bacteria B. Both start with the same number of bacteria. Bacteria A doubles every 2 days, and Bacteria B triples every 3 days. After 12 days, which petri dish will contain more?

    A. Dish A

    B. Dish B

    C. They will contain equal numbers of bacteria.

    D. The problem does not provide enough information.

36. What does r equal in the following equation? $(2r - 12)/6 = 4$

    A. 3

    B. 12

    C. 18

    D. 48

37. A man that is 6 feet tall casts a shadow that is 2.5 feet long. If the height of an object and the length of its shadow are proportionate, how tall is a building that casts a shadow 30 feet long?

    A. 12.5 feet

    B. 33.5 feet

    C. 72 feet

    D. 450 feet

38. You are graphing the number of employees of a startup company versus the year. The graph follows a straight line, where the company started in 2004 (thus had 0 employees at the start of the year) and then in 2006 had 250 employees. Assuming the slope of the line stays the same, how many employees will the company have in 2009?

    A. 500

    B. 625

    C. 750

    D. 975

39. Triangle ABC is inscribed in a semicircle with a radius of 5 units. Line segment AB has a length of 6 units. What is the length of line segment BC?

    A. 4

    B. 8

    C. 11

    D. 16

40. An art teacher is putting together a project where students will construct cubes out of popsicle sticks. If each side of the cube is to be 2 popsicle sticks long, how many total popsicle sticks are used for each cube?

    A. 8

    B. 16

    C. 24

    D. 64

41. What is the y–intercept and x–intercept of the following equation? $-2x + 7y = 14$

    A. y–int: –2, x–int: –7

    B. y–int: 2, x–int: –7

    C. y–int: 7, x–int: –2

    D. y–int: –7, x–int: 2

42. In a set with 6 unique elements, if each element is multiplied by 3, which of the following statements are true?

I. Mean is multiplied by 3.
II. Median is multiplied by 3.
III. Probability of lowest element chosen is multiplied by 3.

    A. I only.

    B. I and II only.

    C. I, II, and III.

    D. Not enough information.

43. Christine's father is 3 times her age, and, 4 years ago, he was 4 times older than she was then. How old is Christine now?

    A. 4

    B. 12

    C. 15

    D. 18

44. Use the table below to answer the question that follows.

Earnings Plan	Payment Structure
1	$55,000 base salary
2	$25,000 base salary + 15% of sales
3	$35,000 base salary + ⅛ of sales

Ralph has been offered a job, and he can choose from the three earnings plans. If he sells $200,000 worth of merchandise, which plan will give him the highest salary for his first year?

    A. Plan 1

    B. Plan 2

    C. Plan 3

    D. All three plans allow Ralph to earn the same amount in his first year.

45. From the histogram to the right, how many sick days in a year would be required to reach the 70th percentile?

    A. 6

    B. 7

    C. 8

    D. 9

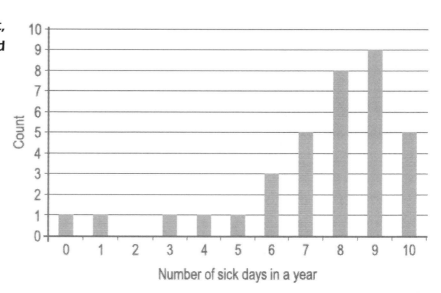

46. Solve for x in the following system of equations:
$$-3x + 2y = -13$$
$$3x = y + 11$$

   A. –2

   B. 3

   C. 9

   D. 11

47. The teacher has declared that they will give at most 20 A's to their class of 40 students. You also know that there are at least as many B's as C's and that only 5 students received either a D or F. What is the minimum number of B's that the teacher will give out?

   A. 7

   B. 8

   C. 15

   D. Not enough information.

48. Use the incorrect work sample below from a student who was asked to calculate the distance between (5, 5) and (–5, –5) to answer the questions that follow.

        Vertical distance: 5 – (–5) = 10

        Horizontal distance: 5 – (–5) = 10

        Total distance: 10 + 10 = 20

Which of the following strategies would help this student visualize the correct solution?

   A. Drawing a square with corners at (0,0), (0,5), (5,0), and (5,5), then rotating the square until it has corners at (0,0), (0, –5), (–5, 0), and (–5,–5).

   B. Drawing a circle with the two points placed along the circumference

   C. Drawing a right triangle with the hypotenuse connecting the two points

   D. Drawing two parallel lines that each have a length of 5 units.

49. A cylindrical can is measured to have a base radius of 4 cm ± 1 cm and a height of 7 cm ± 2 cm. The volume of the can is calculated based on these measurements. What is the difference between the maximum and minimum possible volumes?

   A. 45π

   B. 60π

   C. 90π

   D. 180π

50. The teacher is about to grade the last exam for her small class of 12 students. The first 11 student's scores were all promising results between 80 and 100. The last student has not been performing well all year and has missed most of the homework assignments, so the teacher is concerned that the student failed the exam. If the student received below a 50, which statistical measure will be affected the least?

   A. Standard Deviation

   B. Range

   C. Mean

   D. Median

1. D This problem has many steps. First, determine the price of the sweater after the first markdown. $80 x 10% = $80 x 0.10 = $8.

Now subtract that discount from the original price. $80 – $8 = $72

Then, determine the price of the sweater after the second markdown. $72 x 25% = $72 x 0.25 = $18.

Subtract to find the new price. $72 – $18 = $54

Finally, to find the percentage of the original, you must divide 54 by 80. 54 ÷ 80 = 0.675 = 67.5%

2. C A: $7/8$: Convert the fraction to a decimal by dividing 7 by 8. $7/8$ = 0.875.

Now, subtract from 1 to find distance from 1.   1 – 0.875 = 0.125

B: 1.12
1.12 – 1 = 0.12

C: 0.9^2
0.9^2 = 0.9 x 0.9 = 0.81
1 – 0.81 = 0.19

D: $7/6$: Convert to a decimal by dividing 7 by 6.
7 ÷ 6 = 1.1666...
1.1666... – 1 = 0.1666...

Answer C has the largest distance from 1.

3. C A. The smallest positive number for N is 1. Therefore, the smallest that N–1 can be is 0, it can never be negative. N+1 is positive if N is positive, therefore, this answer choice will never be negative.

B. N+1 and N+2 will both be positive, and a positive times a positive is positive. Eliminate B.

C. The smallest positive number is 1. If N=1, then N(N–2) = 1(1–2) = 1(–1) = –1. Answer C.

D. N is positive, positive times positive= positive. Eliminate D.

4. B Set this problem up as a ratio. The variable y represents the number of cups of raisins that are needed.

$$\frac{\text{Raisins}}{\text{Brown sugar}} = \frac{\frac{3}{4}\text{ cups}}{\frac{2}{3}\text{ cups}} = \frac{y\text{ cups}}{2\text{ cups}}$$

You can solve for the variable y by cross–multiplying.
$3/4$ cups x 2 cups = $2/3$ cups x y cups
$3/4$ x 2 = $2/3$ y
$3/2$ = $2/3$ y

Multiply both sides by $3/2$ to get y by itself.
$3/2$ x $3/2$ = $2/3$ y x $3/2$
$9/4$ = y
2 $1/4$ = y
2 $1/4$ cups of raisins

5. C   Let's break this problem down to figure out how many bananas each monkey stole.

Monkey A steals 9 bananas.
The number A stole has been given.

Monkey B steals 3 less than 4 times what A stole.
First, find 4 times A and then subtract 3.
$4(9) - 3 = 36 - 3 = 33$

Monkey C steals the difference of A and B.
$33 - 9 = 24$

Monkey D steals 2 more than twice C.
Multiply 24 by 2 and then add 2.
$24 \times 2 + 2 = 48 + 2 = 50$

Now, find the sum.
$9 + 33 + 24 + 50 = 116$
116 total bananas

6. B   First, figure out Vanessa's typing rate.
"Vanessa can type 3 words for every 2 that Beth types."
Therefore, Vanessa can type $\frac{3}{2}$ times faster than Beth.
Vanessa's rate = $\frac{3}{2}$ x Beth's rate
= $\frac{3}{2}$ x 40 words per minutes
= 60 words per minute

Next, determine the amount of time that Vanessa typed.
Vanessa typed 4200 words, and she can type 60 words per minute.
If you divide the number of words by her rate, you will determine the time it takes.

Time Vanessa typed = Number of words ÷ Typing rate
= $4200 \div 60 = 70$ minutes

Finally, determine how many words Beth can type in 70 minutes.
Number of words Beth types = Beth's rate x Beth's time
= 40 words per minute x 70 minutes = 2800 words

7. C   Distance from B to C= x
Distance from A to B= $\frac{1}{2}$ x
Distance from A to C = A to B + B to C = x + $\frac{1}{2}$ x = $\frac{3}{2}$ x
Distance from C to D= $\frac{1}{2}$ ($\frac{3}{2}$ x)= $\frac{3}{4}$ x
Distance from A to D= A to B + B to C + C to D= x + $\frac{1}{2}$ x + $\frac{3}{4}$ x= $2\frac{1}{4}$ x

8. B   Let's first determine how many units are type A and then determine how many of those are not defective.
There are 500 units total. 40% of the total units are type A.
Type A units = 40% of 500 = 40% x 500 = $\frac{40}{100}$ x 500 = 200

There are 200 type A units. We know that 5% of those are defective. You can either calculate the number of defective ones and subtract from the total or find 95% of the type A units which are the ones that are not defective.

Defective Type A units = 5% of 200 = 5% x 200 = $\frac{5}{100}$ x 200 = 10

10 defective type A units. 200 total type A units. Therefore, 190 units are type A that are not defective.

9. C   Let's examine each answer to see how you would solve it.

A: A concert lasts three and a half hours and you missed a half hour. How much of the concert did you see?
This problem would be solved by using the following equation: $3.5 - 0.5 = 3$
Eliminate answer A

B: The base of a triangle is 0.5cm and the height is 3.5cm, what is the triangle's area?
The area of a triangle is found by multiplying ½ x base x height.
Area = ½ x 0.5 x 3.5
Eliminate answer B

C. The length of the wooden plank is three and a half feet and you need pieces that are half a foot long, how many pieces can you get from the plank?
In this case, you want to divide the total plank into pieces. The total plank is 3.5 feet and each piece is 0.5 feet. You must divide to find the total number of pieces.
$3.5 \div 0.5 = 7$
Answer C is correct.

D. Jimmy's house is 5 miles from Susie's. If Jimmy can run 3.5 miles per hour, how long will it take him to reach Susie's?
Distance = rate x time. Therefore, to figure out the time, you divide the distance by the rate.
time = 5 miles ÷ 3.5 mph
Eliminate answer D

10. A   There are two ways to approach this problem. Leave the numbers in expanded form and add or convert to standard form, add, and then convert back to expanded form.

Method 1: Convert to standard form and then back.
First number: $200,000 + 30,000 + 8,000 + 70 + 6 = 238,076$
Second number: $400,000 + 80,000 + 900 + 10 = 480,910$
Now add: $238,076 + 480,910 = 718,986$

Convert back to standard form:
$718,986 = 700,000 + 10,000 + 8,000 + 900 + 80 + 6$

Method 2: Leave in expanded form and add
When adding numbers in expanded form, it is easiest to start with the smallest place value and work up.
First number: $200,000 + 30,000 + 8,000 + 70 + 6$
Second number: $400,000 + 80,000 + 900 + 10$

Ones Place: 6
Tens Place: $70 + 10 = 80$
Hundreds Place: 900
Thousands Place: 8,000
Ten–Thousands Place: $30,000 + 80,000 = 110,000$

The ten–thousands place went beyond the ten–thousands. Therefore, keep the 10,000 for the ten–thousands place, and bring the 100,000 to the next place.

Hundred–thousands Place: $100,000 + 200,000 + 400,000 = 700,000$

Now, write number in expanded form:
$700,000 + 10,000 + 8,000 + 900 + 80 + 6$

11.D Train A travels 700 miles in the same amount of time that it takes Train B to travel 500. This gives you a rate that you can use to set up a proportion.

The other side of the proportion should be x/1500 because you are trying to calculate the distance that Train A has traveled in the time that it took Train B to travel the 1500 mile track.

Train A/Train B: 700/500 = x/1500

Another acceptable proportion would be: Train B/Train A: 500/700 = 1500/x

12. A Extrapolate from the pattern that is given. The pattern is 4 elements (shapes) long.

You are asked to predict the 61st element. The closest multiple of 4 to 61 is 60 (15 x 4). Since the 60th element would complete a repetition of the pattern, the 61st element is the first element of a new repetition—the first element in the pattern.

Therefore, the 61st object will be a circle.

13. B To find the probability of multiple events, multiply the probability of each individual event. Make sure to keep in mind how one event may affect the sample space and probability of the following events.

Probability red is selected first
= # of red marbles divided by total marbles = $^{20}/_{90}$ = $^2/_9$

Probability purple is selected second
= # of purple marbles divided by total marbles remaining = $^{30}/_{89}$

Probability yellow is selected third
= # of yellow marbles divided by total marbles remaining = $^{40}/_{88}$ = $^5/_{11}$

To find the probability of all three events occurring, multiply the probabilities of each event.
= $^2/_9$ x $^{30}/_{89}$ x $^5/_{11}$

14. C To find the original number, work backwards.
The last step was to divide by 2 to get 26. Therefore, perform the inverse operation of multiplying by 2.
26 x 2 = 52.

The step before that was to add 4. Perform the inverse operation of subtracting 4.
52 – 4 = 48.

The step before that was to multiply by 3. Perform the inverse operation of dividing by 3.
48 ÷ 3 = 16

The step before that was to take the square root of the number. Perform the inverse operation of squaring the number.
16^2 = 256

15. B There are many possible approaches to solving this problem. Also, before starting either method, take a quick scan of your answer choices. Note that they are in terms of fractions instead of decimals – therefore, in your calculations it will be easiest to think in terms of fractions to save yourself conversions. Here are two methods to solving this problem:

Method 1: Determine values of A and B and then find their difference.

On the number line, you can see that there are 8 spaces in between each whole number. Be careful, you want to count the spaces and not the tick marks as each whole number is divided into equal spaces. Therefore, each space represents $\frac{1}{8}$.

A is 6 of the 8 spaces less than 0. Therefore, A is $\frac{6}{8}$ less than 0. Thus, A is equivalent to $-\frac{6}{8} = -\frac{3}{4}$.
B is 4 of the 8 spaces greater than 1. B is $\frac{4}{8}$ greater than 1. Thus, B is equivalent to $1\frac{4}{8} = 1\frac{1}{2}$.

Now, subtract to find the difference between A and B.
$B - A = 1\frac{1}{2} - -\frac{3}{4}$

To solve this subtraction problem, note two things. First, it is the subtraction of a negative number, remember that this is the same as addition of the opposite signed number. Next, you must convert the fractions to common denominators before subtracting.

$1\frac{1}{2} - (-\frac{3}{4}) = 1\frac{1}{2} + \frac{3}{4} = \frac{3}{2} + \frac{3}{4} = \frac{6}{4} + \frac{3}{4} = \frac{9}{4} = 2\frac{1}{4}$

Method 2: Determine difference between A and B and then the value.

Let's first find the difference between A and B on the number line and then find the value of that difference. If we carefully count on the number line, you will count 18 spaces that separate A and B.

Now, we must determine what each space represents. There are 8 spaces between each whole number, therefore, each space is equivalent to $\frac{1}{8}$.

So, there are 18 spaces or $18 \times \frac{1}{8}$ between A and B.
$18 \times \frac{1}{8} = \frac{18}{8} = \frac{9}{4} = 2\frac{1}{4}$

16. C   Let's examine each option.

I. The greatest common factor of two numbers can be equal to one of the numbers.
This is true. If one number divides evenly into the second number, then it would be the greatest common factor of the numbers. Example: the GCF of 8 and 16 is 8.

II. The least common multiple of two numbers can be equal to one of the numbers.
This is true. If one number divides evenly into the second number, then the second number would be the least common multiple of the numbers. Example: the LCM of 6 and 24 is 24.

III. The product of the LCM and GCF of two numbers can equal the product of the two numbers.
This is true. If one number divides evenly into the second number, then the smaller is the GCF and the larger is the LCM. Therefore, the product of the two numbers would be equal to the product of the LCM and GCF. Example: 5 and 10. GCF = 5, LCM = 10, product = 50.

I, II, and III are true.

17. D   First, convert from feet to yards. Then find the area of the wall. Finally, determine the number of rolls of paper that are needed.

15 feet x (1 yd/3 feet) = 5 yards
18 feet x (1 yd/3 feet) = 6 yards

Area = 5 yards x 6 yards = 30 square yards

30 square yards x (3 rolls/20 square yards) = $\frac{90}{20}$ rolls= 4 $\frac{1}{2}$ rolls

The question asks how many rolls Noah will purchase. If he cannot purchase a part of a roll, then round up. Therefore, 5 rolls is the answer.

18. C There are a few ways to approach this problem, though a quick sketch is always a recommended first step. Don't draw a full coordinate plane on your paper, but quick axes to get an idea of where the points fall so that you can quickly estimate the answer. In fact, on some problems a quick estimate is enough to eliminate three answer choices.

Next, let's review the definition of midpoint. This can be seen in the graph to the right.

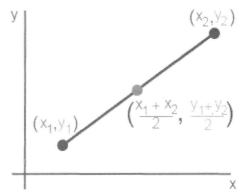

Note, that the endpoints are (x_1, y_1) and (x_2, y_2) and the midpoint can be found by averaging the x–coordinates of the endpoints and the y–coordinates of the endpoints. Now, in addition to algebraically, you should be able to see graphically why the definition of midpoint holds.

Also, remember that the average of two numbers can be found by adding the numbers and dividing by 2.

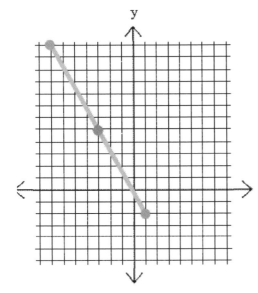

In addition to graphically solving the problem, which is illustrated to the left, let's solve this problem with calculations. The midpoint of a line segment is halfway between the two endpoints. If you were asked to find the midpoint between two numbers, you would find their average. Well, a similar process is used to find the midpoints in the coordinate plane – first you find the midpoint of the x–coordinates and then the midpoint of the y–coordinates.

In this problem, they have given you the midpoint and you need to find one of the endpoints. Well, we know that the x–coordinate of the midpoint, –3, is the average of the x–coordinate of the given endpoint, 1, and the x–coordinate of the unknown endpoint, x.

Remember, to find the average of two numbers, add them and divide by 2. This gives us the following equation:

–3 = (1 + x)/2

Solve for x:

–6 = 1 + x

x = –7

Follow similar steps to find the y–coordinate. The y–coordinate of the given endpoint is –2, the y–coordinate of the unknown endpoint is y, and the y–coordinate of the midpoint is 5. Set up an equation and solve:

5 = (–2 + y)/2

10 = –2 + y

y = 12

Unknown endpoint: (–7, 12)

19.D Start with a quick scan of your answers. Note that all of the answers are solving for angle d in terms of angle c. Therefore, we are going to have to set up some equations and represent d in terms of c. There are two basic facts that you should have memorized with regards to angle measures. The sum of the angles in a triangle add to 180 degrees. The angles on a straight line add to 180 degrees.

Let's set up an equation first with knowing that the sum of the angles of a triangle add to 180 degrees.
$a + b + c = 180$
$30 + b + c = 180$

Next, set up an equation using the fact that the sum of the angles on a straight line is 180 degrees.
$c + d = 180$

If you rearrange the second equation, you can find your answer without having to use the first equation.
$c + d = 180$ Subtract c from both sides.
$d = 180 - c$

20. A To find the average of numbers, you find their sum and divide by the number of numbers. Therefore, we must add the two fractions and then divide by 2.

To add the fractions, we must first find the common denominator, in this case, 120. $17/24 \times 5/5 = 85/120$
$85/120 + 55/120 = 140/120 = 7/6$

Now that we found the sum, we must divide it by 2 to find the average.
$7/6 \div 2 = 7/6 \times 1/2 = 7/12$ feet

Since that isn't in the answer choices, lets convert that to inches.
$7/12$ feet = 7 inches

21. C **Method 1:** The ratio of marbles that Mike has to marbles that David has is 5 to 8. Therefore, the ratio of the difference in the number of marbles to the marbles that Mike has is 3 to 5.

Set up a proportion knowing that the difference in the number of marbles is 12. Also, let m represent the number of marbles that Mike has.

Difference in number of marbles to Marbles Mike has
3 to 5 = 12 to m
$3/5 = 12/m$

Cross multiply and solve.
$3m = 60$
$m = 20$
Mike has 20 marbles.

Method 2: Another way to solve this problem is to write out the possible numbers of marbles that each person has until you find a set of values with a difference of twelve. Assuming that each person can only have a whole number of marbles, the first few possibilities are: 5&8, 10&16, 15&24, and 20&32.

When David has 32 marbles and Mike has 20, David will have 12 more marbles than Mike.

22.B Let's first examine the area. The formula for the area of a circle is $\pi \times \text{radius}^2$
If the diameter triples, the radius also triples.
Therefore, the new area of the circle is $\pi(3 \times \text{radius})^2 = \pi \times 9 \times \text{radius}^2 = 9\pi\text{radius}^2 = 9A$

The formula for the circumference of a circle is $\pi \times \text{diameter}$
Therefore, the new circumference = $\pi(3 \times \text{diameter}) = 3 \times \pi \times \text{diameter} = 3C$

9A, 3C

23. A   If Triangle PQR is an isosceles triangle, then two angles must be equal. The question tells you one of the angles. Therefore, that angle is equal to a second angle, or it is the one different angle. Remember, that in a triangle, all the angles add up to 180°.

One possible triangle: angle P equals another angle. Therefore, two angles equal 70°. To find the third angle, subtract the sum of the two angles from 180. $180 - (70 + 70) = 180 - 140 = 40$.

Another possible triangle: angle P is the different angle. Therefore, the other two angles, Q and R, must be equal. Let the variable y represent the measure of angle Q, which also equals the measure of angle R.

$70 + y + y = 180$
$70 + 2y = 180$
$2y = 110$
$y = 55$

The diagram to the right shows the two possible isosceles triangles.

Angle Q can not equal 20°.

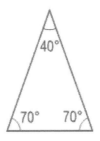
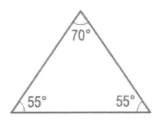

24. B   The trickiest part of this problem is visualizing the door's dimensions. Draw a diagram to help with this. Label all of the dimensions in terms of the original width because that is the quantity for which you are asked to solve.

The original width should be labeled with a variable. We'll use w.
The original length is equal to 3 times the width: 3w.
The new width is doubled: 2w.
The new length is doubled: $2 \times 3w = 6w$.

The area of a rectangle is determined by length times width, so the formula is: $2w \times 6w = 108$ sq. feet

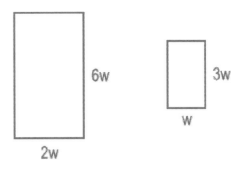

$12w^2 = 108$ sq. feet
$w^2 = 9$ sq. feet
$w = 3$ feet

25. C   The one formula to remember when dealing with travel problems is that: Distance = Rate x Time

For any algebra word problem, assign a variable to the unknown. In this case, the unknown is the average speed of the airplane, let's assign r to represent this value.

Now, we must set up equations. For the trip from San Francisco to Boston, the airplane was flying at a rate of r, but the wind was going against the plane, thus the rate was (r–50). The distance the plane flew was then the rate x time = (r–50) x 6

For the return trip, the airplane was flying at a rate of r, and the wind was helping the plane go faster, therefore, the rate was (r+50). The distance the plane flew back was then the rate x time = (r+50) x 5

The distances were the same in each case, so we can set the two equations equal to each other.

(r–50) x 6 = (r+50) x 5	Set distances equal to each other
6r – 300 = 5r + 250	Distribute on both sides
6r = 5r + 550	Add 300 to both sides
r = 550	Subtract 5r from both sides

26. D   Let's figure out the rate of each painter. The painter can paint a wall 10m x 10m in 2 hours. Therefore, he can paint 100 sq m in 2 hours, or to reduce that, 50 sq m in 1 hour.

Now, we have 2 painters.
The rate of one painter is 50 sq m in 1 hour, if you have 2 painters working at the same rate, then they can paint 100 sq m in 1 hour.

The wall is 40m x 40m.
The area of the new wall is 40m x 40m = 1600 sq m.
The two painters rate is 100 sq m in 1 hour, therefore, to paint 1600 sq m, it will take 16 hours.

27. A   The first step is to put in the additional information provided in the problem into the venn diagram. We are told that 5 students participate in only yearbook, so that is added to the yearbook circle in the area that does not overlap with any other activities. We also know that the total number of students who participate in sports is 30, but we don't know the breakdown between those who participate in sports and music and sports and yearbook, therefore, just enter 30 into the entire sports circle.

Now, we know that the total number of students who participate in activities is 50 and there is only one empty space left in our venn diagram, which is those who participate in music. Therefore, subtract each of the other quantities from 50 to see how many students remain.

$50 - 30 - 12 - 5 = 3$
There are 3 students who participate in only music.

28. A   You are told that each triangle is equal to 2. Let's substitute 2 for each triangle. In addition, let's use variables instead of shapes to help simplify the problem. Let s represent each square and c represent each circle.

$s + s + s + s + 2 + 2 = c + c$
$s + s - c - c - c = 2 + 2 + 2$

Now, simplify each equation.
$4s + 4 = 2c$
$2s - 3c = 6$

Two equations and two unknowns can be solved in many ways. Let's use substitution with the first equation.
$4s + 4 = 2c$
$2s + 2 = c$

Now, you can substitute the value for c into the second equation.
$2s - 3c = 6$
$2s - 3(2s + 2) = 6$
$2s - 6s - 6 = 6$
$-4s - 6 = 6$
$-4s = 12$
$s = -3$

Now, plug the value for s into any equation.
$c = 2s + 2 = 2(-3) + 2 = -6 + 2 = -4$

The problem asks us to find the sum of one circle and one square.
$c + s = -4 + -3 = -7$

29. A If a number is divisible by both 5 and 3, then it must be divisible by 15. Now, we need to find out how many integers between 600 and 700 are divisible by 15.

Starting with 600, since 15 divides evenly into that, count the numbers divisible by 15:

600, 615, 630, 645, 660, 675, 690
7 integers

30. A The easiest way to visualize this problem on a graph. If the diameter of the circle is 8, then the radius is 4. From the center at (–2,–2), go out 4 in each direction, and then draw the circle.

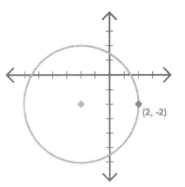
(2, -2)

The point on the circle with the largest x–coordinate is going to be 4 points from the center in the positive direction and with the same y–coordinate. 4 points away is at (–2+4, –2) = (2,–2)

31. A Take the words and translate them into an inequality.

The sum of 4 times a number and 21 is greater than 45
4y + 21 > 45

The sum of 4 times a number and 21... less than 73
4y + 21 < 73

Combine the two inequalities into one statement.
4y + 21 > 45 and 4y + 21 < 73
45 < 4y + 21 < 73

Now, solve by isolating the variable.
45 < 4y + 21 < 73   Subtract 21 from all sides.
24 < 4y < 52   Divide by 4 on all sides
6 < y < 13

32. D Let's start with examining the statements in the question stem. There are at least as many nickels as quarters. This tells us that the number of nickels is greater than or equal to the number of quarters.

There are at least as many nickels as dimes. So, the number of nickels is greater than or equal to the number of dimes.

A. There are an equal number of dimes and quarters.
This is not necessarily true. All the problem tells us is how the number of quarters compares to nickels and how the number of dimes compares to nickels. We have no information on how the number of dimes and quarters compare. For instance, this scenario would be a counterexample:
6 Nickels, 5 Dimes, 4 Quarters – This scenario makes the original statements true, but not answer A.

B. There are at least as many quarters as dimes. This is again not necessarily true. The same explanation for part A holds. We do not know how the number of quarters and dimes compare. The same scenario presented in A is also a counterexample to this answer choice.

C. The number of nickels is at least as much as the sum of the number of dimes and quarters.
We do know that the number of nickels is at least as much as the number of dimes and the number of nickels as at least as much as the number of quarters, but nothing about the sum of the number of dimes and quarters. For example, in the above scenario with 6 Nickels, 5 Dimes, and 4 Quarters we see that this statement does not hold true.

D: None of the Above.

33. B Note that the formula for finding the surface area of a rectangular prism is provided on the TAP.

Method 1: Find the surface area of original and new prism.

The surface area of any object is the sum of the areas of all the faces. A rectangular prism has 6 faces that are all rectangles.

Two faces have dimensions: l by w. The area of each of those faces is lw (multiply dimensions to find area of rectangle).

Two faces have dimensions: w by h. The area of each of those faces is wh.

Two faces have dimensions: h by l. The area of each of those faces is hl.

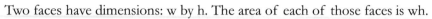

Total Surface Area of original Prism = lw + lw + wh + wh + hl + hl = 2lw + 2wh + 2hl

New prism:

Two faces have dimensions: 2l by 2w. The area of each of those faces is 2l x 2w = 4lw.

Two faces have dimensions: 2w by 2h. The area of each of those faces is 2w x 2h = 4wh.

Two faces have dimensions: 2h by 2l. The area of each of those faces is 2h x 2l = 4hl.

Total Surface Area of New Prism = 4lw + 4lw + 4wh + 4wh + 4hl + 4hl = 8lw + 8wh + 8hl

Surface Area of New Prism = 8lw + 8wh + 8hl = 4(2lw + 2wh + 2hl) = 4(Surf Area of Original Prism)
Surface area quadrupled when dimensions of prism doubled.

Method 2: Analyze what happens when dimensions are doubled.

The surface area is the sum of the areas of all faces of an object. The area is always expressed in square units as it involves multiplying dimensions.

Therefore, if you double only one dimension, area is doubled. But, we are mutiplying all dimensions by 2, and therefore the effect is times 2 x times 2 or times 2 squared or times 4.

As area of each face would be quadrupled, then the sum of each of those areas would also be quadrupled. So, surface area is multiplied by 4 or quadrupled.

34. C First, you can tell that the graph represents an AND statement since only the overlapped portion is shaded. Or would mean all areas that represent either statement are shaded.

Let's look at the line y = x, which has the positive slope. All the points below that are shaded. Therefore, y ≤ x has been shaded.

Now, let's look at the line y = −x, which has the negative slope. All the points greater than that are shaded. Therefore, y ≥ −x has been shaded.

y ≤ x and y ≥ −x

35. B **Method 1:** The number of bacteria in each dish starts out the same, so call that number x. Dish A doubles every two days and Dish B triples every three days.

Dish A: Start=x, Day 2=2x, Day 4=4x, Day 6=8x, Day 8=16x, Day 10=32x, Day 12=64x
Dish B: Start=x, Day 3=3x, Day 6=9x, Day 9=27x, Day 12=81x
81x > 64x

Method 2: Another way you can think of it, is that you know that they start with the same number of bacteria, so let's call that 1. Then, dish A doubles every two days and dish B triples every 3 days. Let's use the variable d to represent the number of days that have passed.

Dish A will double every two days. So, every d/2 days, the quantity will multiply by 2.   Dish A = $2^{(d/2)}$
After 12 days, d=12. Dish A = $2^{(12/2)} = 2^6 = 64$

Dish B will triple every three days. So, every d/3 days, the quantity will multiply by 3.   Dish B = $3^{(d/3)}$
After 12 days, d = 12. Dish B = $3^{(12/3)} = 3^4 = 81$

36. C   Isolate the variable.

$(2r - 12)/6 = 4$ Multiply both sides by 6.

$(2r - 12)/6 \times 6 = 4 \times 6$

$2r - 12 = 24$ Add 12 to both sides.

$2r - 12 + 12 = 24 + 12$

$2r = 36$ Divide both sides by 2.

$2r \div 2 = 36 \div 2$

$r = 18$

37. C   Set up a proportion between the height of the object and the length of the shadow.

height of man/shadow of man = height of building/shadow of building

$6/2.5 = b/30$

Cross multiply and solve for b.

$6(30) = 2.5(b)$

$180 = 2.5b$

$b = 72$

Building's height = 72 feet

38. B   This problem has given you the coordinate pairs of two points on the line and is asking you to find a third point. Using the first two points, find the equation of the line, then plug in the year 2009 to find the number of employees. In this problem, x = year and y = number of employees.

Two points: (2004, 0) and (2006, 250). Slope is change in y divided by change in x

Slope = $(250–0)/(2006–2004) = 250/2 = 125$

Equation: $y = mx + b$; $y = 125x + b$

Plug in a point to find b.

$y = 125x + b$

$0 = 125(2004) + b$

$b = –250,500$

$y = 125x – 250,500$

Now, plug in x = 2009 to find the number of employees in that year.

$y = 125(2009) – 250,500$

$y = 625$, There will be 625 employees in 2009.

39. B   A triangle inscribed inside a semicircle forms a right–triangle at point B.

We also know that AC is the diameter of the circle, which is equal to twice the radius or $2(5) = 10$ units.

We can use the Pythagorean theorem to calculate the length of BC, called x in the following equation.

$x^2 + 6^2 = 10^2$

$x^2 + 36 = 100$

$x^2 = 64$

$x = 8$

40. C   It is sometimes hard to visualize the number of edges of a cube without a sketch. Therefore, draw a quick sketch of a cube.

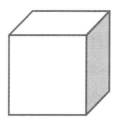

Now, let's count the number of edges. There are 4 around the square in the front of the cube, 4 around the square in the back of the cube, and 4 around the sides of the cube. Therefore, a total of 12 edges.

Each edge is 2 popsicle sticks long. There are 12 edges around each cube.
2 x 12 = 24
24 popsicle sticks are needed.

41. B   The y–intercept is the point on the graph that crosses the y–axis. A point that crosses the y–axis has an x–value of 0. Therefore, plug in x=0 and solve for y.

–2x + 7y = 14
–2(0) + 7y = 14
7y = 14
y = 2, y–intercept = 2

The x–intercept is the point on the graph that crosses the x–axis. A point that crosses the x–axis has an y–value of 0. Therefore, plug in y=0 and solve for x.

–2x + 7y = 14
–2x + 7(0) = 14
–2x = 14
x = –7, x–intercept = –7

y–int: 2, x–int: –7

42. B   **Method 1: Go through each option.** The mean is found by taking the sum of all the elements and then dividing by the total number of elements. If you multiply each element by 3, their sum will also be multiplied by 3. Since the number of elements stays the same at 6, the mean will be multiplied by 3. I is true.

The median is found by listing all the elements from smallest to largest and taking the middle element. Since there is an even number of elements, 6 in this case, the median is the average of the two middle values. However, multiplying each element by 3 will just be the same as multiplying the two middle values by 3 and therefore, increasing their average by a factor of 3. II is true.

The probability of the lowest element being chosen will be 1/6 as each element is unique. If you change the value of each element by multiplying it by 3, the probability of the lowest element being chosen will still be 1/6 as you are choosing 1 element out of 6 options. III is false.

Method 2: Try a sample data set. You could make up a data set with 6 unique elements and determine the mean, median, and probability of lowest element chosen before and after you multiply each element by 3.

Example: Set = {1, 2, 3, 4, 5, 9}
Mean is (1 + 2 + 3 + 4 + 5 + 9)/6 = 4
Median is between the 3rd and 4th elements, so find the average of them: (3 + 4)/2 = 3.5
Probability of choosing lowest element = 1/6

Multiply all elements by 3 = {3, 6, 9, 12, 15, 27}
Mean is (3 + 6 + 9 + 12 + 15 + 27)/6 = 12
Median is between the 3rd and 4th elements, so find the average of them: (9 + 12)/2 = 10.5
Probability of choosing lowest element = 1/6
Statements I and II are true.

43. B   Let's choose the variable c to represent Christine's age now and f to represent Christine's father's age. Now, let's set up equations with the two variables. Translating the words into equations.

Christine's father is 3 times old as her. $f = 3c$

4 years ago, he was 4 times older than she was then. $f - 4 = 4(c - 4)$

Now we have two equations and can solve. You can use any method you want to solve, here we will use substitution. Substitute 3c for f in the second equation and solve for c.

$f = 3c$
$f - 4 = 4(c - 4)$
$3c - 4 = 4(c - 4)$
$3c - 4 = 4c - 16$
$-4 = c - 16$
$c = 12$

Christine's age is 12. That makes her father 36.

44. C   Calculate the amount Ralph will make under each plan, then compare.

Earnings Plan	Payment Structure
1	$55,000 base salary
2	$25,000 base salary + 15% of sales
3	$35,000 base salary + 1/8 of sales

Plan 1: $55,000

Plan 2: First convert the percent to a decimal. 15% = 0.15.
$25,000 + 0.15($200,000)= $25,000 + $30,000 = $55,000

Plan 3: First convert the fraction to a decimal. 1/8 = 0.125.
$35,000 + 0.125($200,000)= $35,000 + $25,000 = $60,000

45. D   To determine the percentile, we first have to figure out the total number of people in the sample. Add the count from each bar and you will see that there are 35 total people.

The question asks for the 70th percentile, so multiply the total number of people by 70% to find out where the 70th percentile would fall.

35 x 70% = 35 x 0.70 = 24.5 or about 25 people would be needed to reach the 70th percentile. Count the number of people with less than or equal to a certain number of sick days.

Sick Days	Cumulative Total
0	1
1	2
2	2
3	3
4	4
5	5
6	8
7	13
8	21
9	30
10	35

The 70th percentile is reached at 9 sick days.

46. B   You can solve the system in a variety of ways. Here I will cover two of the easiest.

Method 1: Substitution by solving for y

Rearrange the second equation to solve for y: $y = 3x - 11$

Plug in the value for y into the first equation:

$-3x + 2y = -13$

$-3x + 2(3x - 11) = -13$

$-3x + 6x - 22 = -13$

$3x = 9$

$x = 3$

Method 2: Substitution with 3x.

Note that the second equation has solved for 3x. You can substitute that value into the first equation and then solve. We know that $3x = y + 11$. Let's substitute that into the first equation and solve for y.

$-3x \qquad + 2y = -13$

$-(y + 11) + 2y = -13$

$-y - 11 + 2y = -13$

$-11 + y = -13$

$y = -2$

Unfortunately, this method now requires an additional step as the problem asks you to solve for x. You must plug in the value for y into either of the original equations to solve for x. Let's use the second equation.

$3x = y + 11$

$3x = -2 + 11$

$3x = 9$

$x = 3$

47. B   You want to find the minimum number of Bs that must be granted. Therefore, we want to maximize all the rest of the grades. We know that exactly 5 students received a D or an F out of the 40 students. That leaves 35 students to receive an A, B, or C.

The teacher has stated that that will give at most 20 A's. Well, using this information and the fact that we want to maximize the number of A's to find the minimum number of B's, we will count the number of A's as 20. Therefore, that leaves 15 students receiving a B or C.

Finally, we are told that there are at least as many B's as C's. This means that the number of B's is greater than or equal to the number of C's. Out of the 15 students, the maximum number of C's is 7 students as this is the highest number that does not invalidate the above statement.

This leaves 8 students as the minimum number of B's that will be given.

48. C   The student incorrectly assumed that to find the distance between two points you should add the vertical distance to the horizontal distance. However, the shortest distance between two points is the straight line that connects the two points, in this case, as can be seen in the diagram to the right, it is the diagonal line between them.

From looking at the diagram, a common way to calculate the distance between two points is to draw a right triangle with the hypotenuse connecting the points. The sides of the right triangle will be the horizontal distance (10 in this problem) and the vertical distance (10 in this problem) and then the hypotenuse or distance between the points can be calculated with the Pythagorean Theorem.

Answer C: Drawing a right triangle with the hypotenuse connecting the two points

49. D   The volume for a cylinder can be found with this formula: Volume = $\pi r^2 h$.
Note that the above formula is on the formula sheet.

Let's calculate the volumes of a cylinder with the minimum dimensions and the maximum dimensions and then subtract.

On the smaller end, the base radius would be 3cm and the height would be 5cm.
$V_{min} = \pi r^2 h = \pi 3^2 5 = 45\pi$

On the larger end, the base radius would be 5cm and the height would be 9cm.
$V_{max} = \pi r^2 h = \pi 5^2 9 = 225\pi$

The difference is $225\pi - 45\pi = 180\pi$

50. D   The first 11 students scores were all rather similar, falling in the range between 80 and 100. Now we are presented with a new possible score that may be less than 50. This score is far from the other scores and is considered an outlier. Now, let's see how this new score will affect the statistical measures.

A. Standard Deviation
The standard deviation measures how much distribution or spread there is in a data set. Before the last student, the data was somewhat centralized between scores of 80 and 100. Now, with this new score, the data will be spread between below 50 and 100, which will increase the standard deviation.

B. Range
The range is found by subtracting the smallest data point from the largest data point. Previously, the smallest and largest data points were between 80 to 100, meaning the range was a maximum of 20. Now, the smallest data point is less than 50, making the range drastically increase.

C. Mean
The mean is found by summing all the elements and dividing by the number of data points. Since this outlier is quite far from the other data points and because there is a small data set, then the mean will decrease by a significant amount. If the data set was extremely large, such as 100 student test scores that were between 80 and 100, and only one student less than 50, then the mean would not be as affected by a single data point.

D. Median
The median is the middle number when all the data points are ordered. The median of the original group of data would be between 80 and 100. A single outlier piece of data would still keep the median between 80 and 100. This additional student's score would not greatly affect the median.

D is correct.

9. Appendix

The following formula sheet will be provided to you during the Test of Academic Proficiency Exam. Please check the ILTS website to ensure that you have the latest version: www.il.nesinc.com. You should be familiar with every definition and formula on this sheet before you enter the exam. Furthermore, you should know when to use it and what type of problems require the use of which formula. You should use a copy of this formula sheet throughout your preparations so you are used to referring to it when needed.

MATHEMATICS DEFINITIONS AND FORMULAS

Definitions

$=$	is equal to	$\leq$	is less than or equal to	$\overline{AB}$	line segment AB
$\neq$	is not equal to	$\pi \approx 3.14$		$\overleftrightarrow{AB}$	line AB
$>$	is greater than	$\angle$	angle	AB	length of $\overline{AB}$
$<$	is less than	$\lrcorner$	right angle	$\frac{a}{b}$ or $a : b$	ratio of a to b
$\geq$	is greater than or equal to				

Abbreviations for Units of Measurement

	U.S. Customary			**Metric System**				
Distance	in.	inch	**Distance**	m	meter	**Time**	sec.	second
	ft.	foot		km	kilometer		min.	minute
	mi.	mile		cm	centimeter		hr.	hour
				mm	millimeter			
Volume	gal.	gallon	**Volume**	L	liter			
	qt.	quart		mL	milliliter			
	oz.	fluid ounce		cc	cubic centimeter			
Weight	lb.	pound	**Mass**	g	gram			
	oz.	ounce		kg	kilogram			
				mg	milligram			
Temperature	°F	degree Fahrenheit	**Temperature**	°C	degree Celsius			
				K	kelvin			
Speed	mph	miles per hour						

Conversions for Units of Measurement

	U.S. Customary		**Metric System**
Length	12 inches = 1 foot	**Length**	10 millimeters = 1 centimeter
	3 feet = 1 yard		100 centimeters = 1 meter
	5280 feet = 1 mile		1000 meters = 1 kilometer
Volume (liquid)	8 ounces = 1 cup	**Volume**	1000 milliliters = 1 liter
	2 cups = 1 pint		1000 liters = 1 kiloliter
	2 pints = 1 quart		
	4 quarts = 1 gallon		
Weight	16 ounces = 1 pound	**Weight**	1000 milligrams = 1 gram
	2000 pounds = 1 ton		1000 grams = 1 kilogram

Geometric Figures

Square

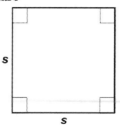

Area = s^2

Perimeter = $4s$

Rectangle

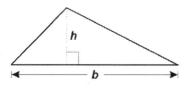

Area = ℓw

Perimeter = $2\ell + 2w$

Triangle

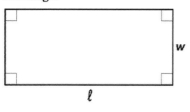

Area = $\frac{1}{2}bh$

Right triangle

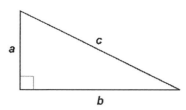

Pythagorean formula: $c^2 = a^2 + b^2$

Rectangular solid

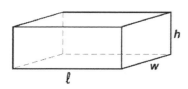

Surface area = $2\ell w + 2\ell h + 2wh$

Volume = ℓwh

Circle

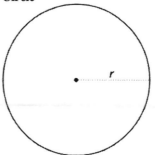

Area = πr^2

Circumference = $2\pi r$

Diameter = $2r$

Sphere

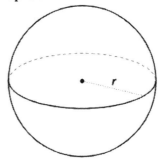

Surface area = $4\pi r^2$

Volume = $\frac{4}{3}\pi r^3$

Cube

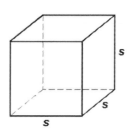

Surface area = $6s^2$

Volume = s^3

Right circular cylinder

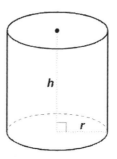

Surface area = $2\pi rh + 2\pi r^2$

Volume = $\pi r^2 h$

Absolute Value: The magnitude or distance a number is from zero. It is always expressed as a positive number. Example: The absolute value of 7, written as |7| is 7. |-3| = 3.

Acute angle: An angle that has a measure between 0 and 90 degrees.

Area: The two-dimensional space inside an object.

Associative: Property that states for problems containing just addition or just multiplication, grouping of numbers does not affect the result.

Bisector: A line that cuts an angle in half.

Chord: A line that begins at one point on a circle and ends at another but does not necessarily pass through the center.

Circumference: The perimeter of a circle which is equal to the product of π and the diameter of the circle.

Combination: The number of ways a group of elements can be chosen from a larger set of elements when the order of the chosen elements does not matter.

Commutative: Property that states for problems containing only multiplication or only addition, order does not matter.

Complementary: Angles that add up to 90 degrees.

Congruent: Two polygons that are congruent have the same size and shape. All the sides and angles of the shapes will be equal.

Coordinate Plane: Shows relationship between two variables with a horizontal number line called the x-axis and a vertical number line called the y-axis.

Counting Numbers: Positive numbers: 1, 2, 3, 4. Also called natural numbers.

Denominator: The part of a fraction that lies below the line. It serves as the divisor of the numerator.

Diameter: Any line that begins at one point on a circle, passes through the center, and ends at another point on the circle.

Difference: The result of a subtraction problem.

Dilation: A transformation for which an object's coordinates are all increased proportionately.

Direct Variation: When the value of a variable is equal to a constant multiplied by another variable. $y = kx$

Distributive: A property indicating a way in which multiplication is applied to addition of two or more numbers. Each term inside a set of parentheses can be multiplied by a factor outside the parentheses. $a(b + c) = ab + ac$

Dividend: A number to be divided. For example, in the division problem 16 ÷ 8 = 2, 16 is the dividend.

Divisor: The number by which a dividend is divided. For example, in the division problem 16 ÷ 8 = 2, 8 is the divisor.

Divisible: Whether a number is capable of being divided. In other words, if a number is divisible by 3, then 3 is a factor of that number.

Domain: A description of all the inputs or x-values for which a function has a valid output.

Equilateral: An equilateral polygon has sides of equal length.

Even Number: Any integer that is divisible by 2.

Expanded Form: Writing a number as the sum of the value of each of its digits.
Example: 321 in expanded form = 300 + 20 + 1

Factors: An integer that divides evenly into a number with no remainder. Example: 4 is a factor of 12.

Factorials: The factorial of a positive integer is equal to the product of all positive integers less than or equal to that number.

Function: A specific type of relation for which each independent variable produces exactly one dependent variable.

Greatest Common Factor (GCF): The GCF of two numbers is the largest factor that they share. Example: GCF of 18 and 24 is 6.

Identity: The identity of addition is 0. Therefore, any number plus zero will equal itself. The identity of multiplication is 1. Therefore, any number times 1 will equal itself.

Improper Fraction: Fractions with numerators that are greater than or equal to the denominator.

Integers: -3, -2, -1, 0, 1, 2, 3. Integers include negative, zero, and positive numbers. Any number that must be expressed as a fraction or decimal is not an integer.

Indirect Variation: When the value of a variable is equal to a constant divided by another variable. $y = k/x$. If two variables vary indirectly, then they are inversely proportional.

Irrational Numbers: Any number that cannot be expressed as a fraction, such as decimals that do not terminate or repeat. The square root of 2 and pi are examples of irrational numbers.

Isosceles Triangle: A triangle that has exactly two equal sides and exactly two equal angles.

Least Common Denominator: The least common multiple of all the denominators in an addition or subtraction problem involving fractions.

Least Common Multiple (LCM): The LCM of two numbers is the smallest non-zero multiple that they both share. Example: LCM of 15 and 20 is 60.

Mean: The average of a set of numbers which is equal to the sum of the numbers divided by the number of numbers.

Median: The middle number in a set of numbers.

Mixed Number: A number containing both a fraction and a whole number. For example, 3 4/5 is a mixed number.

Mode: The most frequently occurring number or piece of data in a set of data.

Multiples: A multiple of a number is equal to that number times an integer. Example: Multiples of 12 include 12, 24, 36, and 48.

Natural Numbers: Positive numbers: 1, 2, 3, 4. Also called counting numbers.

Number Line: A straight line used for representing positive and negative numbers.

Numerator: The part of a fraction that is above the line. The numerator signifies the number to be divided by the denominator.

Obtuse angle: An angle that is greater than 90 degrees but less than 180 degrees.

Odd Numbers: Any integer that is not divisible by 2.

Order of Operations: Often called PEMDAS. For problems with multiple operations, this is the standardized order in which operations must be carried out. The order is Parentheses, Exponents, Multiplication and Division from left to right, and Addition and Subtraction from left to right.

Parallel Lines: Lines that never intersect and have the same slope.

Perimeter: The distance around the edge of an object.

Permutation: The number of ways a group of elements can be chosen from a larger set of elements when the order of the chosen elements matters.

Perpendicular Lines: Lines that intersect to form four 90 degree angles.

Pi: Constant that is equal to the ratio of any circle's circumference to its diameter. It is an irrational number but can be approximated as 3.14.

Prime Number: Any number that has only itself and 1 as its factors. Examples: 2, 7, 23

Probability: The number of favorable outcomes divided by the number of possible outcomes.

Product: The result of a multiplication problem.

Pythagorean Theorem: A relation among the three sides of a right triangle which states that the square of the hypotenuse of a right triangle is equal to the sum of the squares of the other two sides.

Quadrant: The four areas of the coordinate plane. The quadrant in the upper right is called quadrant I and the quadrants are counted counterclockwise.

Quotient: The result of a division problem.

Radius: The distance between the center of a circle and any point on the circle itself.

Range: Set of y-values or outputs of a function.

Ratio: A means of comparing one expression containing numbers or variables to another.

Rational Numbers: Any number that can be expressed as a fraction. This includes decimals that terminate or repeat. Examples: -3.451, ⅔

Real Numbers: All rational and irrational numbers.

Reflection: A transformation that involves flipping an object around an axis creating a mirror image of an object.

Relation: A patterned relationship between two variables.

Remainder: The portion of the dividend that is not evenly divisible by the divisor. For example, when 13 is divided by 5, the remainder is 3.

Right angle: An angle that equals 90 degrees.

Rotation: A transformation that involves turning an object about a pivot point.

Sample Space: The set of all possible outcomes.

Scalene Triangle: A triangle with sides of different lengths. In addition, all angles of a scalene triangle will be different.

Scientific Notation: A way of writing numbers as products consisting of a number between 1 and 10 multiplied by a power of 10.

Similar: Figures that have the same shape are similar. They can be different sizes and positions as the result of uniform scaling (enlarging or shrinking) or transformations (rotation, reflection, or translation). When two figures are similar, the ratios of the lengths of their corresponding sides are equal.

Slope: The change in the y coordinate divided by the change in the x coordinate for a line. This is often referred to as "rise over run".

Sum: The result of an addition problem.

Supplementary: Angles that add up to 180 degrees.

Surface Area: The sum of the areas of all of the faces of an object.

Tangent: A line on the outside of a circle that touches the circle at only one point.

Translation: A transformation that involves the movement of an object without changing it in any other way.

Volume: The three-dimensional space filled by an object.

Whole Numbers: 0, 1, 2, 3, 4, ... Includes zero and the counting numbers.

X-axis: The horizontal axis of a two-dimensional coordinate plane.

Y-axis: The vertical axis of a two-dimensional coordinate plane.

Y-intercept: The point at which a line crosses the y-axis.

Made in the USA
Lexington, KY
30 November 2017